THE GOOD IN THE RIGHT

THE GOOD IN THE RIGHT

A THEORY OF INTUITION AND INTRINSIC VALUE

Robert Audi

PRINCETON UNIVERSITY PRESS   PRINCETON AND OXFORD

Copyright ©2004 by Princeton University Press
Published by Princeton University Press,
41 William Street, Princeton, New Jersey 08540
In the United Kingdom: Princeton University Press,
3 Market Place, Woodstock, Oxfordshire OX20 1SY

All Rights Reserved

Library of Congress Cataloging-in-Publication Data
Audi, Robert, date
The good in the right : a theory of intuition and intrinsic value / Robert Audi.
p. cm.
Includes bibliographical references and index.
ISBN: 0-691-11434-X
1. Ethical intuitionism. 2. Ross, W.D. (William David), 1877–1971.
Kant, Immanuel, 1724–1804—Ethics. I. Title.

BJ1472.A83 2004
171'.2–dc21   2003051738

British Library Cataloging-in-Publication Data is available

This book has been composed in Electra
Printed on acid-free paper. ∞
www.pupress.princeton.edu
Printed in the United States of America
10 9 8 7 6 5 4 3 2 1

To my family, with gratitude

Contents

Preface

THIS BOOK HAS DEVELOPED both from my teaching in ethics over many years and from numerous exchanges of ideas in ethical theory on both sides of the Atlantic. Particularly in recent years, intuitionism has re-emerged as a major position in ethics. Appeals to intuitions in discussing moral questions have long been common—even if not always so described—but there has also been renewed exploration of intuitionism as an ethical theory that uses intuitions as data for moral reasoning and makes a basic commitment to the power of intuition as a rational capacity.

By the turn of the century, intuitionism had become both theoretically richer and more interesting to students of ethics than most recent writers in the field have realized. It is also plausible and attractive to ethically oriented professionals outside philosophy—for instance in business, engineering, journalism, law, and medicine. This emerged quite clearly in a number of post-doctoral seminars I have directed since the 1980s for professional school faculty in those and other fields. These professors teach both ethics and their own specific subject to students in graduate or pre-professional programs, and in their teaching and writing in ethics they found W. D. Ross's intuitionism at once theoretically straightforward and, in many cases, more readily applicable to practical moral problems than virtue ethics, Kantianism, or utilitarianism.

If those who teach ethics in the professions and apply ethical positions to concrete moral problems have found Ross's intuitionism an invaluable resource, many moral philosophers have tended to find it theoretically too thin even where it is plausible and, in its apparently strong epistemological and metaphysical claims, unacceptable. In part, the problem is that intuitionism in the twentieth century could not escape the shadow of G. E. Moore, who, for instance, posited non-natural properties, maintained the indefinability of goodness, and appealed to a strong notion of self-evidence in defending his many assertions about the intrinsically good. One aim of this book is to get Ross as far as possible out from under Moore's shadow and, to some extent, the shadow of H. A. Prichard.

My wider purpose is twofold: to respond to the theoretical concerns of philosophical critics of intuitionism and to develop an overall intuitionist position that represents a theoretical advance beyond Ross's view but is at least as useful as his in approaching moral problems in everyday life. To do this without writing a long book, I confine technical matters and some responses to contemporary critics of intuitionism mainly to the notes, and I forgo considering certain alternative views of major contemporary authors. My hope is that the book will be both readily accessible to nonspecialists and, in some of its implicit treatments of contemporary ethical questions and its many references in the notes to historically and currently important writers, responsive to the theoretical concerns raised by the ethical theory I develop.

ACKNOWLEDGMENTS

This book has profited from discussions with many colleagues, students, and audiences. I have particularly benefited from critical comments on earlier versions. Roger Crisp, Brad Hooker, Joseph Mendola, Michael Meyer, Walter Sinnott-Armstrong, Mark Timmons, Peter Tramel, and Michael Zimmerman insightfully commented on drafts of the entire manuscript. Their comments were of great help, and I benefited further in discussing some of the issues with them. Panayot Butchvarov, Ruth Chang, James Dreier, Hugh McCann, Derek Parfit, Geoffrey Sayre-McCord, Russ Shafer-Landau, Philip Stratton-Lake, Mark van Roojen, and Patrick Yarnell provided detailed comments on an earlier version of one or another chapter, and continuing discussions with them, especially with Parfit and van Roojen, have also proved helpful to me. Many others — more than I can name here (and including anonymous readers) — helped me through responding to one or more of the papers or seminars that provided background for the book, or in conversations or correspondence concerning their related work. Among these I should particularly like to thank John Broome, Garrett Cullity, Jonathan Dancy, Stephen Darwall, John Deigh, James Felt, Robert Frazier, Berys Gaut, Allan Gibbard, Irwin Goldstein, John Greco, Kent Greenawalt, James Griffin, Philip Kain, Stephen Kalish, Robert Kane, Ralph Kennedy, Christopher Kulp, Scott LaBarge, Win-chiat Lee, Noah Lemos, Jimmy Lenman, Mark Mathewson, Patrick Murphy, Lawrence Nelson, Martha Nussbaum, Michael Perry, Louis Pojman, Nelson Potter, William Prior, Elizabeth Radcliffe, Bruce Russell, Thomas Scanlon, John Skorupski, Michael Smith, Robert Solomon, Nicholas Sturgeon, and Jay Wallace. In addition, Michael DePaul, Bernard Gert, John Haldane, Gilbert Harman, Frances Kamm, Christine Korsgaard, David McNaughton, Alfred Mele, Thomas

Nagel, Onora O'Neill, Joseph Raz, Bruce Russell, Ernest Sosa, Eleonore Stump, Judith Thomson, Ralph Wedgwood, Paul Weithman, and Nicholas Wolterstorff provided critical responses to some of the ideas that appear in the book, as well as related ideas of their own that have been a positive resource in my work. For help and advice at many different stages I heartily thank Ian Malcolm and his staff at Princeton University Press. I particularly want to thank Lauren Lepow, whose expert copyediting enabled me to improve the text in many places.

For permission to use, in revised form, material published in my essays, I am grateful to a number of editors and publishers. No chapter, however, consists of a previously published work, and material appearing earlier has been substantially revised and significantly expanded. "Ethical Reflectionism," which appeared in *The Monist* 76, no. 3 (1993); "Intuitionism, Pluralism, and the Foundations of Ethics," published in *Moral Knowledge?*, ed. Walter Sinnott-Armstrong and Mark Timmons (Oxford University Press, 1996); "Moderate Intuitionism and the Epistemology of Moral Judgment," which appeared in *Ethical Theory and Moral Practice* 1, no. 1 (1998); and "Moral Knowledge and Ethical Pluralism," in *The Blackwell Guide to Epistemology*, ed. Ernest Sosa and John Greco (Basil Blackwell, 1999) are reflected in the parts of Chapters 1 and 2 that concern W. D. Ross and what I call Rossian intuitionism. "A Kantian Intuitionism," published in *Mind* 110, no. 439 (2001), is reflected fully in Chapter 3, and the same holds for "Prospects for a Value-Based Intuitionism," in *Intuitionism: Re-evaluations*, ed. Philip Stratton-Lake (Oxford University Press, 2002), in relation to Chapter 4; but both Chapters 3 and 4 contain much that did not appear in those papers. Chapter 5 is not based on any previous work.

My colleagues and students at the University of Nebraska, Lincoln, at Santa Clara University, and in the post-doctoral seminars I have directed since the 1980s have been of great intellectual value to me in producing this book. My research support from these two universities has been generous, and I am also grateful for a Visiting Fellowship at Oriel College in the University of Oxford during Trinity Term of 2001 and for a quarter as A. C. Reid Lecturer at Wake Forest University that same year. That Term in Oxford provided me occasions to discuss many of the central issues treated in the book with philosophers both in Britain and on the Continent.

May 2003
Lincoln, Nebraska

Introduction

MORAL PHILOSOPHY is driven by two quests. One is theoretical, the other practical. Philosophers and others who think seriously about ethics want to understand morality: its language and concepts, its requirements and ideals, its evidences and arguments, its connections with human psychology, and many other topics. But they also want to contribute concretely to our morality and to enhance our ability to realize moral standards. This requires determining what those standards are, what they require in specific situations, what factors tend to prevent our fulfilling them, what punishments may be needed for certain violations, and much more. Neither quest can succeed without empirical information, but practical ethics requires much more of that than theoretical ethics. It is also less philosophical, in at least one way; its success depends less on philosophical sophistication. We should not be surprised, then, that moral philosophers have tended to devote most of their energies to theoretical ethics.

There is, however, widespread dissatisfaction with ethical theories and some dissatisfaction with moral philosophy of any kind. This is often perceptible on the part of many non-philosophers who are concerned with the second, practical quest; but there are also many philosophers, including some practitioners of theoretical ethics, who are dissatisfied with ethical theory as they see it. This point applies especially to the dominant kinds of ethical theory in the modern period: utilitarianism and Kantianism. The resurgence of interest in virtue ethics is in part a result of this dissatisfaction.

Another result of dissatisfaction with the recently dominant ethical theories is a renewed interest in intuitionism. Intuitionism has been a force in the history of ethics since at least the eighteenth century, but there are a number of reasons for its growing prominence. One important point is that it speaks directly to both of the driving quests in moral philosophy. It has a theoretical side expressible in a fairly simple metaethics; but in its richest forms it also has a normative core that is, at least in its best-known version, developed by W. D. Ross, close to the kinds of generally uncontroversial everyday judgments that any ethical theory seeks to account for. These are the kinds of judgments that match our "intuitions," or, on reflection, at least seem intuitive.

There are subtler reasons for renewed interest in intuitionism. For one thing, a half century's responses to W. V. Quine's attack on the a priori, and indeed on the power of reason to reveal significant truths, have restored in many philosophers a certain sense of epistemological freedom. I am not suggesting that the existence of substantive a priori truths is now uncontroversial. But it is probably uncontroversial that the concept of the a priori has not been clearly shown to be incoherent, or the category of the a priori proven to be either empty or populated only by incontestable truths of formal logic. There is thus more space for a rationalist intuitionism. I hasten to add that there is in any case an empirical branch of intuitionist theorizing, not dependent on any appeal to self-evidence, though it is like rationalist versions of intuitionism in taking some moral judgments to be non-inferential.

This brings us to a second point that partly explains why intuitionism should be an attractive option now. We have also recovered from the attack on the possibility of non-inferential knowledge, something that intuitionism in any major form, whether rationalist or empiricist, is committed to positing for certain moral propositions. Even a noncognitivist metaethics can sustain something similar: a kind of non-inferential justification for moral attitudes. Once that is appreciated, intuitionism can be seen as, in some perhaps attenuated form, a possible position even for those who reject realism in ethical theory.

If these points are sound, one might wonder why there are not more intuitionists—or at least more avowed intuitionists. One reason concerns the notion of self-evidence. What does it come to, and are the kinds of moral principles Ross articulated really self-evident? Second, if they are self-evident, how can there be so much moral disagreement? Third, can moral judgments, given the cognitive background and the sensitivity they often require, really be non-inferential and thus not dependent on premises? And if so, why does the apparently direct grasp of truth in question not lead to dogmatism? If we know something without depending on premises, we would seem to have nothing in the way of reasons to offer to anyone who disagrees. Fourth, why should the short list of principles intuitionists have proposed be the only basic ones? Fifth, what unifies or explains them? And finally, how can we reasonably resolve the kinds of conflicts of moral duties Ross acknowledged as common?

There are, then, both theoretical problems facing intuitionism and difficulties in working out a good intuitionist normative framework—a set of principles stating our moral obligations. This book deals with these major theoretical problems and, on the basis of an integration of everyday intuitionist principles with a wider moral philosophy, puts forward a set of such principles that incorporates but also extends the set proposed by Ross.

Chapter 1 introduces ethical intuitionism, beginning with Sidgwick's account of the position and proceeding, through Moore, Prichard, and Broad, to the position of Ross, which was the most prominent intuitionist view throughout most of the twentieth century.

Chapter 2 sets forth a position that constitutes a broadly Rossian intuitionism, but is developed further than Ross's view, in part by extension in some places, in part by rectifying some errors, and in part by meeting difficulties faced by Ross's intuitionism. It should be obvious that if intuitionism can be taken this far beyond what Ross gave us, it is considerably more plausible than many of its critics have thought and may serve some purposes, particularly those of everyday moral judgment, quite well.

Some ethical thinkers may be content to work with a Rossian intuitionism and may take it to be as systematic a position as we can hope for in ethics. But in the light of the intuitionist resources described and defended by the end of Chapter 2, we can advance the overall intuitionist position by integrating it with an interpretation of Kant's categorical imperative— a project that also serves to clarify and strengthen some major elements in Kantian ethics. This is the work of Chapter 3, which attempts both to preserve the major elements in Rossian intuitionism and to strengthen that view by incorporating it in a broadly Kantian framework.

From the vantage point of the integration between Rossian intuitionism and the framework of the Kantian categorical imperative, Chapter 4 pursues the connection between intuitionism as a deontological (duty-based) position and the theory of value, and thus between the right and the good. The result is a value-based Kantian intuitionism that seeks to combine the best elements in Rossian intuitionism with a version of the categorical imperative understood in the light of a theory of value that provides unifying grounds for all of the moral principles in question, from the loftily general categorical imperative "downward" to quite specific standards of conduct. The Kantian intuitionism defended in Chapter 3 can be developed without conceiving it as groundable in the theory of value proposed in this chapter, but the two combined provide a more plausible, more comprehensive ethical theory.

Even with all of this theoretical work accomplished, there remain problems for the normative position that best suits an overall intuitionist ethics. Chapter 5 explores a version of that kind of theory. The result is to reinterpret and revise some of Ross's principles and to expand his list to include further principles having a similar intuitive plausibility and a comparable basis in the value-oriented Kantian framework developed earlier in the book. That work will complete my presentation of ethical intuitionism: it is a resourceful theory that provides at least as promising a route as any other approach to success in both of the driving quests of moral philosophy.

1

Early Twentieth-Century Intuitionism

IF WE UNDERSTAND intuitionism broadly, as the view that at least some basic moral truths are non-inferentially known, and in that very minimal sense known intuitively, the view is very old. It would go back at least to Thomas Aquinas.[1] It is, however, with the seventeenth- and eighteenth-century British moralists that the view as we know it now began to take shape.[2] John Stuart Mill criticized this "intuitive school" in the opening chapter of *Utilitarianism*, but devoted little space to it. Mill's great utilitarian successor, Henry Sidgwick, by contrast, discussed intuitionism at length, and it is with him that we should begin in order to understand intuitionism in the twentieth century and especially in W. D. Ross. Ross's statement of the view is the primary one for the twentieth century and is still defended.[3] I shall also consider G. E. Moore and, more briefly, H. A. Prichard and C. D. Broad, to provide for understanding Ross in particular and intuitionism in general. My main subject, until Chapter 5, will be intuitionism in ethical theory, which concerns the nature, basis, and justification of moral judgments. But much of what emerges in the theoretical discussion will help in developing a plausible intuitionist normative ethics—roughly, a set of standards governing everyday conduct—and the account of Ross in this chapter and the next will consider specific moral principles in the context of explicating his theory. Ross's list of these became so well known that for most of the twentieth century, 'intuitionism' often designated his overall metaethical *and* normative position. Chapter 5 will articulate a normative view that modifies and extends Ross's normative position and will thereby complete the construction of the overall intuitionist ethics this book presents.

1. HENRY SIDGWICK: THREE KINDS OF ETHICAL INTUITIONISM

Sidgwick treats intuitionism in some detail in several parts of his monumental *Methods of Ethics*, the seventh and last edition of which appeared in 1907. This book in some ways marks a transition from nineteenth- to twentieth-century ethical theory, and it perceptibly influenced at least the majority of the later philosophers in the intuitionist tradition. In Chapter 8 of Book 1 Sidgwick distinguishes three kinds—"methods," in his terms—of intuitionism. I take these in turn.

He characterizes the "intuitional" position as "the view of ethics which regards as the practically ultimate end of moral actions their conformity to certain rules or dictates of Duty unconditionally prescribed."[4] These dictates include "ultimately valid moral imperatives . . . conceived as relating to particular acts."[5] Moreover, "Writers who maintain that we have 'intuitive knowledge' of the rightness of actions usually mean that this rightness is ascertained simply by 'looking at' the actions themselves without considering their ultimate consequences" (p. 96). Sidgwick seems to apply this point to both *kinds* of action and particular actions, i.e., act-types and act-tokens. The types are actions anyone might perform, even if they are specified in some detail, say as breaking a promise to help an uncle weed his garden. The tokens are deeds done by a particular agent at a particular time, such as the keeping of the promise just described, by a specific agent at a definite time.[6] To accommodate intuitionism as regards act-types, particularly where their consequences are relevant to their moral status, Sidgwick says that we must "admit a wider use of 'Intuition' as equivalent to 'immediate judgment as to what ought to be done or aimed at' " (p. 97).

In an extreme form, intuitionism "recognises simple immediate [i.e., non-inferential] intuitions alone and discards as superfluous all modes of reasoning to moral conclusions: and we may find in it one phase or variety of the Intuitional method—if we may extend the term 'method' to include a procedure that is completed in a single judgment" (p. 100). Later, he calls this the "Perceptional" phase of intuitionism (p. 102), apparently to capture the analogy with both the immediacy of perceptual judgments grounded in sensory experience and their focus on a specific case.[7] The kind of immediacy he has in mind is mainly the non-inferential character of the judgment. His reference to a method "completed in a single judgment" allows, however, that the agent reflect before judging. Doing so does not entail that the intuitive judgment that completes the application of the "method" is inferential. Nonetheless, the description of a prominent form of intuitionism as holding that "rightness is ascertained simply by 'looking at' the actions themselves," even with Sidgwick's signal quotes, has colored the general conception of the view. It has doubtless contributed to the impression that for intuitionism we "just see" what we ought to do.

Sidgwick thinks that all moral agents probably have "experience of such particular intuitions" and that these form "a great part of the moral phenomena of most minds" (p. 100). Still, many such agents feel a need for "some further moral knowledge"; for

> these particular intuitions do not, to reflective persons, present themselves as quite indubitable and irrefragable . . . the same conduct will wear a different moral aspect at one time from that which it wore at another . . . Furthermore, we become aware that the moral perceptions of different minds, to all appearance equally competent to judge, frequently conflict: one condemns what the other approves. (P. 100)

The point is not that intuitions do not commonly constitute knowledge; it is apparently that they still seem to need support from something else, perhaps something more general, that is "certain and irrefragable."

This felt need provides an incentive to move to "a second Intuitional Method: of which the fundamental assumption is that we can discern certain general rules with really clear and finally valid intuition. It is held that such general rules are implicit in the moral reasoning of ordinary men" (p. 101). The moral philosopher functions, on this view, "to perform this process of abstract contemplation, to arrange the results as systematically as possible, and by proper definitions and explanations to remove vagueness and prevent conflict" (p. 101). This is the kind of system Sidgwick sees as intended by the phrase 'Intuitive or *a priori* morality'—a reference that might identify the target of Mill's animadversions (in the introductory section of *Utilitarianism*) on what he called the "intuitive school." Here Sidgwick uses the name 'Dogmatic Intuitionism', presumably to highlight its assumption that we can have "finally valid" intuitions regarding the common-sense moral principles in question.

It is not surprising that Sidgwick sees philosophers as wanting more than this second kind of intuitionism can supply. His description of the felt need is echoed in current literature and worth quoting at length:

> Even granting that these rules can be so defined as perfectly to fit together and cover the whole field of human conduct, without coming into conflict and without leaving any practical question unanswered,—still the resulting code seems an accidental aggregate of precepts, which stands in need of some rational synthesis . . . From this demand springs a third phase of Intuitionism, which, while accepting the morality of common sense as in the main sound, still attempts to find for it a philosophic basis . . . to get one

8

CHAPTER ONE

or more principles more absolutely and undeniably true and evident from which the current rules might be deduced, either just as they are or with slight modifications . . . (P. 102)

This phase of intuitionism is the philosophical form (p. 102). It can both synthesize and provide evidential grounds for everyday moral rules. It is this "philosophical intuitionism" that Sidgwick favors. It seeks to account for highly general moral principles that constitute a basis for the less general ones recognized by the dogmatic intuitionist, and it provides a method of correction both of formulations at that middle level and of moral judgments concerning particular actions. In concluding this chapter he says, "So far I have been mainly concerned with differences in intuitional method due to difference of generality in the intuitive beliefs recognised as ultimately valid. There is, however, another class of differences . . . as to the precise quality immediately apprehended in the moral intuition" (p. 103). This quality is one he tries to capture in explicating philosophical intuitionism in Book 3.

Given that Sidgwick sees philosophical intuitionism as synthesizing common-sense moral principles, and given that he often talks as if these are plainly true, one might think that he takes intuitions—in the usual psychological sense in which they represent non-inferential cognitions— as, if not infallible, then invariably true. But he is more cautious: he acknowledges

> an ambiguity in the use of the term 'intuition'; which has sometimes been understood to imply that the judgment or apparent perception so designated is *true* . . . by calling any affirmation as to the rightness or wrongness of actions 'intuitive', I do not mean to prejudge the question as to its ultimate validity . . . I only mean that its truth is apparently known immediately, and not as the result of reasoning . . . any such 'intuition' may turn out to have an element of error, which subsequent reflection and comparison may enable us to correct; just as many apparent perceptions through the organ of vision are found to be partially illusory and misleading. (P. 211; cf. p. 215)

In addition to noting the fallibility of intuition, Sidgwick grants that we are "often liable to confound with moral intuitions other states of mind essentially different from them" (p. 102); and he makes clear that these impostors, which include "vague sentiments" or current opinions to which familiarity has given "an illusory air of self-evidence," are far from infallible.

An important counterbalancing element in Sidgwick's acknowledgment of the fallibility of moral intuitions is his restriction of the sources of their error. Of the propositions that are objects of moral intuitions, he says, "such ethical propositions, relating as they do to matter fundamentally different from that with which physical science or psychology deals, cannot be inconsistent with any physical or psychological conclusions. They can only involve errors by being shown to contradict each other" (p. 213). This possibility of logical conflict is one basis of his point that intuitions may embody "an element of error."

Sidgwick also notes a different source of possible error: some ethical beliefs may be caused in a way that makes their falsehood "probable" (p. 212). Factual errors, for instance, can cause erroneous intuitions or false intuitive judgments. These are points about the possibility and causes of error, not about how error is to be established. Causation by prejudice might also make it probable that a judgment is false, but would not entail this. The positive implication in what he says is that intuitions are non-empirical and hence not in potential logical conflict with empirical claims, even if empirical data can make error in some intuition probable. But in the context this implication is not developed. Sidgwick is more concerned with how we can ascertain and rectify error. Let us pursue this.

If intuitively believed moral propositions can be mutually inconsistent, and if, when these inconsistencies occur, we are to deal properly with them, the need for the synthesis called for by philosophical intuitionism comes to the fore. With this point in mind, Sidgwick concludes, "if the formulae of Intuitive Morality are really to serve as scientific axioms, and to be available in clear and cogent demonstrations, they must first be raised—by an effort of reflection which ordinary persons will not make—to a higher degree of precision than attaches to them in the common thought and discourse of mankind in general" (p. 215). This is a task of refining and qualifying common-sense morality, not of abandoning it. It is this task that he undertakes in the final nine chapters.

The standard to be met in this task is self-evidence, a status intuitionists have generally attributed to some moral propositions. The axioms we seek, then, are such that when their content is "made explicit their truth is self-evident and must be accepted at once by an intelligent and unbiased mind" (p. 229). This conception of self-evidence is central for most later intuitionists and is still often held or presupposed. Explicating the conception further, Sidgwick says:

Just as some mathematical axioms are not and cannot be known to the multitude, as their certainty cannot be seen except by minds carefully prepared . . . when their terms are properly understood, the perception of their absolute truth is immediate and irresistible. Similarly, if we are not able to claim for a proposed moral axiom, in its precise form, an explicit and actual assent . . . it may still be a truth which men before vaguely apprehended, and which they will not unhesitatingly admit. (P. 229)

There are at least three important points here. First, even what is self-evident may not seem true to those whose understanding of it is inadequate. Second, given an adequate ("proper") understanding of a self-evident proposition, its truth is non-inferentially seen (this truth is "immediate"). Third, reaching the kind of understanding in question *entails* seeing the truth so understood: perceiving it is indeed "irresistible."[8] Sidgwick is clearly implying that despite their axiomatic status moral axioms (and perhaps self-evident propositions generally) (1) need not be *obvious*, yet (2) are non-inferentially knowable, and (3) are (doxastically) *compelling*, in the sense that when we consider them with proper understanding, we must believe them.

Chapter 13 of Book 3 shows what use Sidgwick, as systematic philosopher, makes of philosophical intuitionism. He formulates "real ethical axioms—intuitive propositions of real clearness and certainty" (p. 373). One is

the self-evident principle that the good of any one individual is of no more importance, from the point of view (if I may say so) of the Universe, than the good of any other . . . And [second] it is evident to me that as a rational being I am bound to aim at good generally . . . From these two rational intuitions we may deduce . . . the maxim of Benevolence . . . each one is morally bound to regard the good of any other individual as much as his own . . . (P. 382)

What we have, in effect, is a movement from philosophical intuitionism to utilitarianism: "The Intuitional method rigorously applied yields as its final result the doctrine of pure Universalistic Hedonism . . . Utilitarianism" (pp. 406–7).

For all his criticism of intuitionism, then, Sidgwick's ethical theory exemplifies the view, though in a utilitarian version. He rejects what he calls dogmatic intuitionism; but he apparently agrees with perceptual intuitionists that we commonly have non-inferential knowledge of singular moral judgments. Moreover, to his general principles from which he derives utilitarianism he seems to accord something like the epistemic status that "dogmatic" intuitionists ascribe to everyday moral principles. Although we are not entitled to take a dogmatic *attitude* in affirming them, they are self-evident.

2. G. E. MOORE AS A PHILOSOPHICAL INTUITIONIST

In the light of Sidgwick's threefold categorization of intuitionist positions as perceptional, dogmatic, and philosophical, we can see both why Moore contrasts himself with intuitionists and why he is nonetheless commonly counted among them. In his Preface to *Principia Ethica*[9] he says,

> The Intuitionist proper is distinguished by maintaining that propositions of my *second* class—propositions which assert that a certain action is *right* or a *duty*—are incapable of proof or disproof by any enquiry into the results of such actions. I, on the contrary, am no less anxious to maintain that propositions of *this* kind are *not* 'Intuitions' than to maintain that propositions of my *first* class [propositions about the good] *are* Intuitions . . . when I call such propositions 'Intuitions' I mean merely to assert that they are incapable of proof . . . (P. x)

Three points deserve emphasis here. First, in granting that there are broadly ethical intuitions, he agrees with Sidgwick's philosophical intuitionist—who is not taken by Moore to be an "Intuitionist proper"—that some broadly ethical propositions are self-evident (pages as early as vii–viii indicate that this is his view despite the 'merely' just quoted). Second, intuitions are unprovable not because they are either obscure or possibly false, but owing to special characteristics (to be described shortly). Third, although Moore is speaking of intuitions as *propositions* that are intuited, he also countenances intuition in the attitudinal, psychological sense common in Sidgwick's writing. In this sense an intuition is not a proposition but a cognition: not an abstract content but a propositional attitude, presumably a belief, that *has* such a content.

The distinction between the attitudinal and propositional senses of 'intuition' is important. Nothing in the notion of an intuition in the attitudinal sense entails that its object must be of a specific kind, much less unprovable. But the Moorean use of 'intuition' for unprovable self-evident propositions invites the contrary view and may have led some philosophers to think that intuitionism is committed to it. In a common sense of the term among ethical intuitionists, an intuition is something like a non-inferential belief or non-inferential judgment (possibly an occurrent judgment, as where one assentingly considers a proposition). Its object need not be a self-evident proposition, but such propositions would be paradigms of the intuitively knowable.

The propositional use of 'intuition' is now uncommon, and I will use the term only in the attitudinal sense. One might think that Moore believed propositional intuitions to be the only appropriate *objects* of intuitions in the attitudinal sense. But (as I explain below) it is unlikely that he held this, and certainly no such assumption is warranted by the usage of 'intuition' in major twentieth-century intuitionist writings.

What, for Moore, is a self-evident proposition? Here is one of his most explicit remarks on this: "The expression 'self-evident' means properly that the proposition so called is evident or true, *by itself* alone; that it is not an inference from some proposition other than *itself*" (p. 143). He has in mind self-evident propositions ascribing (intrinsic) goodness to one or another kind of thing such as pleasure in singing beautiful songs or contemplating virtuous deeds: "such propositions are all of them, in Kant's phrase, 'synthetic': they all must rest in the end upon some proposition which must be simply accepted or rejected . . . This result may be otherwise expressed by saying that the fundamental principles of Ethics must be self-evident" (p. 143). In saying that self-evident propositions must be "simply accepted or rejected," he gives the impression that they are *unarguable*. This is easily taken to suggest that they should be obvious to anyone who understands them. Neither point strictly follows from the self-evidence of a proposition (as Chapter 2 will show), but the impression has become a common part of many philosophers' conceptions of the self-evident.

On the question of how the self-evident is related to intuition, Moore is not altogether clear. Consider one passage central to his view. Maintaining that intuition is not "an alternative to reasoning," he says, "Nothing whatever can take the place of *reasons* for the truth of any proposition: intuition can only furnish a reason for *holding* any proposition to be true: this however it must do when any proposition is self-evident, when, in fact there are no reasons which prove its truth" (p. 144). Here Moore quite naturally uses 'intuition' in a psychological sense. If, however, we think of a self-evident proposition as *an* intuition (in the propositional sense), and so as "incapable of proof," we can see why Moore construes it as such that there are no reasons that prove its truth. If there were such probative reasons for it, then reasoning from them could prove it.

Nonetheless, there is a sense of 'evidence' in which Moore allows that we may have evidence for such a proposition; for he speaks of the "evidence or proof" of a self-evident proposition as "lying in itself" (p. 143) and adds, "Again that a proposition is evident to us may not only be the reason why we do think or affirm it, it may even be a *reason* why we ought to think it or affirm it . . . it is a logical reason for the rightness of holding the proposition" (pp. 143–44). This last point, concerning what we ought to think, explains how he can speak of "reasoning" in holding self-evident propositions, which are unprovable: we can reason from a proposition's being evident to us to the conclusion that we ought to hold it, even though this reasoning does not constitute a proof of it.

There are, then, "three meanings of 'reason' [that] are constantly confused" (p. 144). Moore does not name any of these other than the first: "logical reasons," reasons why a proposition is true. These might better be called *ontic reasons*, since they are apparently something like facts in virtue of which the proposition is true. Call reasons why we "ought to think" a proposition true *evidential reasons*, since they provide a justification in virtue of which we ought to think it true. His third case is that of a "reason why we *do* think it true" (my emphasis). Call this an *explanatory reason*; it is apparently a psychological element that explains why we hold a belief. How are these Moorean reasons related? Clearly, a psychological reason can be an evidential reason as well. But what is the relation between ontic ("logical") and evidential reasons?

I quoted Moore as speaking of "evidence or proof" (p. 143). He does not equate these; but he seems to presuppose that from premises constituting *conclusive* evidence a proof is possible. In any case, he strays from his main point, which is that there is no "logical reason" for a self-evident proposition. The move from the ontic to the epistemic domain is, however, natural for him. For one thing, his explication of the self-evident as "evident or true, *by itself* alone" is not, as one might expect, ontic. It does not cite, for instance, the absence of a reason why some self-evident proposition is *true*, or propose any other ontic point. Instead, his explication is epistemic: the point is that the proposition is "not an inference from some other proposition" (p. 143).[10] The phrase 'evident or true' also invites a conflation of the epistemic and the ontic; to say that a self-evident proposition is 'not an inference' favors an epistemic reading of his notion of self-evidence, but Moore quickly goes on to specify ontic reasons as the kind ruled out by self-evidence.

It is difficult to avoid the conclusion that Moore did not properly distinguish and adequately connect two related ideas: that self-evident propositions are not *true* in virtue of any ontic reason, such as one that explains their truth, and that they are not *knowable* on the basis of any evidential reason, at least where that is the kind of reason from which a proof, as opposed to a non-inferential apprehension, is possible.

There is, to be sure, *some* plausibility in each thesis. As to the first, we might grant Moore that insofar as we think of a proposition as true on account of some fact or state of affairs in virtue of which it is true, we also tend to think of it as "derivative" rather than as self-evident, as with the kinds of theorems of logic we must come to believe through proofs ("derivations").[11] As to the second, paradigms of self-evident propositions are not known inferentially, and in some cases (say, that if $x = y$, then $y = x$) they seem such that there *is* nothing more "basic" to serve as a premise for knowing them inferentially. But neither the idea that no self-evident proposition is true in virtue of some ontic reason nor the claim that none is knowable on the basis of some evidential proposition is clearly correct, and I shall later argue that both are mistaken. It is an interesting question whether Moore would have better argued for the latter, epistemological thesis, which is probably more important for his view, had he been clearer.

In one way, Moore is reminiscent of Sidgwick's dogmatic intuitionists in holding that genuine intuitions—at least on the assumption that they are self-evident—cannot be proved and "must be simply accepted or rejected." But there is at least one difference. Although Moore takes "an intuition" to be a self-evident proposition and incapable of proof, he apparently does not think that *intuitions*, which are cognitions, can have only self-evident propositions as objects (see, e.g., p. 108). In this Moore is like Sidgwick. But whereas with Sidgwick there is some question whether the self-evident might be provable and thus known *both* inferentially and— though not at the same time—by intuition, Moore takes the self-evident to be such that there can be no reasons for it, and it must be apprehended—thus grasped non-inferentially—if it is to be known. On this important point, as we shall see, Prichard and Ross held the Moorean view.

3. H. A. PRICHARD AND THE REASSERTION OF DOGMATIC INTUITIONISM

We have seen that both Sidgwick and Moore reject "dogmatic intuitionism," which posits intuitive moral knowledge only for common-sense moral propositions. These contrast with grand theoretical assertions, such as the principle of benevolence, or with axiological propositions about intrinsic value, say that aesthetic pleasure is intrinsically good, which are not directly moral, if moral at all. Prichard may be seen as asserting his own brand of dogmatic intuitionism against both Sidgwick and Moore, among many others.

Prichard's famous "Does Moral Philosophy Rest on a Mistake?" indicates both a commitment to positing non-inferential intuitive knowledge and an insistence that basic moral obligations cannot be known non-inferentially. Illustrating the first commitment, he says,

> We recognize, for instance, that this performance of a service to X, who has done us a service, just in virtue of it being the performance of a service to one who has rendered a service to the would-be agent, ought to be done by us. This apprehension is immediate, *in precisely the sense in which a mathematical apprehension is immediate*, e.g. the apprehension that this three-sided figure, in virtue of its being three-sided, must have three angles . . . and it is only stating this fact from the other side to say that in both cases the fact apprehended is self-evident.[12]

Sidgwick had made a similar mathematical comparison (and is fruitfully compared with Prichard on the analogy intended). But it is Moore, in his contention that a genuine intuition cannot be proved, who comes to mind when Prichard expresses the second point just referred to—and the main point of the article:

> [I]f, as is almost universally the case, by Moral Philosophy is meant the knowledge which would satisfy this demand ["to have it *proved* to us" that we ought to do certain things], there is no such knowledge, and all attempts to attain it . . . rest on the mistake of supposing the possibility of proving what can only be apprehended directly in an act of moral thinking. Nevertheless, the demand is inevitable until we . . . realize the self-evidence of our obligations, i.e., the immediacy of our apprehension of them. (P. 16)

If we seek an argument for this unprovability view, we do not easily find one, at least in Prichard. But an argument is certainly needed. Even if we grant that "our apprehension" of the principles is immediate, in the sense that we who adequately understand them see their truth noninferentially, it does not follow that *every* apprehension of them—or at least every case of knowing or justifiedly believing them—must be immediate. Perhaps the analogy to elementary mathematical propositions, such as the very simple geometrical proposition Prichard cites, makes it seem that no argument for the unprovability thesis is needed. But surely the very simple, luminously self-evident mathematical propositions in question can be grasped far more easily than their intended moral analogues. They are not good examples to support the claim that the self-evident as such is unprovable.

Whether or not Prichard thought he needed an argument for his unprovability claim, he has a potentially relevant argument in a later paper. Arguing against Bishop Butler (among others), whom he takes to have held that the reason why we ought to do anything whatever is "the conduciveness of the action to our happiness or advantage," he says:

> It is easy to see that if we persist in maintaining that an action, to be right, must be advantageous [a project he also ascribes to Plato's attempt to do "moral philosophy"], we cannot stop short of maintaining that it is precisely advantageousness and nothing else which renders an action right . . . But this is obviously something which no one is going to maintain, if he considers it seriously . . . our doing so, so far from helping us, would render it impossible for us to vindicate the truth of our ordinary moral convictions. For whenever in ordinary life we think of some particular action as a duty, we are not simply thinking of it as right, but also thinking of its rightness as constituted by the possession of some definite characteristic other than that of being advantageous to the agent . . . e.g. *fulfilling* the *promise* we made to X yesterday.[13]

The argumentation here cries out for explication and defense. So far as I can tell, Prichard is presupposing that if there is a way of knowing that obligatory actions conceived simply as such have a further morally relevant property, or at least one that morally justifies performing them, then that property must be what *renders* them obligatory, and we must think of them as obligatory in virtue of having that property. If he was influenced by Moore's contention that for self-evident propositions there is no "logical reason," in the sense of an ontic ground that renders them true, this preemption thesis might well be expectable.[14] For plainly he has no doubt of the self-evidence of the moral principles in question; he might naturally think, then, that apart from a reason for their truth—and there is none— there is no way of showing that the obligatoriness they affirm of various kinds of deeds, such as promise-keeping, *must* have a further characteristic.

Is there a good argument for Prichard's view here? Despite arguing against Plato's, Butler's, and Kant's cases for the advantage thesis, he does not even consider the possibility of a kind of deontic overdetermination wherein two evidentially independent properties, such as being divinely commanded and according with a version of the categorical imperative, are each sufficient to render obligatory the kinds of action that are such. They can play this role, moreover, without our having to *think* of the action as a duty. Foundations need not be visible from the structures they support.

Prichard also seems to presuppose that obligatoriness and advantage cannot be common results of the same grounds, such as a realization of virtues of character. Yet realizing those virtues might be both to our advantage—since it fulfills our nature and is sufficient to achieve a good "external" result—and obligatory in itself or even the ground of obligation. One could then appeal to the notion of realizing virtue to explain and to prove both the truth of certain common-sense moral principles and the claim that adhering to them is ultimately to one's advantage.[15]

Suppose, however, that we grant Prichard's claim that one cannot show obligatory actions to have a necessary consequence of a morally relevant kind unless we take their production of that consequence as their ground. Does it follow that moral philosophy rests on a mistake? I think not, either on the epistemological question of some kind of provability of everyday moral principles or (as Chapter 4 will argue) on the ontological question of their groundability. There could still be a way to prove that certain kinds of actions are indeed obligatory (and, as I shall argue in Chapter 2, it could also be true that there can be intuitive, non-inferential knowledge of their obligatoriness). For they might have a ground that can be known to be such and from which their obligatoriness can be deduced. This was indeed the position of Sidgwick and Moore. As a dogmatic intuitionist, Prichard was bound to deny it. But the argumentative strategy he mounts here (or, to my knowledge, anywhere) does not refute them.

Whatever the cogency of Prichard's arguments against the project of providing for knowledge of duty on the basis of certain premises, Ross apparently accepted them, and the effect of that both on the development of intuitionism in the twentieth century and on its perception among non-intuitionist moral philosophers has been profound. Before we consider Ross, however, we would do well to examine the formulation of intuitionism offered by C. D. Broad.

4. C. D. BROAD AND THE CONCEPT OF FITTINGNESS

It would be easy to miss the significance of Broad's portrait of intuitionism in his *Five Types of Ethical Theory* because it is offered in the course of his discussion of Sidgwick, and Broad does not directly endorse intuitionism. He aims, however, to "state a form of intuitionism which is not open to Sidgwick's objections and is not flagrantly in conflict with common sense."[16] This section, together with Broad's discussion of Sidgwick and his conclusion in the book, leaves little doubt that he regards intuitionism in this form as plausible. The theory is presented in four segments.

Broad first describes an agent called upon to decide whether to do something as being in the "initial phase" (p. 218). Here the question is how to affect the course of events, though Broad does not say that all such agents actually ask themselves this question. Second, in making such a decision there is an important matter of fittingness: "Fittingness or unfittingness is a direct relation between an action or emotion and the total course of events in which it takes place . . . the action might be fitting to certain factors of a certain phase but unfitting to other factors" (p. 219). For instance, if a candidate for office has done me a favor, then "to prefer him to a better qualified candidate would fit one aspect of the situation, since it would be rewarding a benefactor; but it would be unfitting to other factors in the situation, since it would be an act of bad faith . . . as an elector" (p. 219). The suggestion is that, overall, the action ill-befits the whole course of events in question, including the period after the selection. One's final duty is thus to abstain from it.

How are we to determine the overall fittingness of an action relative to something else, such as a previous deed? This brings us to Broad's third main point about the intuitionism he portrays:

> By analogy with mechanics we may talk of the 'resultant fittingness' and the 'component fittingnesses'. But, unfortunately, there is no simple general rule, like the parallelogram of forces principle, by which the resultant fittingness can be calculated from the component fittingnesses. (P. 220)

Even when we determine the resultant fittingness, however, there is a further variable: utility. To ascertain this, we "consider simply the intrinsic goodness or badness of such a course of events" (p. 220), i.e., the course of events yielded by performing the action. With the notion of utility added to that of fittingness, Broad comes to his fourth main point, an articulation of a conception of right and wrong actions:

> the rightness or wrongness of an action in a given initial situation is a function of its fittingness in that situation and its utility in that situation. The pure Deontologist would deny that its utility or disutility was relevant . . . The pure teleologist would deny that there is such a relation as direct fittingness. (P. 221)

As compared with the kind of intuitionism Sidgwick criticizes (the dog-matic kind), this kind avoids two mistakes: first, that of identifying rightness with fittingness and thus failing to see that utility is relevant; second, that of taking too simpleminded a view of fittingness (p. 222). To avoid these, the intuitionist must "moderate his claims . . . He will be confined to state-ments about the *tendencies* to be wrong" (p. 222). Using the example of lying, Broad mentions the special case of lies warranted by the need to shield a third party. There is an immediate unfittingness of lying (relative to, say, the situation of a normal request for information); but, on the joint basis of considerations of fittingness and utility, the act is right.

Broad implies, however, that knowing the basis of the resultant fit-tingness of an action is one thing, and knowing a rule by which to describe how the fittingness (partially) grounds the rightness of an action it warrants is quite another. He concludes that "it is very doubtful whether any general rules can be given for balancing one kind of fittingness against another or for balancing fittingness on the whole against utility on the whole" (p. 222). Here he apparently speaks for himself; and his point about the diffi-culty of giving general rules is one that (as we shall see) Ross develops in more detail.

In his conclusion, Broad lays out some epistemological points that also suggest he speaks for himself in putting forward the intuitionist view just described. Noting that he thinks it is "very likely, though not absolutely certain, that Ethical Naturalism is false, and that ethical concepts are *sui generis*" (p. 281), he goes on to describe them as a priori and to maintain that "there are necessary propositions connecting ethical with non-ethical characteristics" (p. 282). He is apparently not allowing for the possibility that such necessary propositions are empirical. But even if he is, he goes on to make a rationalist claim of a kind characteristic of the major intu-itionist views: "there are self-evident propositions of the form: 'Such and such a type of intention or emotion would necessarily be fitting (or un-fitting) to such and such a kind of situation'. In any possible world it would be fitting to feel gratitude toward one's benefactors . . ." (p. 282). In his terminology (explained above), the point is that there are self-evident prop-ositions about the tendencies of an action. "But it does not follow that any propositions about *total rightness* are self-evident," since overall fittingness is a matter of resultant "fittingnesses," and since the rightness of an action "will also depend on the intrinsic goodness and badness of its conse-quences" (p. 282).

The rationalism of this view should not be exaggerated. In calling moral concepts a priori, for instance, Broad is not denying *any* role to experience, particularly in giving us understanding of the concepts that figure in self-evident propositions. Like other rationalist moral philosophers, he thinks that "Reason needs to meet with concrete instances of fitting or unfitting intentions and emotions before it can rise, by Intuitive Induction, to the insight that *any* such intention or emotion would necessarily be fitting (or unfitting) in *any* such situation" (p. 282). The point seems akin to the idea that experience provides raw material for acquiring a priori knowledge but is not its foundation. It can be a genetic basis for such knowledge without being an epistemic basis for it.[17]

There are strong parallels between the view Broad states here and Ross's. In part because Broad published this work in the same year Ross published *The Right and the Good* (1930), it is not evident from their published work up to that time what influence either might have had on the other. Interesting though that question is, however, it is not important for this book. The comparison between the two positions, by contrast, is important, and at this point we can best proceed by considering the more developed intuitionism presented by Ross.

5. W. D. ROSS AND THE THEORY OF PRIMA FACIE DUTY

In Ross's presentation of intuitionism, we have the view in a form in which it is still widely regarded as a competitor with the best alternative contemporary moral theories. This probably does not hold for any other historically influential intuitionist position,[18] and the point warrants more attention to Ross in this book than is appropriate for any other intuitionist. This is not to suggest that Ross's position cannot be improved by incorporating elements of other intuitionist views—and of non-intuitionist views. But in a treatment of the early twentieth-century formulations of the position we can appropriately give the largest share of attention to Ross and indeed to *The Right and the Good*.

Two Common Uses of 'Intuitionism' in Moral Philosophy

Partly because of Ross's influence, there are currently two main uses of the term 'intuitionism'. In one use, intuitionism is conceived as an overall kind of ethical theory; in the other, it is a moral epistemology taken to characterize such theories. In a third use, built on the first, intuitionism is an overall kind of ethical theory taken *together with* a set of specific normative principles, such as those offered by Ross. His ethics is intuitionist on all three counts, but it is the first two that mainly concern me until Chapter 5.

In the first, overall conception of intuitionism as an ethical theory—the conception that moral philosophers most often have in mind in referring to intuitionism without qualification—the view has three main characteristics. (1) It is an ethical *pluralism*, in the sense that it affirms an irreducible plurality of basic moral principles (Sidgwick and Moore, to be sure, are not generally considered pluralists about the right as opposed to the good, but they are usually specifically cited if their versions of intuitionism are under discussion). (2) Each principle centers on a different kind of *ground* for action, conceived as a factor implying a prima facie moral duty and knowable by ordinary moral agents. The ground might itself be an action, like making a promise; a cognition, such as noticing that a person will bleed to death without one's help; or an accessible fact, such as the possibility that one can contribute to the well-being of others. It is *in virtue of* grounds of these sorts that one has the duty in question. (3) Each moral principle is taken to be in some sense intuitively known by those who appropriately understand it.

By way of interpretation, we might think of (1) as structural and logical; it affirms a plurality of basic principles affecting different kinds of conduct, none being considered deducible from any other or from some master principle. It thus denies, against both Kantian and utilitarian theories as Ross represented them, that there is just one basic moral principle. (2) is ontological: each principle is grounded on a different kind of element that constitutes a basis of the obligation the principle expresses. (3) is epistemological; it locates the basic principles with respect to their knowability. Other important elements in at least the most plausible intuitionist positions will soon emerge, but (1)–(3) are central for the positions most commonly called 'intuitionist'.

It is noteworthy that (1)–(3) do not entail ethical non-naturalism—roughly the view that moral properties are not "descriptive."[19] I do not take non-naturalism as *basic* in an intuitionist ethics as such, and it will become clear in this and later chapters how few distinctively intuitionist—or at least Rossian—claims depend on it. But the major intuitionists have denied naturalism; and in part because of Moore's influential case against it, intuitionism is typically considered a non-naturalist view, and the main points in this book will be compatible with so interpreting it.

In the second, epistemological conception of intuitionism, the view is roughly the thesis that basic moral judgments and basic moral principles are non-inferentially knowable and that, for those who justifiedly hold them non-inferentially, they are justified by, and constitute knowledge on the basis of, the non-inferential deliverances of reason. Reason is often conceived as a rational, intuitive "faculty," but it is not confined to apprehension of self-evident truths. It may be better understood in language that is relatively neutral psychologically: as the mental capacity crucial for understanding logical and mathematical truths, a capacity viewed as differing in crucial ways from sense perception and other possible routes to non-inferential knowledge or justification.

A number of writers, particularly critics of intuitionism, take it to imply the stronger thesis that the intuitive faculty in question yields indefeasible knowledge of self-evident moral truths. One concern of this chapter is whether this stronger conception applies to Ross as opposed to, say, Prichard and the dogmatic intuitionists described by Sidgwick.

The position of Ross is widely regarded as intuitionist in both the overall and epistemological senses, hence as pluralist and as implying that we have intuitive moral justification and intuitive moral knowledge.[20] My chief concern with Ross in this chapter is his intuitionist moral epistemology. Chapters 2–4 will address the ways in which an intuitionist theory should be conceived as pluralistic. This epistemology is, however, fundamental in intuitionism as an overall ethical view even if intuitionism is not conceived as necessarily pluralistic,[21] and an examination of the epistemology will ultimately lead us to a fruitful discussion of the pluralism of the view.[22] We can best clarify and appraise this epistemology by first examining the basic elements of Ross's ethical theory.

The Rossian Conception of Prima Facie Duty

In *The Right and the Good* Ross proposed, as fundamental both to philosophical ethics and to everyday life, a now famous list of prima facie duties: duties of fidelity (promise-keeping and also honesty, conceived as fidelity to one's word) and reparation, of justice and gratitude, of beneficence and self-improvement, and of non-injury.[23] In calling these duties prima facie, Ross meant to make at least two points: positively, that each duty indicates a kind of moral reason for action and, negatively, that even when we acquire such a duty, say by making a promise, the act in question need not be our final duty, since a competing duty, for instance to attend a sick child, might override the original one.[24]

Overridability of a prima facie duty does not imply that it ever lacks *moral weight*. One should, for example, regret breaking a promise, and perhaps must make reparations for this, even when it was right. The point is simply that a prima facie duty is not necessarily final. Hence, to know that one has it is not sufficient for knowing what, finally, one should *do*. In Broad's terminology, that an act is (for instance) a promise-keeping makes it immediately fitting, but entails only a tendency for it to be right. Whether it *is* right is (for Broad) a matter of its resultant fittingness and its utility. Ross can agree on the first point and, depending on how "utility" is understood (e.g. as a matter of how beneficent the act is), possibly on the second.

A word of further explication is in order. Because it is only under certain conditions that a prima facie duty indicates a final duty—roughly, a duty "all things considered"—prima facie duties are sometimes called *conditional duties*.[25] This may misleadingly suggest that we have prima facie duties only when they *prevail*, i.e., constitute final duty. Worse yet, it may suggest that the *content* of prima facie duties is conditional, as where you promise to pay a bill *if* your friend does not. Here, there is a condition for your *having* the duty to pay, at all: your conditional duty becomes "operative" only if your friend does not pay. But many prima facie duties are not conditional in content. Moreover, whether, if you have a conditional duty, it is prima facie rather than final, is left open by its conditionality. Prima facie duties, far from being possessed only conditionally, are *necessarily* possessed provided their grounds are present.

To illustrate, if you promise to pay the bill (period), then you thereby have a (non-conditional) prima facie duty to do so; and you still have this duty even if a conflicting duty, say to save a life, overrides your prima facie duty to keep the promise. This is why one needs an excuse for not keeping the promise and may owe an explanation to the unfortunate promisee. Without a satisfactory excuse, one is to some degree morally deficient. Given a strong enough conflicting duty, however, *keeping* a promise can be wrong. This shows that prima facie duties are not unconditionally *binding*. There are, then, three notions of conditionality to keep distinct: conditionality of content, of possession, and of bindingness. Prima facie duties are not necessarily conditional in content; they are never conditionally possessed if their grounds are present, since those grounds entail the duties in question; and—as such—prima facie duties are never *unconditionally* binding. All this can be seen more clearly if we consider such duties in more detail.

The central idea underlying the Rossian notion of a prima facie duty, I suggest, is that of a duty which is—given the presence of its ground—

ineradicable but overridable. The presence of its *ground* is crucial. In virtue of that ground one necessarily has a *moral reason* for action. One could indeed talk of such reasons rather than of duties, and—since it is obvious that there are inconclusive reasons—this terminology has the advantage of creating no presumption, or a weaker presumption, that one ought on balance to do the thing in question. Ross's terminology, however, has other advantages and can serve quite adequately. Duties, like reasons, depend on their grounds. If, for instance, others could not benefit from my help, I would have no prima facie duty of beneficence, since the ground for the duty would be absent; but since they can, I unavoidably have this duty.

Given the presence of its ground, a prima facie duty is ineradicable even where two grounds yield conflicting duties and one prevails over the other, as where the duty to keep a promise outweighs the duty to express gratitude (which could require doing what would ordinarily be a favor but in the circumstances would force one to break the promise). Here one retains a moral reason to express the gratitude and may later acknowledge regret at having been unable to express it at the appropriate time.

A ground that is present at one time, however, may, without being overridden, cease to exist at another time. Consider the duty to keep a promise. Where the promisee releases us from a promise, or where the fulfillment of the duty becomes impossible in a certain way, say because the person we had a duty to help has died, there is no longer any such duty (though there may be a related one, such as a duty to make reparations for getting ourselves into a situation in which we can no longer keep a promise). Here, the prima facie duty is *cancelable* by removal of that ground. By contrast, overriding conditions do not cancel the duty they override. A duty's being overridden by one or more conflicting prima facie duties implies that its ground is outweighed, but not that the ground is removed. A superior counter-force blocks, but does not eliminate, the force it overpowers.

It may strike some readers that, contrary to a widespread impression, many philosophers and others who do applied ethics (practical, as opposed to theoretical, ethics) might be intuitionists. This is true. Appeals to intuitions in resolving moral questions are a pervasive strategy in contemporary ethical discourse, and many who make them are at least implicitly committed to some form of intuitionism in the overall sense described above. But only a small proportion of the many who appeal to intuitions (or, similarly, to considered judgments) as evidence in ethical theorizing would espouse ethical intuitionism. I believe it will become clear that this may be not because of the implausibility of intuitionism as characterized here, but because of certain pronouncements, by Ross and others, that intuitionism does not require. If I am correct, then many of the case-oriented *intuitivists*, as we might call them, may be able to endorse some version of intuitionism in giving a theoretical account of their evidential appeals to intuitions. With that possibility in mind, let us consider one of the Rossian concepts that have caused most resistance to his view: self-evidence.

The Purported Self-Evidence of Rossian Principles of Duty

Ross stressed a number of features of his position, and at least some of these have become part of the common conception (so far as there is one) of intuitionism. Four particularly need emphasis. First, he insisted on its irreducible pluralism: there is no one thing, such as enhancing goodness in the world, that is our only direct, overall duty.[26] Second, he emphasized the self-evidence of the propositions expressing our prima facie duties:

> That an act *qua* fulfilling a promise, or *qua* effecting a just distribution of good . . . is *prima facie* right, is self-evident; not in the sense that it is evident from the beginning of our lives, or as soon as we attend to the proposition for the first time, but in the sense that when we have reached sufficient mental maturity and have given sufficient attention to the proposition it is evident without any need of proof, or of evidence beyond itself. It is evident just as a mathematical axiom, or the validity of a form of inference, is evident . . . In our confidence that these propositions are true there is involved the same confidence in our reason that is involved in our confidence in mathematics . . . In both cases we are dealing with propositions that cannot be proved, but that just as certainly need no proof.[27]

Third—and this point is less often borne in mind by philosophers discussing intuitionism—Ross apparently intended this claim of self-evidence to hold for *kinds* of acts, not particular deeds. He says, for example, "we are never certain that any particular possible act is . . . right," and, clarifying this,

> we apprehend *prima facie* rightness to belong to the nature of any fulfillment of a promise. From this we come by reflection to apprehend the self-evident *prima facie* rightness of an individual act of a particular type . . . But no act is ever, in virtue of falling under some general description, necessarily actually right; its rightness depends on its whole nature and not any element in it.[28]

His positive point, applied to promising, is in part that when one thinks clearly about what it *is* to promise a particular friend to do something, one can see that doing the deed is called for and would be right, barring special circumstances such as a medical emergency.

His negative point, in the Rossian terminology just introduced, is something like this: from a general description of the grounds that yield a prima facie duty, for instance from the description of an act of mine as a promise, it does not follow that the duty (here the duty to keep the promise) is not overridden; nor is it self-evident that it is not in fact overridden, however clear that may be in many cases. It is not self-evident, for example, that no medical emergency will intervene and override my duty to keep the promise, or even that I am not forgetting a weightier duty that, in keeping the promise, I would fail to fulfill. (These points parallel Broad's views, cited above, about immediate vs. resultant fittingness and about the overall rightness of acts.)

The fourth and final point is that in explaining how we apprehend the moral truths in question, Ross appealed to something like what we commonly call intuitions. He said, for instance, that if someone challenges

> our view that there is a special obligatoriness attaching to the keeping of promises because it is self-evident that the only duty is to produce as much good as possible, we have to ask ourselves whether we really, when we reflect, *are* convinced that [as he takes Moore to hold] this is self-evident . . . it seems, on reflection, self-evident that a promise, simply as such, is something that *prima facie* ought to be kept . . . the moral convictions of thoughtful and well-educated people are the data of ethics, just as sense-perceptions are the data of a natural science. Just as some of the latter have to be rejected as illusory, so have some of the former; but as the latter are rejected only when they conflict with other more accurate sense-perceptions, the former are rejected only when they conflict with convictions which stand better the test of reflection.[29]

The last point here, to the effect that intuitions are justifiably rejected only when they conflict with other intuitions (as opposed, e.g., to theoretical claims) may remind one of Sidgwick's similar point (noted above) regarding intuitively held common-sense moral principles. But whereas Sidgwick argued for a general (utilitarian) principle usable in reconciling such conflicting elements or in rejecting any that are mistaken, Ross denies that any principle can accomplish this. Ross's treatment of conflicts of prima facie duties merits exploration in some detail.

Conflicts of Prima Facie Duties

Ross does not make clear whether the imagined conflicts are ever resolvable by appeal to generalizations supportable by intuitions, such as one to the effect that promises to meet with one's students have priority over promises to distribute leaflets. Suppose I discover that keeping a promise to comment on a long manuscript will take vastly more time than anyone could foresee. Something rather general may occur to me (if I follow Ross): that I have prima facie duties of other sorts, arising, for instance, from considerations of beneficence as well as from other promises, say to my friends. As I reflect about my overall duties, my sense that I must prepare the comments may conflict with my sense that I should fulfill other duties. Ross countenances this kind of conflict; but because he treats "the verdicts of the moral consciousness of the best people as the foundation on which we must build" and is thinking of judgments about concrete moral options, he seems to believe that ethical generalizations (other than the basic principles of prima facie duty) do not, *independently* of those judgments and the basic principles, carry evidential weight in such conflicts. One should not, for example, appeal to a second-order generalization that duties of justice are stronger than duties of fidelity. Rather, one should focus on the specific facts in the situation of conflict and, in that light, determine one's actual duty. If long experience shows that by and large duties of justice prevail in such cases, that rule of thumb may thereby acquire some authority; but it has none a priori or even independently of generalization from the verdicts constituted by judgments made in the light of the facts of each case of conflict and with the presupposition of the basic principles of duty.

The task of conflict resolution here is very much like that of using Aristotelian practical wisdom in dealing with a moral problem. For Ross as for Aristotle, a rule may emerge *on the basis of the resolution* one reaches. But there is not necessarily any rule that the agent or anyone else need ever have been aware of, *antecedently* governing each particular case one may encounter. I may, through my reflection on such a conflict of duties, frame a rule for similar future cases; but I do not bring to every case a ready-made rule that, irrespective of my intuitive judgments about the case, tells me what to do.

In this rejection of the view that there are always second-order generalizations available to resolve conflicts of prima facie duties, Ross seems to be, as regards judgments of overall obligation, a *particularist* rather than a generalist, in this sense: in order to determine what generalizations hold, we must attend to particular cases to which they apply, even if it is *repeatable features* of those cases, such as their being acts of relieving suffering, that reveal the general truths we reach through reflection on the cases.[30] This is a point not about what *can* be known, but about the order of knowing, the epistemic order: our basic moral knowledge—of prima facie as well as final duties—comes from reflection on particular cases calling for moral decision, where those cases are properly conceived in terms of their repeatable features.

If Ross's rationalism is in certain ways reminiscent of Plato, his epistemology of moral judgment is more Aristotelian. It is particularist in emphasizing the need to consider the details of each case that calls for moral assessment; and it is holistic in insisting that we take into account all the elements of the case which, in the light of all the applicable prima facie duties, practical wisdom would have us consider.

Our most elemental moral knowledge, then, does not come from reflection on abstract, universal moral propositions. We do not, for instance, apprehend a Platonic form of justice, or grasp the Kantian categorical imperative, a priori, and then apply it to the issue at hand with a view to formulating, on the basis of it, a "theorem" that resolves our problem. That abstract, monistic approach, conceived as making knowledge of even prima facie duties dependent on knowledge of a single paradigm or principle, and as grounding all of those duties in that paradigm or principle or in some single value it expresses, is also precluded by Ross's pluralism. But pluralism is not his only demand. He would also reject even a set of mutually irreducible rules if they were abstractions imposed on particular cases in the way the categorical imperative or a principle of utility might be, rather than derived from reflection on particular cases.

An example of commitment to such a set of rules would be an a priori *hierarchism*, a view on which some of the prima facie duties automatically outweigh one or more others. Ross would reject this because, for him, as for intuitionists in general, there is neither a *complete* ordering of duties in terms of moral weights—a ranking of duties from strongest to least strong—nor even any *pairwise ordering*, an invariable ranking of some pair of the prima facie duties, as where the duty of non-maleficence (say, to avoid killing) is always said to outweigh that of beneficence (e.g. to save life).[31] To be sure, these points do not entail that *no* comparisons between strengths of (prima facie) duties can be proper objects of intuition. Given a typical pattern of facts concerning a babysitter annoyed by a cranky infant, one might have a quite secure intuition that the babysitter's duty not to flog the child to death is stronger than the duty not to administer a soporific dose of vodka.

Some General Features of Ross's Moral Epistemology

We can now compare Ross's view with the common conception of intuitionism (in moral epistemology) noted earlier. He fits that conception in holding that the basic moral truths—which he takes to be expressed by his principles of prima facie duty—are self-evident. But he does not posit a special rational faculty. He is not committed to the existence of a "part" of the mind, or even a special capacity of reason, required only for moral thought, if indeed he is committed to any bifurcation or modularization of the mind. He talks, to be sure, of moral consciousness and of "apprehension" (roughly, understanding) of those self-evident truths (by 'apprehension' he often means a species of what is commonly meant by 'intuition'). But in presenting his moral epistemology he emphasizes, as did Sidgwick and Prichard, that the prima facie moral duties are recognized in the same way as the truth of mathematical axioms and logical truths. Ross says, for instance,

> We find by experience that this couple of matches and that couple make four matches . . . and by reflection on these and similar discoveries we come to see that it is of the nature of two and two to make four. In a precisely similar way we see the *prima facie* rightness of an act which would be the fulfillment of a particular promise . . . and when we have reached sufficient mental maturity to think in general terms, we apprehend prima facie rightness to belong to the nature of any fulfillment of promise. (Pp. 32–33)

Ross also speaks (e.g., in the same passage) of the relevant moral and mathematical propositions' becoming "self-evident to us" (p. 32). He does not always distinguish apprehending the truth of a proposition that *is* self-evident from apprehending *its self-evidence*.[32] This is an important point, since (if there are self-evident propositions) it should be easy to apprehend the truth of at least some of them, whereas the epistemic *status* of propositions, for example their justification or self-evidence or apriority, requires using theoretical notions and is a paradigm source of disagreement. It should be noted, however, that even apprehension of the self-evidence of propositions does not require having a special faculty. But suppose it did. Does Ross's overall position commit him to our having non-inferential knowledge of the self-evidence, as opposed to the truth, of the relevant principles? I think not. If not, then one apparently common view of intuitionism can be set aside as a misconception. Let me explain.

We might know that a moral principle is self-evident only on a limited basis, say from knowledge that the grounds on which we know that principle to be true are conceptual as opposed to empirical (e.g., observational). We would know its truth *on* these grounds; we would know its self-evidence through knowledge *about* the grounds, knowledge to the effect that they are an appropriate kind for a self-evident truth. For instance, suppose we think we know a moral proposition, say that there is a prima facie duty to keep promises, (a) on the basis of understanding the concepts involved in this proposition and (b) non-inferentially (roughly, without dependence on some premise as evidence). We might plausibly think it follows, from our having this kind of knowledge of the moral proposition, that it is self-evident.

This way of knowing the status of a Rossian proposition expressing a basic prima facie duty requires having concepts of self-evidence, of non-inferentiality, and, in effect, of a priori knowledge. But *none* of these concepts is required simply to know, as intuitivists might take themselves to know, that there is a prima facie duty to keep promises. It is, however, that first-order proposition, the principle that promise-keeping is a duty, and not the second-order thesis that this principle is self-evident, which is the fundamental thing we must be able to know intuitively if a Rossian intuitionism is to succeed in the twofold way in which Ross apparently intended it: as a moral theory and as a practical moral guide to everyday life. As moral agents, we need intuitive knowledge of our basic duties. For any Rossian intuitionism, they are not derivable from non-moral propositions, nor could they be known through regressive or circular inferences or even through pure coherence considerations. We do not, as moral agents, need intuitive knowledge of the status of the principles of duty. We do not need to know that at all. Moral theorists do seek such knowledge, but it may or may not be inferential.

This brings us to the last key point in the most common conception of intuitionism: the idea that it posits *indefeasible justification*—roughly, justification that cannot be undermined or overridden—for any cognition constituting a genuine intuition. Ross as ethical intuitionist is not committed to this general idea, even if he regarded certain kinds of beliefs, say of luminously self-evident principles of logic, as indefeasibly justified. Granted, some intuitionists have sought such a status for the intuitively knowable; recall Sidgwick's suggestion that we need moral knowledge that is "indubitable and irrefragable." I find no equivalent suggestion in Ross.

Once it is seen that in Ross's intuitionism the primary role of intuition is to give us direct, i.e., non-inferential, knowledge (or at least justified belief) of the *truth*, rather than of the self-evidence, of moral propositions (especially certain moral principles), there is less reason to think that moral beliefs resting on an intuitive apprehension of principles are indefeasibly justified. Indeed, given Ross's quite reasonable insistence that a certain mental maturity is needed to apprehend the truth of his principles of duty, defeasibility might be expected. For surely when a maturing person reaches just the minimal threshold for justification, plausible arguments by credible people could defeat it. In the hands of powerful skeptics, such arguments can perhaps defeat much justification that goes well beyond that threshold.

Even if self-evidence were the main element that is intuitively apprehended, Ross would be entitled to hold—and in fact stresses—that there can be conflicts of moral "convictions" in which some are given up "just as" in scientific inquiry some perceptions are given up as illusory (see the quotation above from pp. 39–41 of *The Right and the Good*). If intuitions are sometimes properly given up in this way—and the convictions in question are apparently a species of what are commonly called intuitions—the justification of intuitions is plainly defeasible (subject to being undermined or overridden); and so, at least with respect to moral judgments of particular deeds, defeasibility is to be expected.

We can now see something that does not seem to have been generally noticed by critics of intuitionism and is at least not emphasized by Ross. The view that the justification of moral intuitions is defeasible, even when they are grounded in the careful reflection Ross thought appropriate to them, is quite consistent with his claim that the self-evident truths in question do not admit of proof. That a proposition does not admit of proof is an epistemic fact about *it* and leaves open that a person might have only poor or overridden grounds for *believing* it. It is true that paradigm cases of presumptively unprovable propositions—such as luminously self-evident simple axioms—invite the sense of indefeasibility. But a proposition's having the epistemic status of unprovability does not entail that one cannot lose one's justification for believing it, or fail to become justified in believing it upon considering it, or even fail to find it intuitive and for that reason not come to believe it at all.

It must be granted, however, that by putting us in mind of the simplest logical and mathematical truths, Ross's unprovability claim easily creates the mistaken impression that genuine intuitions are either infallible or justificationally indefeasible or both. Nonetheless, nothing in his theory as set out in *The Right and the Good* is inconsistent with the rather striking disclaimer earlier made by Moore, following his sketch of what constitutes an intuition (and quoted in part above).[33] In calling propositions intuitions, Moore tells us, he means "*merely* to assert that they are incapable of proof; I imply nothing whatever as to the manner or origin of our cognition of them. Still less do I imply (as most Intuitionists have done) that any proposition whatever is true, *because* we cognise it in a particular way or by the exercise of any particular faculty . . . in every way in which it is possible to cognise a true proposition it is also possible to cognise a false one."[34] Apparently, for Moore as for Ross, even if the truth or self-evidence of a proposition can be apprehended by reflection, there need be no special faculty yielding the apprehensions; and whatever the basis of those apprehensions, it is of a kind that can produce mistaken beliefs, including some that one would naturally *take* to be apprehensions of self-evident truths.[35] Anyone aware that mistaken beliefs can arise from apprehensions or intuitions (or in any other way one can "cognise" a proposition) should be willing to regard intuitions (in the psychological sense) as capable of being unjustified or even false.

6. INTUITIONS, INTUITIONISM, AND REFLECTION

If Ross's view is a paradigm of intuitionism, then a widely held conception of intuitionism is inadequate. Above all, he is (by his major views) committed neither to the existence of a special faculty of intuition—such as a capacity peculiar to ethical subject matter—nor to the epistemic indefeasibility of the "self-evident" judgments that reflection yields.[36] The same seems true of Moore. This section will clarify further what an intuitionist like Ross *is* committed to. I begin with a sketch of the notion of an intuition, in the psychological, specifically *cognitive* sense in which it is an element like (and perhaps a kind of) belief. We have not been discussing, and need not take up, intuitions in the *propositional* sense, i.e., propositions of the kind Moore considered unprovable and took to be fitting objects of intuitions in the cognitive sense.

To summarize my negative points about intuitions, I have contended that they need not be infallible or indefeasibly justified; nor need they be, or even be grounded in, deliverances of a special faculty distinct from our general rational capacity as manifested in grasping logical and (pure) mathematical truths and presumably other kinds of truths, ethical and non-ethical. What, then, is distinctive of an intuition?[37]

Four Characteristics of Intuitions

First, an intuition must be non-inferential, in the sense that the intuited proposition in question is not—at the time it is intuitively held—believed on the basis of a premise. Call this the *non-inferentiality (or directness) requirement*. It is not a content requirement; no particular kind of content is implied, even if some kinds, such as self-evident propositions or certain singular moral judgments, readily lend themselves to being intuitively known. The point is not that one *could* not have a premise for what one intuitively believes, but that at the *time* a belief (or other cognition) counts as an intuition, its basis in the person's cognitive system is not inferential. Some intuitionists have emphasized the non-inferentiality of intuitions, and it is at least implicit in Ross and Moore.[38] If we do not grant it, we cannot explain why Ross and Moore do not indicate premises on which intuitive judgments are based or why they should hold that propositions we know intuitively are ever unprovable; for if they took intuition to be potentially inferential and thus potentially based on premises, they would surely have addressed the question whether, for at least some intuitive judgments or some intuitively known propositions, there might be premises that enable us to prove those propositions. They appear to have thought that there are not even premises that ground justified belief of self-evident propositions and thereby a potential inferential basis of the intuitions having those propositions as their content.

Given the close association in some intuitionist writings between the non-inferentiality of intuitions and the *ungroundability thesis*, as we might call it—the view that what is intuitively known cannot be (evidentially) grounded in premises—it is important to stress something about that thesis. It is a view about what can evidence the intuitively known, not about its modality or apriority; it does *not* imply that a proposition intuitively known is necessary or a priori.

Ross apparently believed, however, that the *universal* moral propositions in question (notably his principles of prima facie duty) are both a priori and necessary. But it is doubtful that he regarded as a priori in any sense one's apparently primitive conviction that one has a prima facie duty to keep *this* promise. If he held any aprioristic, rationalist view regarding such

singular moral judgments, it would presumably have been qualified so as
to avoid empirical assumptions. These can be avoided, even for highly
specific duties, by conditionalizing; for instance, one may apprehend the
truth of a concrete generalization like "*If* one sees someone fall off a bicy-
cle and can easily help with a bleeding leg, one (prima facie) ought to do
so." Consider, by contrast, the unconditional proposition that I actually
have this obligation. This presupposes both my existence and that of the
injured person(s) and hence is plainly neither a priori nor necessary. The
conditional generalization, on the other hand, even if one grasps it in
application to an individual case, is not about any actual case. I emphasize
this because, although Ross was a rationalist in his epistemology, much of
his overall intuitionist view—taken as mainly a pluralism committed to
intuitive moral knowledge—does not entail moral rationalism. As important as the rationalist strain in his view is, many elements in that view
do not depend on it.

A second point about intuitions is that they must be moderately firm
cognitions—call this the *firmness requirement*. There may be a gradual
approach to forming an intuition, but we do not have one without a definite sense that the proposition in question holds. Intuitions are typically
beliefs, including cases of knowing. But the term 'intuition' may include
one kind of judgment—such as assentingly saying to oneself that a statement would be dishonest—and other mental events implying belief. A
mere inclination to believe is not an intuition; an intuition tends to be a
"conviction" (a term Ross apparently sometimes used for an intuition) and
tends to be relinquished only through such weighty considerations as a
felt conflict with a firmly held theory or with another intuition. Granted,
some intuitions are easily overcome by doubts or counter-evidences, and
certainly a proposition one is only inclined to believe may be or seem
intuitive. Still, one does not have an intuition with that proposition as its
content until one believes the proposition. We might speak of intuitive
inclinations as opposed to intuitions, and the former need not be denied
some degree of evidential weight. But it would be less than that of intuitions proper: the data would be less clear, just as a view of an unexpected
island in the fog is less clear than it would be in sunlight and provides less
reason to alter one's map. The concepts of intuition and of the intuitive
are not sharp, but nothing in what follows will turn on their vagueness.

Third, intuitions must be formed in the light of a minimally adequate
understanding of their propositional objects—call this the *comprehension
requirement*. That they are formed in this light is doubtless one reason for

their firmness (as least where the proposition in question is genuinely self-evident). Moreover, often intuitions are based on a more than minimally adequate understanding, and this kind of basis of a belief tends both to produce cognitive firmness and to enhance evidential value. We apparently tend to be confident of what we directly see, especially when we understand it well. We are often more confident of such propositions than of what we derive from reasoning, particularly if the reasoning is not self-evidently valid.

As to the required adequacy of this understanding, the standard may be expected to vary with the complexity and perhaps also the modal or epistemic status of the relevant proposition. Ross, like Moore, insists that, before one can apprehend a self-evident moral truth, one must get precisely that true proposition before one's mind. In many passages (including one quoted above) Ross indicates that reflection is required to see the truth of the proposition in question. The more complicated the proposition, or the richer the concepts figuring in it—like the concept of a promise—the more an adequate understanding of that proposition requires.[39] Intuitions are sometimes regarded as arising quickly upon considering a proposition. They need not so arise, and in some cases, such as those in which there is a serious conflict of duties, probably should not so arise. Since the required adequacy of the understanding in question need not be maximal, it may be improved (as well as defeated). There may also be a use of 'understanding' in which certain kinds of inadequacy of understanding of a proposition are compatible with having an intuition of it, but this is not a use appropriate to Ross.

Fourth, I suggest a *pretheoreticality requirement*: roughly, intuitions are neither evidentially dependent on theories nor themselves held as theoretical hypotheses, for instance as propositions posited to explain observable phenomena or embraced by induction from empirical data, such as the proposition that when "intrinsically" more valuable coins are circulated with coins having the same face value but less intrinsic value, the former tend to be hoarded. The point is not that the propositional *content* of an intuition cannot be inferentially justified or in some sense theoretical or even inferentially *held*. It is that although inferential justification is not the only kind possible for the content of an intuition, an intuition *as* such—as a cognition held intuitively—is held neither on the basis of a premise nor as a theoretical hypothesis. (It might seem that if a cognition is non-inferential, it *cannot* be held as a theoretical hypothesis; but that is not so: the *justification* of a non-inferential cognition can derive from justification for other propositions even if they are not premises it is based on, and the kind of explanatory element crucial for such hypotheses is at least not typically appropriate to intuitions.)

If intuitions' being pretheoretical entailed their being *preconceptual*, that would undermine the comprehension requirement: without at least a minimal understanding of the concepts figuring in a proposition, one is not even in a position to find it intuitive. But clearly Ross and other intuitionists intend our "convictions" (intuitions), including those of other people, to be used as data for moral generalization somewhat in the way perceptual beliefs are data for scientific theorizing. Given his understanding of this idea, not only will an intuition not be inferentially based on a theory, or held as a theoretical hypothesis, it will also not epistemically depend on a theory even in the general sense that the theory provides one's justificatory ground (even a non-inferential ground) for the intuition.

The Intuitive and the Theoretical

The independence of theory just described does *not* entail that intuition has a complete independence of theory: an intuition may be defeated and abandoned in the light of theoretical results incompatible with its truth, especially when these results are supported by other intuitions. This is a kind of *negative epistemic dependence* of intuition on theory: the justification of the intuition does not derive from the impossibility of such untoward, hypothetical results, but it can be destroyed by them. Such defeasibility on the part of intuition, unlike the evidential dependence we have considered so far, is not a positive justificatory dependence on any actual theory (and is not naturally called dependence at all); it is a negative dependence on—in the sense of a vulnerability to—disconfirmation by theories, whether actual or possible.[40]

In some ways, the perceptual analogy can mislead. For one thing, an intuition is more like a belief based on a careful observation than like an impression formed from a glimpse, though that impression is equally perceptual and can produce belief. One could, however, speak of sensory "intuitions" in reference to cognitions that rest on observational sense experience in the way perceptual beliefs commonly do when formed under favorable conditions, for instance visual beliefs, acquired in good light, about an island before one. One might think that since my four conditions encompass such cognitions, they are probably too broad; but to build in, say, that intuitions are non-observational cognitions of a conceptual or a classificatory kind, would probably make the conditions too narrow, and the breadth of the characterization is appropriate to our purposes.

The perceptual analogy is also misleading because intuitions need not be about observables: rights and duties are not observable, yet we have intuitions about them. We may see them in the sense of recognizing them, as where one "sees" a right (and that there is a right) to refuse feeding tubes. If what is both non-observable and significantly complex is thereby theoretical, then we certainly have intuitions about theoretical entities; but such "theoretical" intuitions need not be epistemically dependent on any theory.

It is controversial whether, in either intuitive or perceptual cases, there *is* anything pretheoretical to appeal to. But if not—if, for instance, to have concepts sufficient for judging a theory one must be biased by either that theory or another one relevant to judging the theory—then it is not only Ross who has a problem. One would hope that even if every judge has some biases, there are some judges who at least have no biases that vitiate their decisions on the cases they must resolve. Even if no cognition is entirely pretheoretical, perhaps some may be pretheoretical *with respect to* a moral generalization needing appraisal. Granted, this would rule out only theoretical biases. Intuitionists apparently hope that no others are ineliminable, but absence of *all* bias is apparently not part of the concept of an intuition. The effects of biases may indeed help to explain how an intuition can be mistaken. It is not necessary, for purposes of working out a satisfactory intuitionism, that biases always be avoidable. It is enough if, as Ross apparently thought, they are always correctable by further reflection. Such reflection may include comparison with the intuitions of *others*, just as in scientific inquiry one might compare one's observations with those of co-investigators.

Two further points may significantly clarify the sense in which intuitions might be pretheoretical. One (implicit above) is that an intuition's being pretheoretical does not imply that it is indefeasible—not even indefeasible by judgments based on the theory we build from a set of intuitions including the one in question. Recall the case in which I see that keeping a promise is not my final duty because I realize that other duties override my promissory duty. Here, the basis of the other moral considerations is apparently of the same pretheoretical sort as that of the first duty. The second point is that an intuition which is pretheoretical at one time can evolve into a judgment grounded in a theory. A Rossian intuitionism is committed to the existence, at any time when our convictions provide the data for ethics, of pretheoretical intuitions; it is not committed to denying that intuitively held propositions can later be held on the basis of theory-laden assumptions—or that yesterday's intuitions can be given up because they are undermined by today's reflections by "thoughtful, well-educated people." Rossian intuitionism does not require that any evidential propositions be absolutely pretheoretical. Calling a cognition an intuition may commit one to allowing it a certain evidential role, but not to assigning it a specific kind of content or isolating it from integration with, or defeat by, theory.

Let us suppose for the sake of argument that either there are no pretheoretical intuitions or, more likely, *some* of the intuitions needed for confirmation of basic moral principles are in some way theoretical. We can still distinguish between theories that bias the appraisal of a moral principle and theories that do not. If, for instance, a theory of the psychological make-up of persons is needed for the capacity to have certain moral intuitions—for example the intuition that locking a child in a small dark closet for failing to dry the dishes is prima facie wrong—this need not vitiate the appraisal. The intuition may depend on a theoretical (here, psychological) understanding of the fears caused by being locked in a dark closet, but neither the kind nor the level of the relevant theory undermines the justifiability of the intuition. We might, then, distinguish between what is *relatively* and what is *absolutely* pretheoretical: the former is simply pretheoretical relative to the issue in question, say the moral status of the act-type, locking a child in a dark closet. Perhaps a relative notion of the pretheoretical is all that intuitionism needs to meet the objection that theoretical dependence vitiates the justificatory role it claims for intuitions.

If intuitions are both non-inferential and pretheoretical, one might wonder to what extent they represent rationality, as opposed to mere belief or even prejudice. Here it is crucial to recall Ross's requirements of adequate maturity and "sufficient attention." We should also keep in mind that he saw prima facie duties as appropriately *grounded*. One may not, then, simply insist that someone has a duty, or ought to do something, and claim that one "just sees" it. For every duty there is a ground, and Ross's theory implies that people are entitled to ask what constitutes the ground of a duty, to compare it with similar grounds in respect of whether the putative duty is implied, to search for reasons to think that the duty is overridden even if it does exist, and so forth. The intuitionist thesis that some knowledge of what we ought to do is intuitive and non-inferential implies neither that it is not reflective nor that it cannot be supported by argument or refuted by relevant considerations to the contrary.

Even the brief treatments of the intuitionists presented in this chapter bring out certain prominent features of ethical intuitionism. All five philosophers, Sidgwick, Moore, Prichard, Broad, and Ross—and indeed, all of the major versions of intuitionist theory—affirm the possibility of non-inferential knowledge of certain broadly ethical propositions, at least propositions about the good even if not (as with Moore) propositions stating specific obligations; and each philosopher, despite differences in terminology, takes certain general moral principles to be self-evident and (again excepting Moore) considers some singular moral judgments, such as self-ascriptions of promissory duties, to be intuitively and non-inferentially justifiable. There is far more to say about these claims and about the character of Ross's theory in particular. The next chapter will explore how Ross's position may be extended and strengthened. This will require clarifying the notions of intuitive knowledge and self-evidence and distinguishing between the claims he made for his own ethical view and what he was committed to by the central tenets of his intuitionism.

2

Rossian Intuitionism as a Contemporary Ethical Theory

THE INTUITIONISM Ross developed in *The Right and the Good* remains the statement of the position most often illustratively referred to by writers in ethics, and something close to it is defended by a number of contemporary moral philosophers.[1] But as we saw in Chapter 1, his statement of the view leaves both questions of interpretation and some serious problems. There are difficulties concerning the sense in which intuitions are non-inferential, problems in understanding the notion of self-evidence, and a number of philosophical worries confronting intuitionism as a rationalist moral epistemology. This chapter develops a moderate intuitionism that may be called *Rossian* because of its continuity with Ross's stated view, but departs from him on several important points. I first formulate the core of his theory with an eye to constructing a modified version. The next task is to articulate a conception of self-evidence that makes a more moderate intuitionism possible. Using that conception, we can explore the resources and varieties of this position and consider how well such a moderate intuitionism accounts for moral judgment and its role in rational action.

1. THE ROSSIAN APPEAL TO SELF-EVIDENCE

Three elements in Ross's intuitionism are appropriate to the metaethics of any full-blooded version of intuitionism: the claim of irreducible plurality for basic moral principles; the association of each principle with a different kind of ground of duty; and the thesis that each principle is in some sense intuitively knowable by those who appropriately understand it. On the normative side, Ross proposed, as fundamental in both moral practice and ethical theory, the prima facie duties of fidelity, reparation, justice, gratitude, beneficence, self-improvement, and non-injury.[2] As noted in Chapter 1, he took the associated principles to be self-evident and rejected any a priori hierarchy among them.[3]

The Self-Evidence of Prima Facie Duties

We might begin by reiterating Ross's essential self-evidence claim:

> That an act, *qua* fulfilling a promise, or *qua* effecting a just distribution of good . . . is *prima facie* right, is self-evident . . . in the sense that when we have reached sufficient mental maturity and have given sufficient attention to the proposition it is evident without any need of proof . . . just as a mathematical axiom, or the validity of a form of inference, is evident . . . In both cases we are dealing with propositions that cannot be proved, but that just as certainly need no proof.[4]

One crucial role of intuition as a rational capacity is to enable us to apprehend self-evident propositions, which are among the objects of *intuitions*, conceived as cognitions. Ross takes it as both self-evident and intuitive, for instance, that promises are prima facie binding:

> I venture to think that most people . . . cannot accept as self-evident, or even as true, the theory that would require them to do so ["get rid of our view that promise-keeping has a bindingness independent of productiveness of maximum good"]. In fact it seems, on reflection, self-evident that a promise, simply as such, is something that *prima facie* ought to be kept . . . the moral convictions of thoughtful and well-educated people are the data of ethics, just as sense-perceptions are the data of a natural science. Just as some of the latter have to be rejected as illusory, so have some of the former; but as the latter are rejected only when they conflict with other more accurate sense-perceptions, the former are rejected only when they conflict with convictions which stand better the test of reflection.[5]

Two elements need emphasis. Ross speaks of our grasping (or apprehending) the *truth* of the relevant moral and mathematical propositions. But he also speaks of what, in my view, he conceives as our apprehending their *self-evidence*. One indication of this latter focus is his taking us to be aware that we are dealing with propositions which are not in need of proof—*proof-exempt*, we might say.

It may not have occurred to Ross that exemption from proof does not entail the impossibility of proof nor, indeed, even the weaker status of ungroundability. He is influenced, I believe, by the dialectic of argument with other philosophers about what is self-evident, and he is not concentrating on the more basic question of how we can know the truth, as opposed to the self-evidence, of first-order moral propositions.

Such a shift of focus from non-inferential knowability to ungroundability is particularly easy if one thinks that the relevant kind of proposition, if true, *is* self-evident. For then one might not usually expect to find, and would certainly not normally seek, premises for it; or, like Moore and Ross, one would think there can be no such premises—and, as a philosopher, would want to explain why we lack premises by maintaining that the proposition in question is self-evident. Even a decade later, we find a similar affirmation of unprovability in A. C. Ewing. Although his intuitionism is in some ways more moderate than Ross's, Ewing says, of the intuitive grasp of a self-evident entailment, that "such *immediate* reasoning would only be another name for what is commonly called intuition. The connection between *p* and *q* would still be something that you could not *prove* but either saw or did not see."[6]

Two Orders of Apprehension

One reason it might be natural for Ross not to distinguish (or at least not to distinguish explicitly) between apprehending the truth of a proposition that *is* self-evident and, on the other hand, apprehending *its self-evidence*[7] is that on the conception of self-evidence prevailing when he wrote, self-evident propositions are those whose *necessity* is grasped when they are properly understood. This conception is apparent in at least one passage from Broad cited in Chapter 1, and it goes back at least to Kant.[8] If we so conceive self-evident propositions, we are already supposing that understanding them entails *apprehending their necessity*, hence their *modal* status; and particularly if we think of the self-evident as (synthetic) a priori, as Ross and other intuitionists did, then it is natural to suppose we also grasp their *epistemic* status—particularly their self-evidence.

Self-evident propositions have also been considered so luminous that one cannot grasp them *without* believing them.[9] Where they are seen as irresistible in this way, one might easily think they wear necessity on their sleeve, even if one does not hold that understanding them *depends* on grasping their necessity. But seeing the epistemic status of propositions, say their warrant or self-evidence, is a quite different matter from seeing their truth or even their necessity. Even if every self-evident proposition is necessary and can be seen a priori to be so,[10] the distinction between apprehending truth or necessity and apprehending self-evidence remains. The truth of at least some self-evident propositions is easy to apprehend;

but apprehending (or otherwise realizing) self-evidence or even necessity is second order and requires conceptual sophistication.

Furthermore, self-evidence is not a property that in general one can non-inferentially know a proposition to have. Perhaps we can non-inferentially know that it is self-evident that if one person is taller than a second, the second is shorter than the first. But if so, this could be because it fits paradigms with which we associate the notion of the self-evident. Our belief here could also non-inferentially derive from the testimony of someone else. For many self-evident propositions, to know that they are self-evident we must know something about such factors as how they are properly understood or about their modal status, or both, and must infer that they are self-evident from propositions about these elements. Such knowledge requires a degree of conceptual sophistication, or at least certain technical concepts, not needed for knowledge of Rossian principles of duty. In any case, neither a Rossian intuitionism nor any other plausible version of intuitionism commits one to positing *non-inferential* knowledge of the self-evidence, as opposed to the truth, of the relevant principles.

We can now see why one apparently common conception of intuitionism, especially of Ross's, is a mistake. His view does not imply that ordinary moral agents know or would accept the self-evidence of its principles, nor even that moral theorists can know their self-evidence *non-inferentially*. It is first-order moral propositions, such as the principle that there is a prima facie duty to keep promises, and not the second-order thesis that such principles are self-evident, which are the fundamental kind of thing we must be able to know intuitively if a Rossian intuitionism is to succeed.

As to the positive role of self-evidence in the theory, we might consider the concept of self-evidence, by contrast with that of truth, to be an epistemically explanatory notion more appropriate to the metaethics of intuitionism than to its formulation as a normative view. Ross did not deny this, but his exposition leaves unclear the contrast I am stressing, and critics of intuitionism have often not appreciated that one can defend the normative view with a weaker metaethical theory than Ross's and adopt it in practice without taking any particular epistemological or metaphysical position at all.

This is not to slight the importance of the concept of self-evidence for Rossian intuitionism as an *overall* view in ethics. The application of the concept of self-evidence to a proposition explains both how it can be known (roughly, through understanding it) and why its justification requires no premises. Ross naturally wanted to indicate not just *that* his principles are true and knowable but *why* they are. Still, one might surely know the former, intuitively or otherwise, without knowing the latter.

It is, then, one thing to hold, as intuitionists do, that moral agents have intuitive knowledge of their duties (or at least intuitively justified belief as to what their duties are); it is quite another to maintain that they have or need higher-order knowledge or intuition. Neither intuitionists as moral theorists nor we as moral agents need intuitive knowledge of the modal or epistemic status of the principles of duty. Moral agents do not need *any* such second-order knowledge. This latter point can hold even where they know those principles to be true. The possession of first-order knowledge does not imply possessing second-order knowledge that one has it. As to moral theorists, if their purposes sometimes require having that second-order knowledge, it need not be intuitive or otherwise non-inferential.

As indicated in Chapter 1, even cognition grounded in genuine intuition may not be indefeasibly justified. Despite the impression one might get from critics of intuitionism, the view does not imply such cognitive impregnability. Ross may, however, have presupposed it for special cases, and positing it is invited by his comparing the self-evidence of principles of prima facie duty with that of mathematical axioms and valid rules of inference. Nonetheless, for ethical intuitionism as a normative theory, the primary role of intuition is to give us direct, i.e., non-inferential, knowledge or directly justified belief of the *truth* of certain moral propositions. Neither knowledge of the self-evidence of basic moral propositions nor indefeasible justification for believing those propositions is required for guiding moral conduct. They are not required even for one kind of plausible response to ethical skepticism, which raises a regress problem. Skeptics will press the question of what justifies a moral judgment. For any proposition offered in reply, they will go on to ask what justifies it; and so forth. Suppose that in reply one can cite a self-evident proposition. We can be amply justified in believing such a proposition, and in stopping the regress by adducing it, even if we cannot justify claiming it *to be* self-evident. Epistemologists may undertake that higher-order task; but justifying everyday moral judgments does not depend on their success, any more than building a sound structure requires fending off an attack on it.[11]

To be sure, self-evidence may be plausibly argued to entail necessity. Suppose it does. Even the necessary truth of what we believe does not imply that our *justification* for it is indefeasible: we can lose our justification for believing a theorem that is both necessary and a priori because our "proof" of it is shown to be defective. Granted that any Rossian (hence rationalist) version of intuitionism is committed to the self-evidence of basic moral principles, neither intuitionism in general nor Ross's theory in particular need claim that ordinary moral agents must *know* their self-evidence or have indefeasibly justified beliefs of them.

Conclusions of Inference versus Conclusions of Reflection

If I have eliminated one significant element from Ross's view and thereby provided a more moderate intuitionism, on a related matter I want to claim somewhat more than he did and thereby clarify the notions of intuitive knowledge and intuitive justification. There is a sense in which, although an intuition (or an intuitive judgment) is not grounded in a proof or argument, it *can* be a conclusion formed though rational inquiry or searching reflection. A conclusion, in the most general sense, is a proposition arrived at in a certain way or, in its psychological sense, a judgment or other cognition having such a proposition as its object. There are many kinds of routes to conclusions.

Consider reading a poem with a view to deciding whether its language is artificial. After two readings, one silent and one aloud, we might judge that the language is indeed artificial. This judgment could be a response to evidential propositions that occur to one, say that the author has manipulated words to make the lines scan. But the judgment need not so arise. If the artificiality is subtler, there may just be a stilted quality in the poem. In this second case, one judges from a global, intuitive sense of the integration of vocabulary, movement, and content. Call the first judgment of artificiality a *conclusion of inference*: it is premised on propositions noted as evidence. Call the second judgment a *conclusion of reflection*: it emerges from thinking about the poem as a whole, but not from one or more evidential premises. It is more like a response to viewing a painting or to seeing an expressive face than like an inference from propositionally represented information. You respond to a pattern: you notice a stiff movement in the otherwise flowing meter; you are irritated by an inapt simile; you find words dictated by metrical needs rather than warranted by content.

Drawing a conclusion of reflection is a kind of wrapping up of the question, akin to concluding a practical matter with a decision. One has not added up the evidences and inferred their implication; one has obtained a view of the whole and thereby broadly characterized it. Far from starting with a checklist of artificialities, we can compose the relevant list only after studying the poem.

Similarly, consider appraising a letter of recommendation described as strong. After a careful reading, we might judge that it is really not strong. One way to arrive at such a judgment is in response to evidential propositions that strike us, say that the writer puts all of the praise in the mouths of others and endorses none of it. But the letter could exhibit a subtler evasion of commitment: a labored description of progress from poor to good performance, an excess of points that balance the praise, an indirectness about the high commendation. One might then simply feel an element of reservation. In this second case, one might judge by a global, intuitive sense of the integration of vocabulary, detail, and tone. The first judgment about the letter, then, is a conclusion of inference, the second a conclusion of reflection: it emerges from taking in the letter as a whole, but not from noting evidential premises.[12]

This is a good place to stress that intuition is not limited to any one kind of propositional object, and to bring out a related distinction. Particularly because the paradigms—or at least the most influential examples—of intuition in the philosophical literature are apprehensions of logical and mathematical truths, there is a tendency to think intuitions have self-evident propositions as their objects. This conception is unduly narrow. Moreover, quite apart from this narrow conception, there is a tendency to think of intuitions as *focally grounded*: as based simply on a grasp of the proposition taken in abstraction from one's grounds for it. But the literary and testimonial examples illustrate a sense in which intuitions may be *globally grounded*: based on an understanding of the proposition seen in the context of the overall grounds for it.

The distinction between focally and globally grounded intuitions is not sharp. The same holds for a related contrast between abstract and concrete intuitions. There are cases in which an intuition with quite abstract content, like a concrete one with a global content, is grounded in part on a conception of a single concrete illustrative case. The sight of a soldier in an occupying army violently slapping an old man may serve as a paradigm by which the wrongness of injury is memorably seen. It must also be granted that even when our basis for an intuition is highly abstract, we at least normally *can* construct illustrative cases. There is no a priori limit to the richness of detail that can figure in the grounding of an intuition. Granting that no concrete details need figure in such abstract intuitions as that if no As are Bs, then no Bs are As, it is commonly very different with moral judgment, especially where such judgment emerges only upon reflection.

By distinguishing conclusions of reflection from conclusions of inference, intuitionism can account both for our need to reflect in order to reach some moral judgments and for the way in which reflective equilibrium can enhance—or its unobtainability can undermine—our justification for an "intuitive" moral judgment and for at least some moral principles.[13] Just as two details in a poem or a letter can conflict in relation to an interpretation I give, one supporting it and the other not, moral principles might conflict in relation to a decision I make. A moral principle might also have overwhelmingly counterintuitive implications in certain concrete instances. These cases all illustrate a kind of disequilibrium. Comparison and inference may be needed to reach equilibrium among an intuition and other cognitions, and the intuition thus contextualized may be better grounded as a result of the effort, even though, being an intuition, it is not based on inference from premises.[14]

Moreover, given how intuitions are understood—as deriving from the exercise of reason and as having evidential weight—conscientious intuitionists will try to factor into their moral thinking, especially on controversial issues, the apparent intuitions of *others*.[15] This point may in part explain why Ross appealed repeatedly to "what we really think" and compared intuitions in ethics with perceptions in science.[16] Intuitions, then, are not properly conceived as arbitrary or as isolated from like cognitions on the part of others. Many have a basis in reflection and are shared by people who differ greatly in experience and outlook.

By no means all moral intuitions, even concerning matters the agent considers important, are conclusions of reflection. People differ in intuitive reactivity. Some are quick to judge or decide, others are deliberate, still others are slowed by ambivalence. A given person may also change over time, even in responding to the same proposition. I grant that in principle, where one arrives at a conclusion of reflection, one *could* figure out why and *then* formulate, in explicit premises, one's basis for so concluding. This is a point easily missed if we picture intuitions as having self-evident contents, especially if these are conceived as basic in a sense that precludes their being ever known inferentially. The point is also easily overlooked if one is thinking only of focally grounded intuitions and, as is easy in that case, neglecting the rich grounds that may be provided by the kind of reflection that underlies intuitions which constitute conclusions of reflection. Still, the point that a ground of intuitive judgment *can* be formulated through articulation of one's basis for judging does not entail that the ground must do its justificatory work in an inferential way.

On the conception of intuition I am developing, then, it is, in the "faculty" sense, chiefly a non-inferential cognitive capacity, not a non-reflective one. The cognitions in question—intuitions—manifest the capacity so conceived in at least two ways. We might speak of intuitions in the *experiential (occurrent) sense* where they are conscious, experienced cognitive responses, such as arise in a moral assessment of an accusation; this is a kind of "intuiting" of a proposition, though it may be at least partly based (in a non-inferential way) on a property intuition whose object is one or more of the relevant properties or concepts or both. By contrast, an intuition in the *dispositional sense* is roughly the holding of a belief conceived as an intuition in the sense explicated in Chapter 1, as where a once occurrent intuition is retained in memory and is no longer in consciousness.[17] Understanding of the relevant proposition is of course required for any of these cognitions to possess intuitive justification, and, often, understanding comes only with time.[18] Achieving understanding may be so labored that a truth it finally reveals, even non-inferentially, *seems* not to be true and is either not believed or not believed with strong conviction.

2. TWO TYPES OF SELF-EVIDENCE

Two types of self-evidence, a hard and a soft kind, are especially relevant to understanding intuitionism. Before describing them, I want to sketch a general conception of a self-evident proposition. Taking off from the idea (which Sidgwick, Moore, and Prichard all express in passages cited in Chapter 1) that a self-evident proposition is one whose truth is in some way evident "in itself," I construe the basic kind of self-evident proposition as (roughly) a truth such that an adequate understanding of it meets two conditions. First, in virtue of that understanding, one is justified in believing the proposition (i.e., has justification for believing it, whether one in fact believes it or not)—this explains why such a truth is evident *in*

itself. Second, if one believes the proposition on the *basis* of that understanding, then one knows it.[19] Thus (abbreviating and slightly altering the
characterization), a proposition is self-evident provided an adequate understanding of it is sufficient both for being justified in believing it and for
knowing it if one believes it on the basis of that understanding.

Belief and Understanding

The first point is easily underemphasized or denied because it is natural
to conceive the self-evident as believed without question, and even as such
that one cannot help believing it when one considers it. But this conception is mistaken. As this first point indicates, it does not follow from the
self-evidence of a proposition that if one (adequately) understands (and
considers) the proposition, one *does* believe it. This non-belief-entailing
conception of self-evidence is plausible because one can fail initially to
"see" a self-evident truth yet later grasp it in just the way one grasps the
truth of a paradigmatically self-evident proposition: one obvious in itself
the moment we consider it. Take, for example, a self-evident proposition
that is perhaps not immediately obvious: the existence of great-grandchil-
dren is impossible apart from that of four generations of people. A delay
in seeing something, such as the truth of this, need not change the character of what one sees.

There is no need to deny that, upon comprehendingly considering a
self-evident proposition which they adequately understand, rational persons *tend* to believe it. But they need not believe it. In some cases we can
see *what* a self-evident proposition says—and thus understand it—before
seeing *that*, or how, it is true. As this indicates, it is important not to identify
the self-evident with the obvious. It is obvious (to anyone suitably posi-
tioned) that this paper is printed; but that is perceptually evident, not self-
evident. The proposition *itself*, as opposed to acquaintance with what it
describes, contains too little information to reveal its truth. By contrast, it
is self-evident, but not (unqualifiedly) obvious, that if one proposition entails a second, and the second entails a third, and the second or the third
is false, then the first is false.[20]

The notion of adequate understanding is multidimensional. I cannot
attempt a full analysis of it, but I have several clarifying points. First, it
is to be contrasted with mistaken, partial, and clouded understanding.[21]
Moreover, adequate understanding of a proposition is more than simply
getting the general sense of some sentence expressing it, as where one can

parse the sentence grammatically, indicate something of what it means through illustrative examples, and perhaps correctly translate it into another language one knows well. Second, adequacy here implies not only seeing what the proposition says but also a kind of *knowing how*. One must know how to use it in description and reasoning; for instance, one must be able to apply it to—and withhold its application from—an appropriately wide range of cases. Similarly, one must be able to see some of its logical implications, to distinguish it from a certain range of close relatives, and to comprehend its elements and some of their relations.[22] An *inade-quate*—as opposed to limited—understanding of a self-evident proposition does not in general suffice to justify believing it, nor should beliefs of the proposition based on such an understanding be expected to constitute knowledge.

It is also important to recognize quite different kinds of understanding, as opposed to understanding that has the appropriate scope and depth just described. Adequacy of understanding manifests itself in different ways in each case. There are both occurrent and dispositional uses of 'understanding'. The former are illustrated by comprehending a proposition one is entertaining (and so has in mind), the latter by such propositional comprehension as we retain in memory, say after our attention turns elsewhere. A distinct, weaker dispositional use is illustrated by 'Talk to her; she understands such theories', uttered where one has in mind something like this: she has never entertained them, but would (occurrently) understand them upon considering them.

Leaving further subtleties aside, the central point is that in the above characterization of self-evidence, 'understanding' may bear any of the indicated three senses, so long as 'justification' is understood accordingly. There are thus three cases. If we occurrently understand a self-evident proposition, we have occurrent justification for it, roughly, justification grounded largely in elements in our consciousness, such as our awareness of an entailment. If we have strong dispositional understanding of it, we have dispositional justification, roughly in the sense that we can bring justifying elements into consciousness by suitable reflection, including introspection, but not including the kind of inference that produces a new justification.[23] If we have weak dispositional understanding, we have only *structural justification* for it: roughly, although we lack dispositional justification, there is an appropriate accessible path leading (perhaps by natural inferential steps) from justificatory materials accessible to us to an occurrent justification for the proposition.[24] (I shall assume that when knowledge of a self-evident proposition is based on understanding it, the understanding is occurrent or strongly dispositional, but we could devise a conception of such knowledge with a looser connection to understanding.)

Immediate Self-Evidence, Mediate Self-Evidence, and Obviousness

Given the proposed conception of self-evidence, we may distinguish those self-evident propositions that are readily understood by normal adults (or by people of some relevant description, e.g. the mentally mature Ross spoke of) and those they understand only through reflection on them. Call the first *immediately self-evident* and the second *mediately self-evident*, since their truth can be grasped by such people only through the mediation of reflection.[25] This distinction is relative to the selected reference class; but particularly since we are mainly concerned with moral agents, that does not undermine its usefulness in this context.

Since the mediation in question is reflectional and not inferential, the reflection is not a matter of discerning one or more premises and inferring the proposition from them, but rather of reaching the kind of understanding required to see the truth of the proposition "in itself." Still, the reflection may involve drawing inferences that play a special range of roles. For the proposition that it is prima facie wrong to pay people unequally for equal work, there might be inferences about what it means to do equal work and about what one pays *for*, say a material product or a commitment to doing a certain kind of job if the situation demands it. Consider lifeguards, who may do the "same work" if no one needs rescue, yet can do it with different levels of preparedness. The role of inferences is, however, limited largely to clarifying what the proposition in question says: as self-evidence is normally understood, a self-evident proposition is knowable without our relying on any inferential *ground* for it. We may require time to get the proposition in clear focus, but need not reach it by inference from premises. We may have to take a long path through reflection, but need not climb the ladder of inference.

There is, however, at least one role inference can have in facilitating the understanding required for knowledge of the self-evident. Consider the self-evident proposition that if p entails q and q entails r, and yet either q or r is not true, then p is false. Some may instantly see this; but even if one must first infer from it that p entails r (which self-evidently follows from the first part of the if-clause), this proposition is not a *ground* for believing the whole conditional proposition. It is an implicate of a constituent in the proposition and it helps one to see how the whole conditional is true. Call the inference here an *internal inference*. Even if an internal inference is required to know the truth of a proposition, the proposition may still be mediately self-evident. It may thus be far from obvious.

Internal inferences may also be purely clarificatory, say semantically, as where one uses a definition of 'grandparent' to help one see the self-evident truth that first cousins share a pair of grandparents. We might say, then, that knowledge of a self-evident proposition (and justification for believing it) may, for some people, depend *internally* on inference, above all where inference is needed for adequately understanding the proposition; but it may not depend *externally* on inference, where this entails epistemic dependence on one or more premises. Such knowledge and justification are not, then, inferential in the usual sense.

In the light of the distinction between the mediately and the immediately self-evident, the characteristic intuitionist claim that the basic moral principles are self-evident can be seen to require only that a kind of reflection suffices to yield a certain kind and degree of justification for them — the kind and degree of justification that yields knowledge when belief of a true proposition is based on such justification. This justification need be neither maximal in degree (if there *is* maximal justification) nor indefeasible in status. In the light of how much time and thought may be required for such reflection, the intuitionist view may be seen in a wider epistemological context, for instance as less distant from Kant's moral epistemology than one might think, at least if, for Kant, it is the apriority of the categorical imperative that is epistemologically most important, as opposed to the inferential character of our knowledge of it.

Even supposing that, for Kant, knowledge of the categorical imperative is inferential, as one might think from the way he argues for it in the *Groundwork* from considerations regarding practical reason,[26] it should be stressed that Rossian principles of duty, as first-order moral principles, need not be in the same epistemic boat. If they are even mediately self-evident, they should be taken to be knowable non-inferentially. But any (or virtually any) proposition that can be known non-inferentially can also be known inferentially, say on the basis of a carefully constructed argument for it.[27] Ross, apparently following Moore and Prichard, implicitly denied this,[28] but there is no need for intuitionism, either as a moral epistemology positing intuitive knowledge of moral principles, or as an ethical pluralism, to deny it.[29]

Hard and Soft Self-Evidence

To see why this point has often been missed, contrast two types of self-evidence. *Hard self-evidence* belongs to self-evident propositions that are (a) strongly axiomatic, roughly in the Aristotelian sense that there is nothing epistemically prior to them (hence nothing better justified or, in a sense, "better known"), as perhaps holds for such simple logical truths as the proposition that if no philosophers are bigots, then no bigots are philosophers; (b) immediate (in the temporal sense explained above, understood relative to minimally rational moral agents), as is the logical truth just cited; (c) indefeasibly justified; and (d) compelling, i.e., cognitively irresistible given a comprehending consideration of them. *Soft self-evidence* belongs to self-evident propositions that have none of these properties; this seems so for all those expressing Rossian duties (whether those he formulated or any others deserving the name). Between the hard and soft kinds of self-evidence there are intermediate varieties, but it is apparently hard self-evidence that, despite Ross's qualifications, has most influenced the common conception of the notion as employed by intuitionists.

The paradigms of self-evidence in the literature tend to approximate the hard sort, and for many readers Ross's comparison (following earlier intuitionists) of his principles to mathematical axioms and valid forms of inference evokes such paradigms and, with them, the mistaken idea that calling a principle self-evident puts it beyond dispute or even justificatory argument. There are, to be sure, many degrees of approach to hardness, and even soft self-evidence is not very soft—such propositions are, as most plausibly understood, a priori and necessary. Moreover, even a proposition having hard self-evidence might not be immediate for all who encounter it in a language they understand; and soft self-evidence, as we have seen in examining intuitionism, is commonly mediate.

The kind of self-evidence to which a moderate intuitionism is committed lies quite far at the soft end. The propositions in question can be known independently of premises, but they are not the kind of strong axioms that cannot be known on the basis of anything "deeper." They are also withholdable, and even disbelievable, even given comprehending contemplation. This, in turn, allows that skeptics—or proponents of moral theories inconsistent with intuitionism—can refuse to accept them without lacking an adequate understanding of them. As applied to Rossian intuitionism, this possibility makes adequate room to explain disagreement in certain moral matters and certainly in matters of ethical theory.

As long as basic moral principles *can* be known (or at least justifiably accepted) independently of relying on premises, morality can be understood and practiced as intuitionists understand it. Their goal, in part, is to account for the spontaneity with which moral agents can often make warranted moral judgments. For this, the soft self-evidence of the applicable moral principles is quite enough. In some ways, basic actions are similar. Life would be very different if we could not move our legs except by doing something else, such as activating a machine that moves them. But we *can* do such things, and at times may find it desirable. The possibility of moving our legs in a secondary way does not, however, change the nature of our primary leg movements. So it can be with knowledge of basic moral principles.

It is only ethical theory (of a certain kind), and not everyday moral thinking, that must provide for the possibility of overdetermined justification or knowledge of moral principles by virtue of their being supported independently by both intuitive and inferential grounds. Providing for this possibility is (as I argue in Chapter 3) in no way hostile to any major intuitionist purpose. Indeed, so long as the basic moral principles *can* be directly known (or justifiedly accepted) in the way they can be if they are self-evident, they may be considered *epistemically autonomous*. If they are, and if, as Ross perhaps thought, they are a complete set of ethical "axioms," then there is a sense in which ethics as a domain of reason is also autonomous. It is not detached from the theory of practical reason, and it perhaps can receive support from non-moral principles; but it can also command rational allegiance without such support.

3. RESOURCES AND VARIETIES OF
MODERATE INTUITIONISM

If the arguments of this chapter add to the plausibility of a moderate rationalistic intuitionism, they also suggest how intuitionism can be detached from rationalism. I favor a rationalist version, but much of what is important in the view does not require rationalism. It is therefore important for completeness to outline a non-rationalist version. I begin with this possibility and then proceed to describe some important aspects of intuitionism in general.

The Possibility of a Non-rationalist Intuitionism

Consider intuitionism in the weak (and rough) sense of the view that an irreducible plurality of basic moral judgments can be intuitively and non-inferentially justified. Such a view can be non-rationalist, taking intuitions to be non-inferential responses to perceptual experience and thereby resting on empirical grounds for moral judgments or principles. On one view, intuitions might be construed as deliverances of a moral sense, regarded as much like a perceptual faculty. Moral *principles* would likely be taken to be justified inductively on the basis of intuitions whose objects constitute premises; the principles would not then be construed as self-evident, so on that score an empiricist intuitionism would contrast with a Rossian version.[30]

Can an empiricist intuitionism account for the strength that intuitive moral justification may have? Recall two points. First, it is only general principles that even rationalist intuitionists take to be self-evident, and an empiricist might accept the same ones and simply take them to have strong empirical justification. Second, and more important, since (for reasons indicated earlier) the major intuitionists are not committed to denying, and tend to grant, that justification for believing moral propositions is defeasible, a further obstacle to their being empirical is eliminated.[31] Moral justification (or moral knowledge) could be held to come from a broadly perceptual faculty (perhaps an empathic one), or from an intuitive sense of obligatoriness, or from some other empirical source sensitive to moral properties, whether directly or through sensitivity to their grounds. These two kinds of sensitivity need explanation.

If there is a direct cognitive sensitivity to moral properties, then if it is perceptual, we should take such properties (say, the obligatoriness of relieving someone's suffering) to be connected with moral judgment in some broadly causal way. A "perceptual" intuitionist need not, however, conceive moral properties themselves as natural and may also consider them non-causal. Nonetheless, for naturalists and non-naturalists alike, moral knowledge could be conceived as quasi-perceptual. For where a morally sensitive agent responds to the natural properties that are (I assume) the *base* on which the relevant moral properties supervene, or are, in Ross's perhaps preferable terminology, "consequential," the evidence required to sustain knowledge is both present and properly reflected in cognition.

Consider a sensitive moral agent who sees someone gleefully whipping an infant with a leather belt. Seeing this would evoke both moral emotion and a negative judgment, say indignation and the judgment that the act is vicious. Given the ground of this judgment—the perception of the flogging—the judgment apparently represents moral knowledge if anything does. The ground of the wrong itself is a natural event: the injury constituted by the flogging. As Ross might say, it is *in virtue of* the act's being a flogging (hence having a perceptible property of the act) that it is wrong. In responding to this ground, the judgment reflects, in a non-inferential way, the basis of the wrong, and that basis, in turn, supports the truth of the judgment. This point can be accepted by empiricists as well as by rationalists.

The Evidential Role of Moral Emotion

It is no accident that the kinds of grounds that evoke and justify moral judgment in such cases also tend to arouse moral emotion. Indignation, for example, or the sense of injustice, or the feeling of moral satisfaction that may come with resisting temptation can be fitting or unfitting to circumstances in roughly the same way as judgments. This holds for any plausible intuitionist view, rationalist or empiricist. So does the point that moral indignation and other emotions may have non-inferential *evidential* value. This is certainly possible where the emotion is produced as an appropriate response to the relevant base properties, such as flogging or lying, properties that would directly support the corresponding moral judgment.

The evidential role of emotion is not limited to cases in which it is a direct response to perception of the situation in question, as opposed to being based on a judgment about that case. But an emotion grounded in certain cognitions, including those preserved in memory as well as those made in circumstances that the agent is appraising, might also provide a non-inferential ground of moral judgment. Imagine recalling an incident in which one person criticized another and, as the details come back, getting more and more disapproving until a judgment emerges from the contemplated pattern of events, say that the first belittled the second. The pattern might produce an emotion that also warrants the further judgment that the first was unfair to the second, and it can warrant either judgment without yielding beliefs of supporting premises. Emotion can sometimes interpret people or situations before a search for propositional evidence can find the crucial points, or even where it cannot.

Intuitionism, because of its strong historical association with rationalism and with the often cut-and-dried operation of intuitive judgment portrayed by such writers as Prichard, has often seemed too intellectualist to take account of the role of emotion in grounding or refining moral judgment. But if moral properties are taken to be consequential on natural ones, as intuitionists have generally held, then emotions arising from perception of, or from judgments about, those grounding properties can play a significant evidential role. That role can be accounted for by rationalist as well as empiricist forms of the view.

Epistemically Internalist and Epistemically Externalist Intuitionisms

We have seen that the moral sensitivity that yields intuitive judgment need not be geared directly to a base property. Intuitive judgment may also be a response to something that is produced by one or more base properties in a way that adequately evidences the moral property in question, as indignation might. Granted, indignation can have some other genesis, such as a prejudiced assessment. This does not imply that it never has evidential value. Given that it is (arguably) a necessary truth that whipping an infant implies wrong-doing, the judgment that it is wrong is objectively well-grounded and can express justified belief and indeed knowledge.

There are at least two ways to conceive the justification of a judgment that is evidenced by a direct or indirect sensitivity to the kinds of natural properties that underlie moral properties. On reliabilist lines, the judgment that the whipping is wrong is well-grounded because it is based on a reliable belief-generating process: one with a high (possibly perfect) ratio of true to false beliefs as products. One might, for instance, judge an action on the basis of a sensitivity to the property of producing a negative balance of happiness to unhappiness in a certain context, say among a group of family members or where only a small number of people are concerned and all are observable (taken unrestrictedly, this property is unlikely to play the required role). By contrast, on (epistemologically) internalist lines, the judgment might be well-grounded by virtue of being based on an appropriate internal ground, say a sensory experience that, through an appropriate connection with moral standards, justifies believing that the whipping is wrong. Thus, given a visual experience of a whipping with its characteristic signs of welts and stings, we would accordingly judge the act wrong. Both the moral standards in question and the beliefs about the whipping would be construed as justified on internalist lines.

The difference between the two epistemological approaches is mainly in the internalist's but not the externalist's requiring internal accessibility (roughly, accessibility to introspection or reflection) of justifying grounds. The internalist appeals to an experience that is not necessarily veridical and so does not entail the truth of the belief; reliabilism, as an externalist view, appeals to a ground that is not necessarily experienced and so, even if it more often than not produces true beliefs, can apparently also produce true beliefs without the agent's having a sense of any factor that justifies beliefs.[32] If one brain can reliably "read" another in a way that leads to true moral judgments about the person in question, the agent with the neural detectors can have moral justification or knowledge even apart from having any sense of what justifies the judgments. The reliabilist's intuitions might thus be less articulate than the internalist's, but both kinds would be non-inferential.

In the light of the ways in which both epistemically externalist and epistemically internalist moral epistemologies can exploit the consequential relation between moral and natural properties as providing for an objective non-inferential ground for moral knowledge, we can see in more detail how intuitionism can be developed along empiricist as well as on rationalist lines. (I have in mind a strong relation such that the base properties *determine* the supervening, or consequential, ones.[33]) The empiricist versions take the consequential relation to be empirical; the rationalist versions take it to be a priori.

There are related metaphysical considerations. Although the consequential dependence of moral on natural properties might be thought to constitute a non-reductive naturalism, its non-reductive character is paramount: it allows a metaphysical and ethical non-naturalist like Ross to exploit the objectivity of the consequential relation to argue for the possibility of genuine moral knowledge without either construing that knowledge as empirical or taking the properties that are its primary object to be (in any straightforward way) perceptual, or even natural. Injustice, for instance, can be objectively grounded in unequal treatment even if the property of injustice is not itself a natural one, and even if the knowledge that the kind of unjust act in question is wrong is not empirical. Rationalists and empiricists tend to disagree on the modality, not the objectivity, of the grounding relations basic for moral judgments. The former take the relations to be conceptual and a priori; the latter, whether they think it conceptual or not, conceive it as empirical.[34]

A Contextualist Conception of Intuitionism

One could also defend intuitionism along contextualist lines. The central point would be that contextual features of a cognition determine its justification. Since these features need not operate through inference, intuitive non-inferential justification and knowledge are not precluded.[35] In the context of a friend's asking help loading a car for a family vacation, I may be justified non-inferentially and indeed without reflection in believing I should help, whereas I might need both deliberation and inference if the context were that of an obvious abandonment of spouse and children. My justification is, as on Ross's intuitionism, defeasible.

This defeasibility can be missed if one does not keep in mind that, for any moderate intuitionism, it is basic moral principles and not singular moral judgments that are self-evident. For contextualism, even the former might be contextually grounded (say in terms of prevailing social practices) rather than a priori—though contextualism can also be combined with an empiricist or rationalist account of what it is *about* a context of non-inferential justification that renders it justificatory.

As with Rossian intuitionism, a contextualist intuitionism may also hold that singular moral judgments need not be intuitive or otherwise non-inferential, say because some of them arise only through a process of deliberatively comparing conflicting obligations and concluding on the basis of premises that one or another prevails. In some cases, we might have little confidence in such a judgment; in others, it might come to seem intuitive as we review the various considerations through which we arrived at it.

A context-sensitive judgment could be a conclusion of reflection rather than of inference. For an intuitionist contextualism, moreover, *some* non-inferentially justified moral judgments must be countenanced. How close the view is to a Rossian version will depend chiefly on the kinds of contextual elements it represents as determining justification. If they are elements of understanding on the part of the agent, the view is likely to be quite Rossian; if they are culturally varying elements that tend to preclude a priori justification, it will be less Rossian.

4. DISAGREEMENT, INCOMMENSURABILITY, AND THE CHARGE OF DOGMATISM

Although an intuitionist view in moral epistemology can be defended along empiricist lines, it is best conceived, given the overall views of its major proponents, as a rationalist position, and my answers to some objections to it will stress the rationalism of the reconstructed Rossian intuitionism developed above—construed in outline as the view that we have intuitive justification both for some of our particular moral judgments and for a plurality of mediately self-evident moral principles.

Self-Evidence, Consensus, and Agreement in Reasons

A common objection to intuitionism centers on the claim that the basic principles of ethics are self-evident. If so, why is there so much disagreement on them?[36] Call this the *dissensus objection*.

First, since soft (hence mediate) self-evidence is the only kind that intuitionists need (or commonly do) claim for basic moral principles—in which case the principles may be far from obvious—we should not expect ready consensus on them, or even a high degree of consensus after some discussion. Indeed, given the complexities of understanding 'prima facie', some people have difficulty understanding Ross's principles in the first place. Without adequately understanding them, one has little or no reason to assent to them; and—given that they attribute pervasive duties to us and are to that extent demanding—there is some reason to expect resistance to granting them.

Second, at least among philosophers, some hesitation in accepting the principles may come from *thinking* of this as requiring endorsement of their self-evidence, which is after all the status intuitionists have prominently claimed for them (or of their necessity, a property that has commonly been taken to be grasped *in* seeing the truth of an a priori proposition). But I have stressed that the second-order claim that they are self-evident need not also be self-evident in order for them to have this status themselves; and, unlike Ross, I argue that it should be expected not to be self-evident.

Third, even if there is disagreement on the truth or the epistemic or modal status of the Rossian principles, there need not be disagreement about the basic *moral force* of the considerations they cite. For instance, whether or not we accept Ross's principle concerning promising, we might, both in our reflection and in regulating our conduct, take our having promised to do something as a basic moral reason to do it—*basic* in the sense that its reason-giving force does not derive from some other reason. This is a case of agreement *in* reasons. A parallel point holds for the beneficence principle. We might take the fact that driving home now would strand a friend to die in a house about to freeze from lack of fuel, as a basic reason not to do that: it is a failure in beneficence and may even imply injury. There are at least three levels of response to reasons in such matters: *accepting* reasons, accepting them *as* reasons, and *conceptualizing* them as reasons. Let us take these in turn.

(1) If I do something simply because I promised to, I am like a Rossian "plain man." In consciously doing the deed because I promised to, I am manifesting my acceptance of promising as providing a reason. That I promised to do the deed is my reason for doing it; and I unselfconsciously accept its reason-giving status. (2) If a student is late for an appointment and I think it was because he lingered to talk, but he tells me that it was owing to an unexpected illness, I accept this reason as such; I am contrasting it with other possible explanations of his lateness and construing it as (normatively) excusatory. But since my concern is only whether I should, say, comment or admonish, I do not need to conceptualize (as opposed to merely comprehending) his statement *as* offering a reason. (3) If, by contrast, I consider the general question whether disliking people is a reason not to recommend them for a job, I am conceptualizing a variable *as* a reason. My focus is in part the property (or status) of being a reason. At the first two levels, and especially at the first, we can exhibit agreement with others *in* reasons for action—*operative agreement*, as we might call it—without agreeing *on* them, say on their epistemic status.

There are also at least three cases of agreement on reasons. One is agreement on what *constitutes* a reason in the kind of context in question; this requires conceptualizing some element as a reason. A second case is agreement on some *principle* expressing reasons. This may or may not require such conceptualization, since it may be formulated only in terms of, say, duties. But it is general in a way agreement in accepting a reason need not be. A third case is agreement on how much *force* a reason has relative to other considerations; this, too, is general but may or may not require such conceptualization.

Agreement on reasons, then, requires a view about reasons or their status; it is coincidence in beliefs *about* reasons. Agreement in reasons, as where two children each flee from a bully in response to the same threat,

may not even require the concept of a reason, as opposed to a responsiveness to the considerations that constitute reasons. It is a kind of coincidence in such responsiveness. If it does require the concept of a reason,
the agent still need have no general view about the status or varieties of
reasons. I can be moved to nurse a wound that someone gets from falling
on the pavement, even if I do not think of the situation as giving me a
reason to do it. Nor need I think of it that way in order to answer 'Why
are you late?' by citing the victim's need for help. I may in fact consider
this a good answer even apart from subsuming the notion of need here
under that of a reason for action. I am, to be sure, in a position to appreciate, in an intellectual way, the reason I had and to begin to appraise its
force. But no such intellectual reflection is required for responsiveness to
such a reason.

Moreover, someone who is like me in behavioral and even inferential
responsiveness to reasons may have, or be disposed to give, a quite different
intellectual account. In elemental cases that present us with moral reasons
for action, Kantians and utilitarians may respond in similar ways, each
judging that there is, say, an obligation to give a terminally ill patient a true
diagnosis, despite their differing accounts of the basis of the obligation.
Intuitionism builds on this similarity, and its appeal is in part due to the
sense that at the level of agreement in reasons, thoughtful people[37] tend
to have the makings of a common starting point.

Agreement on reasons seems closely connected with intuitive induction
as Ross, Broad, and others saw it. The conceptual progression they portray
might in some cases have the following three stages. Consider the grasp
of an individual ground as supporting a kind of act, say of promising as
calling for doing the promised deed. This grasp is, as manifested in a sense
of duty to do the promised deed, a recognition of a reason. As manifested
in realizing the *truth* that on the basis of the promise one ought to do the
deed, it is at least a minimal recognition of a reason as such—as something
that renders one obligated to act. Third, in the richest of the three cases,
the grasp of a reason manifests itself in believing the principle that promising always gives rise to prima facie duties. This belief represents one kind
of a generalization of the recognition of a reason.

Ross saw intuitive induction as going further than the third stage, yielding at least some apprehension of the *necessity* of the grounding relation;
but although one might reasonably take this fourth step on the basis he
sketches, an intuitionist ethics need not conceive taking it as required for
an ordinary moral agent to be guided by Rossian principles. Moreover,

contrary to what the term 'induction' invites us to think, intuitionism does not have to view intuitive induction as inferential. Intuitive induction is essentially *developmental* in yielding higher-level or more general cognitions (or both) as outgrowths of lower-level or less general cognitions. But the path need not be inferential, even if one could construct an inferential description of the typical routes the intellect follows.

As the examples illustrate, a *commitment* to a view *about* reasons may be implied in taking a consideration *as* a reason. But commitments are not always realized, and this kind may not even tend to be realized unless abstract or philosophical questions arise for the agent. Much moral practice raises no such questions. If there is the kind of wide agreement in moral practice that I think there is, then the most important kind of consensus needed for the theoretical success of intuitionism as a moral theory is in place. It can at least be argued that the truth and non-inferential justifiability of the relevant principles explains, or at least comes closer to explaining than any competing hypothesis, the high degree of consensus among people in wide segments of their everyday moral practice.[38] Non-inferential justifiability is particularly important here: by contrast with, for instance, overarching principles endorsed by utilitarianism, Kantianism, and divine command approaches, Rossian principles do not stand in need of justification by derivation from standards or wider principles viewed as independently grounded. If, however, they are also true, then disconfirmation is (other things equal) less likely to occur and more likely to be defeated if it does.

The Incommensurability Problem

Supposing this response to the dissensus objection succeeds, we must acknowledge a further problem for intuitionism—a problem besetting virtually any pluralistic ethical view. Non-inferential knowledge or justified belief that a consideration morally favors an action is one thing; such knowledge or justification for taking it to be overriding is quite another. One might speak of an *incommensurability problem*, since intuitionism countenances irreducibly different kinds of moral grounds for action, as opposed to, say, just hedonic grounds that can perhaps be aggregatively assessed to determine our obligations. There are at least three crucial points here.

First, intuitionism does not imply that we typically have non-inferential knowledge of *final* duty. We may have to compare the case at hand with earlier ones or with hypothetical cases and then reason from relevant information to a conclusion. Thus, we might note that if we submit a certain appraisal of a proposed grant project, we may seem biased. We may then see the question in relation to conflict of interest. Our final judgment may (though it need not) arise from formulating a sufficient condition for a conflict of interest and judging that the prospective action satisfies it and is thereby impermissible. Incommensurability can allow justified comparative judgments.

Second, it is essential to distinguish higher-order knowledge (or justification for believing) that the duty (or other kind of reason) overrides any competing ones from the first-order knowledge that a given action, say keeping one's promise in spite of a good excuse for non-performance, is obligatory (or required by some other kind of ground). To know specifically that a duty is overriding requires not only using that comparative and theoretical concept, but also making or perhaps even reflecting on a comparison of duties. But one can sometimes know what one is obligated to do, even in a situation of conflicting duties, without making such a comparison or even possessing the kind of comparative knowledge one might get from, say, utilitarian calculation or Kantian deduction. Perhaps I simply see that I must do what is called for by my job, even where I have reason to relieve a friend's distress instead. My final duty can be obvious to me even if I make no comparison to ascertain that I am not missing a better alternative. This is part of what it is to have moral maturity.

Granted, the truth of my judgment that I ought to do a certain thing may, in the abstract, *depend* on comparative merits of my alternatives; granted, too, that my justification may be defeated if I acquire information indicating that some alternative action is preferable. But that a truth depends on a comparative matter does not entail that our knowledge of it requires *making* a comparison, or even forming a belief of a comparative proposition; and that justification can be defeated by a kind of information does not entail that ruling out such information is a *precondition* for having the justification (if it did, a far-reaching skepticism would be at best hard to resist).[39]

It is true that if (for instance) I know that I should help a distressed friend, in a case where I realize that this precludes my keeping an appointment, I am in a *position* to figure out that one of the two duties is overriding, or even to reach the second-order knowledge that I know this comparative proposition. But I do not in such cases automatically know either of these propositions; and if I am not skilled in moral reasoning, it may be difficult for me to do more than sketch an account of why one duty is overriding. That we easily make mistakes in such sketches is one reason why knowledge of overridingness, and particularly of just *why* it obtains, is often hard to come by.

To be sure, if what I know is that I ought to do a particular thing, and if the situation is one in which I am aware of something else I have some (lesser) moral reason to do, my knowledge has a comparative *basis*. But this does not entail my knowing a comparative *proposition*, even if it may give me the materials for justifiably inferring one. Suppose, indeed, that it must give me those materials. It would not follow that I know such a proposition. I need form no belief of it.[40]

My third point here is that the difficulty of achieving knowledge or justification when there are conflicting grounds is not peculiar to ethics. Consider divided evidence, which is common when there are opposing scientific theories, at a generally less technical level, or in detective cases. At times we must suspend judgment or cannot reasonably choose between two competing theories or hypotheses. This does not imply that we never have grounds good enough for knowledge; and the conditions for achieving a degree of justification sufficient to warrant acceptance of a hypothesis are less stringent than for achieving knowledge. So it is in ethics, sometimes with lesser justification than is common in rational ascriptions of guilt or innocence, but in many cases with greater: even when lying would spare someone pain, it can sometimes be utterly and immediately clear that we should not lie. If there is incommensurability, in the sense of the absence of a common measure for all moral considerations, there can nonetheless be *comparability* in the sense implying the possibility of a rational assessment in the context of the relevant facts.[41]

Intuitionists may also contend that final duty is like prima facie duty in being consequential on natural facts. On this (plausible) view, even where there is no single quantitative or otherwise arguably straightforward basis of comparison among conflicting duties, we can describe the various grounds of duty in each case, compare the cases in that respect with similar instances resolved in the past, bring to bear hypothetical examples, and the like. This is the sort of stuff of which practical wisdom in ethics is made.[42]

Metaphilosophical Commitments of Intuitionism

The controversy between empiricism and rationalism as epistemological perspectives is apparently very much with us in ethical theory, despite how few ethical theorists are avowedly committed to either perspective. I want to examine some of the main objections to the kind of intuitionism developed here that are either motivated by empiricism or best seen as objections, not to its appeal to intuitions, but to its underlying rationalism: roughly, to its taking reflection, as opposed to observation, to be capable of grounding justification for substantive truths, such as (if they are indeed true) Rossian moral principles.

If self-evident truths are conceived as not only not in need of external evidence but also necessary, it is understandable that intuitionism might be considered dogmatic. Is it dogmatic, as some have held?[43] It might well be dogmatic to claim both that we have intuitive, certain knowledge of what our prima facie duties are *and* that we cannot ground that knowledge on evidence or in some way support it by examples. But a plausible intuitionism, including Ross's, is not committed to our having "certain knowledge" here—where such certainty implies indefeasible justification.

Moreover, dogmatism, as distinct from mere stubbornness, is a second-order attitude, such as a conviction, on a controversial matter, that one is obviously right. Even holding that basic moral principles are self-evident does not warrant taking a dogmatic attitude toward them or one's critics. The self-evident may not even be readily understood, much less obvious.

Despite Ross's in some ways unfortunate analogy between moral principles and elementary logical and mathematical ones, he leaves room for reflective equilibrium to enhance—or for its unobtainability to reduce or defeat—justification for an "intuitive" moral judgment. If the judgment is incongruous with similar ones, as where one makes opposite moral appraisals of highly similar deeds, or if it conflicts with a plausible principle, as where one judges non-self-defensive aggression to be unobjectionable, this counts against its justification. Further, nothing Ross must hold, qua intuitionist, precludes systematization of his moral principles in terms of something more general (a possibility pursued in Chapter 3); and in at least one place he speaks as if one prima facie duty might be derivable from another.[44] Contrary to what the dogmatism charge suggests, such systematization might provide both reasons for the principles and an additional source of correctives for false or merely apparent intuitions. An intuition can be mistaken, and a mere prejudice can masquerade as an intuition.

As suggested earlier, it is incumbent on conscientious intuitionists to factor into their moral thinking, particularly on controversial issues, the apparent intuitions of *others*. This may be why Ross appealed repeatedly to what "we" really think, and stressed the analogy between intuitions in ethics and perceptions in science. Intuitions, then, should not be conceived as arbitrary. Many have a basis in reflection and are shared by people of very different experience. Furthermore, supposing an apparent intuition might sometimes arise as an arbitrary cognition, it would not necessarily have even prima facie justification; and, where a genuine intuition, which presumably does have some degree of prima facie justification, is misleading, it can at least normally be defeated by other intuitions that reflection might generate or by other elements in the reflective equilibrium that a reasonable intuitionist would seek.

Let us now turn to the question whether a moderate intuitionism is committed to implausible epistemic principles. I have contended that intuitionists need not take self-evident propositions to be (epistemically) ungroundable—incapable of being evidenced by anything else. I now want to suggest that quite apart from whether they can be externally evidenced, Ross's basic principles of duty are at least candidates for a priori justification in the way mediately self-evident propositions should be.

Keeping in mind what constitutes a prima facie duty, consider how we would regard some native speaker of English who denied that there is a prima facie duty not to injure—say to stab or burn—other people and meant by this something which clearly implies that doing it would not in general be even prima facie wrong.[45] This is not amoralism—the point is not that the person agrees but would not be *moved*. Rather, such a person apparently exhibits a kind of *moral deafness*, apparently not hearing the moral element at all. Our first thought might be that there is a misunderstanding, say of 'prima facie'. We expect some kind of agreement in reasons here, even if we think there will be disagreement *on* them. Apart from misunderstanding, I doubt that anyone not in the grip of skepticism or a competing theory would deny the proposition, and I believe that any plausible competing theory would tend to support the same moral judgment, though perhaps disguised by different clothing or rationalized in a very different way.

Granted that some skeptical considerations could lead someone who adequately understands a properly formulated Rossian principle to deny it, some can also be brought against non-moral a priori propositions. In any event, they are not necessarily good reasons to doubt either the truth or the apriority of the challenged proposition.[46]

What is perhaps less controversial is that if we do not ascribe to reason the minimal power required in order for a moderate intuitionism of the kind I have described to be epistemologically plausible, then Rossian intuitionism is not the only kind of theory in difficulty. Serious problems would have to be solved before any instrumentalist or empiricist ethical theory is plausible.[47] For one thing, instrumentalists, such as neo-Humeans, must account for their fundamental principles, for instance the principle that if, on our beliefs, an action serves a basic (roughly, non-instrumental) desire of ours, then there is a reason for us to perform the action. Is this proposition empirical or instead a candidate for mediate self-evidence?[48] Unless reason has sufficient power to make principles like Ross's plausible candidates for truth, it is not clear that instrumentalist principles are plausible candidates either.[49]

5. INTUITIVE MORAL JUDGMENT AND RATIONAL ACTION

In defending the epistemology of a moderate Rossian intuitionism, and particularly the view that moral principles can be self-evident, I may appear to be implying that skepticism in ethics can be, if not eliminated, at least dramatically mitigated. But suppose moral knowledge is possible. Would that vanquish moral skepticism? If we take it to include the full range of skeptical positions in ethics, it would not. General moral knowledge, say of principles expressing basic prima facie duties, is possible quite apart from whether there can be knowledge of singular moral judgments—the often self-addressed, action-guiding kind that moral life depends on. I have argued that despite the incommensurability problem raised by the plurality of values, such singular judgments can express knowledge, and certainly justified belief. But is either moral knowledge or justified moral belief extensive enough to provide rational moral guidance for daily life?

A related question arises when we realize that *non-moral* values can conflict with moral ones, and that we should not assume the latter must always prevail.[50] A third problem concerns the gap between moral judgment and action: even assuming that holding a moral judgment entails motivation to act accordingly,[51] such action may be inhibited or may occur for some other reason, such as a motive of self-interest. Then the action earns no moral credit for the agent and may not even be rational (depending on whether the non-moral explaining factor suffices to render it rational). Let us pursue these three problems.

Concerning the possibility of moral knowledge about individual actions, I maintain that although singular moral judgments are not self-evident, they may still be non-inferentially knowable. This point may be obscured because it may seem that intuitionism requires self-evidence as a condition for knowledge or justified belief of singular as well as certain general moral propositions. But it cannot plausibly require this if I am right in taking self-evident propositions to be knowable on conceptual grounds; these grounds would not suffice for knowledge of singular moral judgments, which are existential and depend on contingencies. Nor does intuitionism imply that *only* self-evident propositions are intuitively knowable. A singular moral judgment about a particular person can be intuitively knowable, especially when it is an application of a principle of prima facie duty as opposed to an ascription of final duty.

Varieties of Particularistic Intuitionism

One may also be tempted to think that if, in making singular moral judgments, we are guided by moral principles, and if, after the fact, we can frame a principle to cover the action in question, then we can see the judgments in question as derivable from principles in a way that certifies them as knowledge. This idea neglects a point at the heart of an epistemologically particularistic intuitionism such as Ross's: at least some intuitions regarding concrete cases are epistemically more basic than, or in any event indispensable to, intuitive knowledge of the corresponding generalizations. It may be only when one thinks of a deed concretely and sees that it is wrong that one can see that all deeds of that kind are wrong. This is the sort of thing Broad had in mind in holding that experience of fittingness in particular cases is required before one can "rise to" intuitive induction yielding general knowledge of the kind of case in question.[52]

In calling Ross's intuitionism particularist, I use a term that applies in many domains. My concern is mainly with the notion of duty. I have already suggested that Ross's intuitionism is an *epistemological particularism*. This is roughly the view that cognitions (including intuitions) regarding duty in a concrete instance, such as a situation in which one must aid an injured person, are epistemically prior to cognitions regarding duty in general, particularly to knowledge or belief of a general principle of duty. Intuitive induction is one kind of epistemic process in which knowledge of something particular is prior to, and yields, knowledge of something general that the particular instantiates.

A related view is *conceptual particularism*, roughly the position that cognitions concerning such concrete cases are conceptually prior to cognitions concerning duty in general. On this view, one can acquire the concept of duty only on the basis of acquiring the concept of, say, a duty to keep a promise to trim the rosebush on Saturday; it is from understanding such a concrete duty that we acquire a concept of duty as such. This is not the view that *knowledge* of particular truths about a case of duty yields knowledge of something general about duty; that could hold where the former kind of knowledge embodies a general concept of duty not derived from understanding a particular duty. Conceptual particularism requires that one have a concept of a particular duty as a basis for a general concept of duty.

Conceptual particularism should be distinguished from an empirical thesis we might call *genetic particularism*, the position that in the normal order of learning of concepts and propositions, exposure to concrete cases is prior to understanding general deontic concepts and general principles of duty. This view does not entail conceptual particularism. First, it is empirical and applies only to normal conceptual learning. Second, the *content* of what one learns *initially* through exposure to concrete cases can be conceptual and general: a child who genuinely learns what it is to have a duty to keep a particular promise may at some level be both acquiring the concept of a duty to keep *promises* and learning that promising implies such a duty. Ross (like Broad and others) was apparently a genetic as well as an epistemological particularist; but it is not clear that he held conceptual particularism, and in any case a moderate intuitionist can hold the former two views and not the third.

Genetic particularism does not entail that any specific method of moral thinking is preferable to the others, but it naturally goes with a kind of *methodological particularism*. This is the thesis that moral reasoning, whether in individual cases calling for moral judgment or in theoretical matters, should give some kind of priority to reflection on particular cases, such as those in which one person owes reparation to another.[53] This view can take various forms, depending on the kind of priority, say temporal or, more likely, epistemological priority; and it is likely to be held by intuitivists whether or not they are also intuitionists. I mention this view for the clarity it adds by contrast with the other kinds of particularism; although many intuitionists have implicitly held some version of it, as a methodological view it might be held by non-intuitionists and is not of major concern in evaluating substantive particularist views.

A fifth kind of (ethical) particularism—*normative particularism*—is more controversial among intuitionists. I refer to the view that the deontic *valence* of a consideration (such as one's having promised to do something), i.e., the consideration's counting for or against the action in question (or neutrally), is determinable only in particular cases and is not invariant across different cases. A stronger normative particularism has it that even the *relevance* of a consideration to determining duty is ascertainable only in particular cases.[54] Ross was not a normative particularist in either sense. He held, regarding the grounds of basic duties, an *invariant valence view*: the valence of, say, an act's injuring another person is always negative. The injury is a prima facie reason against it.

A moderate intuitionism can (with Ross) maintain epistemological and genetic particularism, leave open conceptual particularism, and reject normative particularism in favor of the invariant valence view. It is natural to call this position a *moderate particularism*, by contrast with the strong version that endorses all of the particularist theses. But at least the invariance view, as in a sense generalist, may seem inappropriate for any particularist view and perhaps even for ethical intuitionism as such. Let us explore this.

Suppose I promise to pick a friend up at a certain crowded place at ten and I discover just as I am about to drive off that someone intends, when I get there, to detonate a powerful bomb concealed in my car. Is my promising to pick up my friend even relevant to deciding whether to do so? Should we not adopt a contextualist view, as a strong particularist would?[55] A great deal can be said here. I have space for only a few of the major distinctions a moderate intuitionism can bring to bear.

First, it is essential to distinguish the *deliberative relevance* of a consideration, roughly its relevance to making a decision regarding what to do, from its *normative relevance*, its valence (positive, negative, or neutral) in relation to the action(s) in question. My promise to pick up my acquaintance is not deliberatively relevant; I would be at best foolish to bring it into my thinking about whether to do something that would kill dozens of innocent people. It does not follow that it lacks normative relevance. To claim this would be like saying that because it makes no sense to wait for a penny in change at the cost of missing one's flight, the penny has no value. Granted, to *say* that a promise like the one in question has normative relevance is odd. But that may be owing to the pragmatic point that it is highly misleading to call a consideration normatively relevant when, in the circumstances, any normative weight it has is far below the threshold of deliberative relevance.

A further point supporting the normative relevance view is that despite how obviously my promissory obligation is outweighed, I should explain my non-appearance to my friend. Moreover, suppose I discover that I can get the bomb defused in time to pick the friend up a bit late. I should then do this rather than not at all. This point also suggests that a positive reason is overridden in a way that generates a *duty of substitution*, rather than that in the context the promise had no force at all. The promise remains as a ground on which one should try to build something, even when it is clear that one should not do the promised deed. This brings us to a second major point.

Just as we can distinguish considerations above and below the threshold of deliberative relevance, we can distinguish considerations above and below the threshold of ordinary discernibility in the context of decision. A flashlight beam is not visible in bright sunlight; promising to pick up my friend at ten is not readily discernible as a reason to do so in the special case in question. It is so minor given what is at stake that it would not ordinarily occur to one as a reason. But just as we can conceive blocking the sunlight, we can conceive removing the bomb; and there seems no better reason to say that the presence of the bomb changes the force of the promise than to say that the presence of the sunlight changes the brightness of the flashlight.

Indeed, suppose I am certain that the very same people (including my friend and me) will be killed by a different terrorist if I do *not* pick up my friend at ten. For those to whom promising is a serious matter, it may seem better to keep the promise than not: at least I fulfill one more obligation before the end. I say 'may seem' because in this case I allow myself to be *used*, and there is prima facie reason to avoid *that*. A good analogy to the flashlight may require eliminating this element. In principle, however, being below the level of ordinary discernibility does not entail being below the threshold of deliberative relevance (and conversely). A similar point might apply in mathematics. Given a clearly cogent proof of a theorem, competent testimony that it is a theorem may add so little to one's justification as to seem negligible; but given a plausible attack on the proof, such testimony might become an important reason to retain belief of the theorem. Deliberative relevance varies with changes in context and may or may not be proportional to ease of discernibility.

A third pertinent distinction is between the intrinsic valence of a consideration and its overall normative force in the context of a given decision or action. A major case in point is *Schadenfreude*: roughly, taking pleasure in the suffering of another. Can the prima facie duty of beneficence, for instance, provide any reason at all to give someone an opportunity to take pleasure in sadistically beating another person? Plainly, this is the wrong kind of pleasure. Does the invariant valence view allow us to say this, at least if it endorses promotion of pleasure for someone as a (prima facie) reason for action? (It may of course deny that beneficence is manifested in promoting just any kind of pleasure.) It does allow this. To see how, we might focus on the closely related case of pain. Is it not at least in part because of the invariant badness of pain that the pleasure in question *is* the wrong kind? That an act produces pain is a reason to abstain from it. Moreover, we may plausibly hold that the overall state of affairs, someone's taking pleasure in paining another, has a negative value vastly outweighing the positive value of the pleasure in question. This point (which will be developed in Chapter 4) may allow us to say, in some cases, that whatever positive value promoting pleasure may have is below the threshold of deliberative relevance and perhaps even below that of ordinary discernibility.[56]

The fourth distinction relevant here is between two kinds of holism. *Holism regarding judgments of final duty* is roughly the view that where two or more conflicting considerations bear on a prospective action, one can discern one's final duty only in the light of an overall assessment of them. *Holism regarding judgments of prima facie duty* is roughly the strong particularist view that the same point applies to judgments of prima facie duty. Moderate intuitionism (including Ross's, apparently) is committed to the first but not the second kind of holism. Suppose one faces a conflict of duties, with considerations of fidelity and familial beneficence favoring an expenditure for one's children and considerations of both rectification and general beneficence favoring an incompatible expenditure for a special charity. Determination of final duty can be a holistic matter involving a huge variety of considerations even if the relevant prima facie duties are grounded in factors having a constant valence.

A constant valence, moreover, does not entail a constant *weight*; promising to do something, for instance, can invariably be a normative reason to do it, even if some promises provide better reason than others and even if, as circumstances change, the overall weight of a promise in the context of decision can change. We can, then, be holists about final duty and not about prima facie duty.[57]

To be sure, for a strong coherentist theory of justification, *any* kind of justification is a holistic matter. One may, however, embrace a coherence theory of the acquisition and functioning of concepts—*conceptual coherentism*—without holding *epistemological coherentism*, which is roughly the view that the justifiedn6ss of beliefs and other cognitions is grounded in the mutual coherence of the relevant items.[58] We apparently do not acquire concepts one by one, and understanding any of them is essentially connected with understanding certain others. But it does not follow from this conceptual coherence constraint that there are no considerations which, even by themselves, give us prima facie justification. Indeed, just as it is doubtful that we can account for justified belief without giving experience *some* role in generating prima facie justification, it is doubtful that we can even be in a position to decide what act is our overall duty without giving some role to independently accessible considerations generating prima facie duty. In any case, Ross is clearly a foundationalist about the grounds of duty, and a moderate intuitionism is most plausible when placed within a carefully qualified foundationalism regarding prima facie duty.

It should be plain from a number of points made in defending the invariant valence view that it does not imply a *subsumptivist* conception of our knowledge of singular moral judgments, the idea that these judgments are knowable only as applications of generalizations. This conception may also arise from the correct point that in many cases, before we can determine what, overall, we should do, we must be able to see that two or more conflicting (prima facie) generalizations apply to our options. But the applicability of several generalizations to a case does not imply that our final obligation therein is determined by the application of a further, reconciling generalization. That point holds even if such a generalization is in principle formulable after the fact.

Final Duty, Overall Moral Judgment, and Reflective Equilibrium

A more specific claim may be warranted here. Suppose that (all) moral properties are consequential on some finite set of natural ones and that the relevant natural ones and their grounding relations to the moral ones are discernible by ordinary kinds of reflection. Then, given a sound moral judgment in a case of conflicting obligations, we can in principle formulate a generalization that non-trivially applies to similar cases. For the overall obligatoriness we discern will be based on natural properties that we can in principle discriminate and appeal to in framing a generalization.

There is, then, a plausible case for this kind of generalizability in principle. Such generalizability is not, however, a necessary condition for one's forming a justified judgment. One can achieve a sound result whether or not one generalizes on it or even can do so. It could be, for instance, that overall obligation is *organic* (a point pursued in Chapter 4) and that given the sense in which it is, we cannot always specify just what properties ground it. Even if prima facie obligation is entailed by certain natural properties (a view that intuitionists commonly hold), overall obligation apparently requires a more complicated account.

One might question whether final obligation *is* consequential on natural properties. Consider a final obligation to tell the truth, and suppose that it prevails over a conflicting obligation to protect a friend. What natural properties might ground the relational normative property of (moral) *prevalence* or *being weightier*? Ross would insist that there is no one dimension, such as the hedonic, determining the finality of the duty of veracity. It is plausible to hold, however, that a counterpart prevalence will occur in any exactly similar case of conflicting duties. Granting that this does not entail that final duty is consequential on natural properties, how can we explain such generalizability except on the assumption that final obligation *is* consequential on natural properties of the relevant case? It is, moreover, at least in the spirit of a rationalist intuitionism to say that *if* we could formulate and understand all of the relevant variables, we might thereby achieve intuitive knowledge of the resulting—presumably consequential—final duty. But suppose there simply is no closed list of relevant natural properties. If not, then the consequentiality of final duty is difficult to establish. Such consequentiality may yet hold. Compare the beauty of a painting: should we deny that it is consequential on such elements as the colors and shapes and their relations, because we cannot close the list of relevant factors?

If, by contrast, we can formulate and understand all of the variables relevant to determining the finality of a duty, the generalization we might then articulate could turn out to be mediately self-evident or otherwise a priori. One could then plausibly argue that the comparative weights of the relevant duties in the kind of case in question are an a priori matter. This not only would not undermine the idea that final duty is consequential on natural properties, but would in fact extend the scope of intuitionist moral principles beyond the range anticipated by Ross and other intuitionists. Although there would still be no a priori hierarchy ranking some general duties, such as those of fidelity, over others, such as those of beneficence, some judgments of final duty could be instances of more specific comparative moral principles; and we would have more such principles in proportion to our skill at generalizing from the use of practical wisdom.[59]

A further point concerning the epistemic resources of a moderate intuitionism is that in many cases of a singular judgment settling a conflict of duties, there is the possibility of reaching a reflective equilibrium between this judgment and various moral principles and other singular judgments. This equilibrium may contribute to the justification of that judgment. It may also provide, in some cases, justification for a second-order belief that the judgment is justified. It may even make the difference between a judgment with only some degree of justification and one sufficiently well justified to be both a good guide for action and a candidate for knowledge. Here, then, is one way a judgment that begins as a tentative assessment can graduate to the status of justified belief or knowledge.

Given what has now been said, we can address the problem of conflicts between moral and non-moral values. It should first be said that this problem can beset any plausible ethical theory. To be sure, Kant treated ethical considerations as basic in the theory of practical reason and regarded the categorical imperative as grounding moral obligations with absolute authority. But suppose for the sake of argument that it does ground some absolute *moral* obligations; this does not entail that there is no possibility of anyone's ever rationally (and knowingly) doing something that morality does not permit. Regarding utilitarian theories, if (as I shall assume) they ground all reasons for action in whatever they take to have intrinsic value, then unless (implausibly) a utilitarian view takes only one specific kind of value as basic, something like an incommensurability problem can arise. Consider a hedonistic utilitarianism. Even if, contrary to the view of Mill and others (almost certainly including Aristotle), no one kind of pleasure is better than any other, there are problems weighing promotion of pleasures against reduction of pains. To say, however, that the problem besets other views is not to answer the skeptical claim that it is devastating. Let me briefly address that problem.

If the moderate foundationalism that I suggest is crucial for any plausible intuitionism is sound,[60] we can make at least two significant points that bear on skepticism about knowledge or justification. First, if we distinguish between *rebutting* a skeptical view—showing that the case for it is unsound—and *refuting* it, which is showing it to be false by establishing that there *is* the relevant kind of knowledge or justification, then there is reason to think rebuttal is possible. We can consider the various epistemic standards which a skeptic says moral judgment cannot meet and argue that either the standard is too high or the judgment can meet it.[61] Second, although refuting skepticism is harder than rebutting it, refutation may yet be possible provided our epistemic standards are not unrealistically high. For one thing, some paradigms may simply be more intuitive than any competing intuitions that serve skepticism—which, like any other philosophical view, depends on intuitions for its motivation. Surely it is more intuitive that we are justified in judging that flogging infants is prima facie wrong than that no one is ever justified in holding moral judgments. If the former is intuitive enough, it can serve as a partial basis for rebutting and, to a lesser extent, refuting skepticism about the justification of moral judgments.[62]

We can now also address the problem posed by the logical gap between, on the one hand, moral judgment expressing knowledge or justified belief and, on the other, rational action in accordance with such judgment. Skeptics may rightly note that one can justifiedly judge that one should A, yet end up A-ing for a selfish reason and in a way that prevents the action from being rational: the deed might be neither based on the justified judgment calling for it nor rational on any other ground. Why, however, should we assume, as skepticism characteristically does (e.g., in appraising inductive inference), that a logical gap is intrinsically unbridgeable by rational considerations? Consider Kant's view that, in doing obligatory deeds, we cannot always know that some kind of vitiating motivation has not operated.[63] It does not follow that we *never* know, or, especially, that we never have justified belief, that we are acting on a morally sound basis.

The gap between justified moral judgment and action it warrants is not peculiar to intuitionism. Any ethical theory must acknowledge it. Moreover, non-moral propositions can also be believed because of, say, wishful thinking, and merely rationalized by appeal to evidence. But once again, we may resist the skeptical claim that if a thing is possible, then we can know that it is not the case only on grounds *entailing* that it is not; and intuitionists, recognizing as they do various kinds of non-inferential knowledge, are especially likely to deny this.

Quite apart from whether the relevant moral knowledge is inferential, we may plausibly hold that sometimes we are—and have good reason to believe we are—wholehearted in wanting to do a duty and can tell that our sense of this duty is a sufficient motivator of our action.[64] Suppose, however, that we cannot tell, even when we try to monitor our motivation in acting. Suppose further that a prejudice motivates the action and our appeal to an expected good consequence of the deed merely rationalizes it. Still, in virtue of holding a moral judgment constituting knowledge or justified belief that the action is obligatory, we *have* justification for the action. This justification simply does not transfer from our judgment to our deed. This is at least better than neither acting with justification nor even having it.

There is far more to say about the dimensions and prospects of moral skepticism. Here I have simply indicated how moral skepticism might be at least rebutted. I have said too little to carry out such a rebuttal in detail, but I have sketched a strategy of rebuttal open to the position I am defending. The appropriate attitude to adopt in the light of all this is a fallibilist humility, both about whether our moral judgments represent knowledge and about whether we know that the actions we attribute to them are really based on them. This attitude permits moral conviction, but forswears ethical dogmatism.

If I have been roughly correct in this explication and partial defense of a moderate Rossian intuitionism, then it is not difficult to see why intuitionism now occupies a larger place in contemporary ethical theory. Until quite recently, Ross has been seen as more like Moore than he is—for instance, as dogmatic in appealing to self-evidence and as simplistic in his account of knowledge of moral principles. Even apart from this distorted picture of Ross (and in some respects of Moore), there are better grounds for a rationalist moral epistemology than is generally realized. Once we jettison certain baggage that neither intuitionism nor rationalism need carry, some of the major obstacles in the way of a rationalist account of the foundations of ethics are eliminated. These include the ideas that intuitive justification is indefeasible, that it requires a special mental faculty not needed to account for knowledge in general, that for intuitionism we "just see" the truth of basic moral principles, and that non-inferential singular moral judgments cannot be both intuitively justified and defensible with reference to principles. We may clear away other obstacles by noting how a moderate intuitionism conceives self-evidence and can bring to bear the distinctions between hard and soft varieties thereof, between the self-evident and the obvious, and between conclusions of inference and conclusions of reflection.

There is much to commend a fallibilist, intuitionistic moral rationalism that uses reflection as a justificatory method in the ways described here, encompassing both intuitions as prima facie justified inputs to ethical theorizing and reflective equilibrium as a means of extending and systematizing those inputs. Rossian intuitionism is, then, a good theory so far as it goes. For all that, we may still want, and most philosophers will tend to want, a more systematic account of moral obligation than any Rossian intuitionism can provide. We have made room for it by establishing that the self-evident is capable of being evidenced, but we have yet to formulate such an account. That is the main business of the next chapter.

3

Kantian Intuitionism

A MAJOR MERIT of Rossian intuitionism is providing moral principles that directly apply to daily life, principles governing promissory commitment, truthfulness, beneficence, reciprocity, justice, reparation, and much more. In this respect the view has an advantage over other major normative theories. Kantianism and utilitarianism, for instance, require interpretation — and sometimes reasoning that is complex or controversial or both — to yield principles that directly apply to everyday action. From Kant's categorical imperative or Mill's principle of utility, for example, there is often a long, uncharted distance to moral decision. In recent decades, virtue ethics has sometimes seemed preferable to the leading rule theories. But if rule theories appear to their critics rigoristic or too abstract or simply erroneous, virtue theories seem to their critics unclear in application to action, lacking in principles needed to justify or teach moral decision-making, or at best derivative from rule theories.

Intuitionism can help us overcome deficiencies both of virtue ethics and of single-principle rule theories. Nonetheless, many writers in ethics consider it inadequate because it lacks a comprehensive moral theory of a kind that provides an adequate basis for its disparate principles. Rossian intuitionism also shares with virtue theories — and arguably with the other plausible rule theories — great difficulty in providing a good way to resolve conflicts of duties, those "knotty points" in ethics, as Mill called them, that are a central concern of practical ethics.[1]

Sidgwick was conscious of these felt difficulties for moral theories. He saw a need, especially in practical ethics, for moral principles that as it were mediate between overarching moral theory and intuitions about cases. In *Practical Ethics* he called for "middle axioms." Expressing pessimism about agreement on "ultimate principles" (such as the principle of utility), he said, "We must remain as far as possible in the 'region of middle axioms'."[2] He offered no list, but he seemed to mean the sorts of everyday moral principles, such as those prohibiting lying, promise-breaking, and punishing the innocent, that Mill before him called secondary rules and Ross after him called principles of prima facie duty (though Ross did not apply 'middle axiom' to the latter).[3] As a utilitarian, however, Sidgwick was apparently far more optimistic than Ross about the value of using an overarching standard—in this case, utility—to determine in practice what duty prevails when duties conflict. This chapter will show how the modified Rossian intuitionism developed in Chapter 2 can largely answer Sidgwick's call for middle axioms and how it can be integrated with a Kantian moral theory in such a way that the result—a Kantian intuitionism—yields the major benefits of both positions: the moral unification possible through the categorical imperative and other notions prominent in Kant, and the relative closeness to moral practice of Rossian principles of duty.

There are two sorts of benefits we might hope for, either of which might justify my project: for ethical theory, a better understanding of moral obligation and of the justification of moral judgments; for moral practice, an enhanced ability to determine what to do, particularly where we face conflicting duties. Progress toward either goal may easily contribute to achieving the other. I hope to go some distance toward both goals.

1. THE POSSIBILITY OF SYSTEMATIZING
   ROSSIAN PRINCIPLES

One may wonder how, if Rossian principles of prima facie duty are axioms, they can mediate between something more basic and something less so: how can anything be more basic than an axiom? To be sure, self-evidence would qualify the principles as axioms; yet (as we saw) Ross seemed to regard them as basic in a way that would preclude an intermediate status appropriate to mediating between "deeper" axioms and other principles. But (as we also saw) neither the concept of self-evidence nor anything in intuitionism as such precludes systematizing its moral principles by appeal to a more general principle or a comprehensive standard. Ross seems to have failed to see this, as others generally have,[4] perhaps partly because of the influence of paradigms of the self-evident that are—or seem—strongly axiomatic and thus incapable of being evidenced by more basic propositions. But a self-evident proposition is (I have argued) roughly one that is evident *in itself*, in the sense implying that adequate understanding of it, as distinct from inferential derivation of it from prior premises, yields justification for believing it; self-evident propositions need not be (epistemically) *ungroundable* and so not capable of being evidenced by, or derived from, something more basic or having a significant degree of independent support. What counts as an axiom, viewed in itself, may also be a theorem, viewed in relation to some other proposition.

It should help here to make a distinction that Sidgwick and Ross apparently did not make, but could have accepted, between propositions that are axioms and those that are simply *axiomatic*. The notion of an axiom is in one sense relative, as where we speak of the axioms of Euclidian geometry or of a theory. In this sense a proposition is an axiom *with respect to* one or more others it entails, and it is an axiom *for them* (this relation does not require its being self-evident, but usually propositions are not considered axioms without qualification if they are not viewed as at least candidates for self-evidence). In another sense, the notion of an axiom is not relative: any self-evident proposition is axiomatic (though it would be odd to call one axiomatic if we had difficulty seeing its truth). Any self-evident proposition, moreover, is a candidate to ground others it (non-trivially) entails and hence to be an axiom in the relative sense. A self-evident proposition that seems suited for this role, say because it is highly intuitive or in some way "significant"—especially in having such non-trivial consequences as moral principles or philosophical propositions—may not unnaturally be called axiomatic.

These points do not eliminate the vagueness of 'axiomatic', but the term is clear enough to enable us to see how Sidgwick and Ross might have considered propositions axiomatic (as middle axioms might be) even if they did not regard them as axioms in the strong sense in which they apparently understood the axiomatic. Indeed, as Sidgwick conceived Rossian principles, they *are* theorems relative to more basic propositions (though he might not have put it this way). For Ross, however, a genuine axiom, assuming it must be self-evident, cannot be proved and thus cannot be a theorem in the usual sense. It would indeed have to exhibit hard self-evidence and hence be *ultimately basic*: roughly, of a status inconsistent with the existence of any proposition that is more basic, in the sense that it can be justified or known independently of the axiom and entails it. Ross would consider such an "axiom" a theorem.

A further distinction pertinent here is between proving and *evidencing*, in the broad sense of providing (objective) ground for belief. Some propositions might be capable of being evidenced even if not of proof, though Ross might well have said that for a priori propositions the only *kind* of evidencing is proving.[5] I doubt that this is the only kind and have argued that in any case the notion of the self-evident does not entail either unprovability or ungroundability.

Given that the concept of self-evidence does not rule out proof or evidencing by something else, it is noteworthy that Ross at least once spoke as if one of the prima facie duties might be derivable from another.[6] And Ewing, a decade later, spoke of a confusion of "the true proposition that intuitions are not completely established by reasoning with the false proposition that they cannot be supported by reasoning."[7] These remarks seem to acknowledge the possibility that despite many pronouncements to the contrary by some intuitionists, the self-evident can be evidenced by something independent of it. If we can realize the possibility this suggests— namely, a systematization of the Rossian duties by appeal to a more comprehensive set of grounds than Ross appealed to—then contrary to what the dogmatism charge implies, that systematization might provide both reasons for holding the principles and a source of correctives for false or merely apparent moral intuitions or moral principles. If intuitionism can be enriched by even a partial account of why Rossian principles hold, of what they have in common, of why one of them sometimes takes priority over another, of what sort of thinking helps to internalize them, and of related matters that go with a well-developed systematization, then an intuitionist ethical view will be much more plausible.

By rejecting some of Ross's metaethics, then, we can conceive his principles of duty and others like them—Rossian principles, as I am calling them—as candidates for middle axioms: middle because they can be in some way systematized by an overarching moral theory, axioms because they are apparently self-evident and can ground propositions plausibly considered theorems deducible from them. If, however, Rossian principles can be in the middle, what might be at the top?

2. A KANTIAN INTEGRATION OF INTUITIONIST PRINCIPLES

I have already suggested that one reason why Ross did not consider trying to systematize his principles by appeal to an overarching theory is that he conceived the self-evident as unprovable. To be sure, not all systematization requires proof, as opposed to weaker or simply different connections between grounding and grounded propositions, but this may not have occurred to him.[8] In any case, Ross had an ontological reason, as well as this epistemological ground, for rejecting an effort to systematize his principles. At the opening of his chapter on the basis of morally right action, he asks "whether there is any general character which makes right acts right," and, with special emphasis on Moore's "ideal utilitarianism," he mentions egoism and utilitarianism as providing affirmative answers.[9] He answers negatively; but he left—and there remains—much unclarity about what should count as a "general character" underlying the right.

One might think that provability of one proposition from another *entails* certain ontic relations between the content of the former and that of the latter, for instance that if Ross's principles are provable from the principle of utility, then each Rossian duty is constitutively *grounded* in utility. Prichard apparently thought something like this when, in the passage criticized in Chapter 1, he argued that if, in seeking to support principles of duty, we try to show that fulfillment of duty must have a certain kind of consequence, we are grounding duty in the relevant consequential value. But the entailment in question surely does not hold. Epistemic relations need not mirror ontic ones (at least in this simple way). For instance, logically speaking, even if Ross's principles could be known on the basis of both that principle and the principle of utility, Ross's principles could be grounded in a third element, common effects, as it were, of the same causes. We might speculate, moreover, that Ross's preoccupation with providing a rule theory superior to Moore's ideal utilitarianism led him to underestimate the possibility that a Kantian theory would be a better candidate for comparison with his view and even an ally. I want to explore this possibility.

Normative Completeness, Epistemic Completeness, and Conflicts of Duties

In order to see the potential advantages of integrating a Rossian intuitionism with a Kantian theory, we might best begin with a problem for Ross's normative account of duty. He was keenly aware of conflicts both between duties in two or more of his basic categories and between duties in the same category, say between professional and familial promissory duties. He held that no general theory satisfactorily deals with these conflicts and that here practical wisdom is our best resource.[10] In developing Rossian intuitionism and integrating it with a Kantian perspective, I will explore this claim and will argue that the resulting comprehensive theory can take us beyond a Rossian application of practical wisdom in dealing with conflicts of duties. I begin with an outline of some broad characteristics specially relevant to appraising the kind of comprehensive normative theory in question.

Let us call an ethical position, such as intuitionism or utilitarianism, *normatively complete* provided it accounts for every kind of deed that, on balance, we (morally) ought (or ought not) to do, say to abstain from harming others and to keep our promises. Roughly, this is to say that it provides principles or standards in the light of which every overall (i.e., final) moral obligation can be plausibly exhibited as such.[11] Normative completeness is a kind of adequacy condition for a truly comprehensive moral theory. It enables the theory, at least in principle, to take us from knowledge or a plausible assumption of an overall (moral) obligation to a plausible account (and ideally to knowledge) of why the action in question is obligatory.

Suppose for the sake of argument that Ross considered his list of prima facie duties normatively complete. On the one hand, he apparently thought that all our final duties (overall obligations) trace to one or more of the prima facie duties on his list, and hence he might view any final duty as an overriding case of a prima facie duty that he could explain as based on the relevant kind of ground. But, on the other hand, he saw practical wisdom as essential for determining final duty in at least difficult cases of conflicting duties. There is no doubt that it sometimes can determine final duty. But yielding determination of final duty does not necessarily yield explanation of it. Depending on what practical wisdom reveals to us, we might or might not be warranted in claiming that it enables us to explain why the duty it represents as final is so. It might lead us to see exploitation underlying an ostensibly permissible business decision, and we might thereby explain the duty to avoid the act under the heading of non-injury. Practical wisdom might, however, provide only an intuitive judgment of one option's being morally preferable to another, as where reflection gives us a sense that telling a third party about someone's illness would be improper. Further, reflection might yield a general description of the case that enables us to subsume it under a duty; but for Ross, sound moral judgment does not depend on the availability of such a conceptualization.

There is a related kind of completeness that a moral theory may have. Suppose we start not with an obligation, but with (non-moral) facts about our situation: our relations to others, our resources, our capacities, and any other facts we judge potentially relevant to what we ought to do. Suppose our main question is not whether, given an obligation, our theory can account for it, but whether, given the (non-moral, non-normative) facts about our current situation, our theory can tell us what we are (overall) obligated to do. Let us call a moral theory *epistemically complete* provided it enables us, at least in principle, to determine, from (non-normative) facts about our situation—facts that it may help us identify—what we ought (overall) to do. Epistemic completeness is a kind of adequacy, or at least desideratum, in a moral theory that enables it to take us from facts of human life—that we have friends, that killing and deceit are rampant, that children are dying—to what we ought to do. The more readily a moral theory enables us to do this, the better it is, other things equal.

Clearly, both kinds of completeness are important: we should be able to explain and justify ascriptions of obligation, and we thus want a normatively complete theory; we should (at least ideally) be able to determine what we ought to do from the normatively neutral point of view of "the facts," and so should seek an epistemically complete theory. We want knowledge both of what we should do and of why we should do it. Epistemic completeness is needed for a theory to give us the comprehensive moral guidance we seek as moral agents; normative completeness is needed to enable us to explain—and, correspondingly, justify—the moral judgments we arrive at on the basis of the facts that indicate our obligations.

The possibility of completeness of these two kinds should be no surprise. If moral properties are consequential on non-normative ("natural") ones, it is to be expected that an act's possessing the former should be explainable by appeal to its possession of a certain set of the latter. Moreover, given the apparent epistemic dependence of singular moral judgments on knowledge or justified belief regarding the relevant facts—for instance, our being able to know that someone owes reparations to another person only through knowing that the former injured the latter while dashing to catch a bus—it is to be expected that knowledge of specific duties arises (ultimately) from knowledge of the facts that ground them.[12]

Moral theories can achieve these kinds of completeness with varying degrees of success. I believe that in their most plausible versions utilitarianism and Kantianism may be viewed as normatively complete, and at least the former may be considered epistemically complete, though problems of measurement and prediction of, say, happiness and suffering require qualifying this assessment in relation to many actual moral questions. This apparent twofold completeness of utilitarian theories (such as Bentham's and, arguably, Mill's) is a major reason for their enduring attractiveness.

They appear to provide an empirical, factual basis of moral knowledge and a route to acquiring it. To what extent does Rossian intuitionism approach completeness in either sense?

It would take an entire treatise to clarify in detail each of the wide-ranging duties on Ross's list. Intuitionism, however, is not limited to that list (as Ross realized in deliberately not claiming completeness for it).[13] But given the potentially wide scope of Ross's intuitionism, I will tentatively assume its normative completeness and will consider instead the pivotal question of how such a theory provides for resolving conflicts of duties (I defer the question of its epistemic completeness until Section 4). Inability to deal adequately with these conflicts may be the largest obstacle to regarding it as normatively complete. Two kinds of case are crucial. Each indicates different aspects of the notion of normative completeness just described.

Consider first a case in which a worthy charity asks you for a donation. For Ross, there is a prima facie duty of beneficence, grounded in the good one may achieve by donating. If his theory is normatively complete, it can account for this duty. I propose to say that a normative theory has *first-order normative completeness*—as opposed to the kind of overall normative completeness described earlier—provided it accounts for every instance in which, as here, we have a *prima facie* duty and hence (on plausible assumptions) accounts for all our basic duties. Roughly, for each instance of a (first-order) prima facie duty, it can specify something in virtue of which it is a duty. Thus, its list of grounds of prima facie duty will include at least one ground for each such duty. The better the theory, the more readily we can ascertain such a ground for any given prima facie duty we identify.

One might think that this achievement is trivially accomplished since we cannot identify a prima facie duty in the first place without knowing its ground, as where we know we ought to do something in virtue of knowing we have promised to. But this is not so. Moral sensitivity can run ahead of judgment. We may sense a duty, say to help someone, without any good idea of whether the duty derives from a tacit promise or from beneficence or both. We may thus *respond* to appropriate grounds before forming a *belief* that they are present or making the corresponding judgment, here the judgment that we should help. This is one kind of case in which emotion, say compassion or indignation, can be both morally evidential and morally motivating. Emotions may reveal what is right or wrong before judgment articulates it; and they may both support ethical judgment and spur moral conduct.

This case also illustrates the application of a kind of particularism regarding moral judgment, as opposed to the subsumptivist view that justified moral judgment requires regarding an act as of a certain ethical kind (say, a duty of beneficence). The particularism is genetic in taking moral judgment to arise in a certain way from experience of the situation that calls for it (assuming, as Ross explicitly did, sufficient mental maturity on the part of the agent); it is epistemic in implying that this kind of genesis can provide justification. Moreover, even where moral sensitivity does not run ahead of judgment, judgment can be produced by its grounds without our recognition of the process or even of the grounds.[14] Third, we may mistakenly attribute a duty to one ground when it rests on another, as where we think we must make reparations for a wrong but have actually not done one and instead have a duty of fidelity dictating the same effort on someone's behalf, say, helping a friend with a travel plan. A theory having any significant degree of depth accounts, in a way that has appreciable explanatory power, for all the grounds of prima facie duty. This is something Ross apparently tried to do.

Does Ross's intuitionism, conceived as centering on his famous list of duties, achieve even first-order normative completeness? Taken at face value, it apparently does not. Consider my breaking a promise to a friend because I have a stronger obligation (owing to sudden sickness in my child). I ought at least to give my friend an explanation, and the 'ought' seems both moral and overriding. If I do not give it, I fail in some moral respect. But which Rossian duty do I violate? If Ross's view has first-order normative completeness, then in not explaining my failure, I must violate at least one. Explaining to my friend why I have failed is not clearly a case of reparation, as would be my doing the promised deed doubly well later on. One may wonder, then, whether Ross's theory has even first-order normative completeness.

One defense of the theory on this point is this. We might conceive my apologetically explaining my failure as required by the duty of non-injury if not by that of reparation, or by both. I see no reason why Ross could not say this, and I consider it quite plausible. If the claim is sound, it illustrates two interesting points.

First, a Rossian theory can countenance *second-order duties*, such as the prima facie duty to explain a failure to perform a (first-order) prima facie duty. A second-order duty of this kind *derives* from his list, and is broadly what I call Rossian, but is not *on* it. It might perhaps be conceived an instance of one of the listed duties; but this conception would be at best misleading, since those duties have a first-order content, such as avoiding harming others. Failure to explain promise-breaking does not in itself seem to be a case of harming the promisee. Even promise-breaking does not in itself appear to be a kind of harm, as opposed to a wrong.

Second, there is more than one way in which a theory can be complete in accounting for our duties, whether prima facie or final. It might construe all of them as a matter of meeting a single standard, such as maximizing pleasure; but a theory might also account for duties disjunctively. By this I mean it sometimes construes an obligatory action as called for by at least one of two or more duties, say fidelity and non-injury, but does not specify one in particular. It thereby leaves open how many duties we meet by performing the action.[15] A complete moral theory need not, then, be *fully distributive*: it need not enable us to specify, for each obligatory action, exactly which duties it fulfills; its standards may only collectively account for all our duties.

A theory exhibiting first-order normative completeness, even if fully distributive, may not exhibit overall normative completeness, i.e., completeness in accounting for final duty. As we saw in Chapter 2, accounting for that is no easy matter, and Ross did not claim to do it, if indeed he thought it achievable. Might a modified Rossian theory do this? Might it account for, say, the *finality* (roughly, overridingness) of my duty to aid my child (thereby breaking my promise)? It is one thing to account for this prima facie duty; it is much more difficult to account for my final duty. Ross denies that rival theories can provide a general account of overriding,[16] and he himself offers only a rough *procedure* for doing this. His account of morality does not provide a theoretically plausible ground for the finality of a duty, even though finality is something we need to determine whenever we must resolve a conflict of duties or, especially, when we must explain or justify such a resolution.

Let us say that a normative theory that (like any plausible moral theory) countenances conflicts of prima facie duties has *second-order normative completeness* if and only if it accounts for the finality of any (first-order) duty that prevails in such a conflict (and for the equal stringency of two conflicting duties that are equally stringent).[17] The problem for Rossian intuitionism requires more than countenancing *derivative second-order duties*, particularly those that, like the duty to explain why one broke a promise, rest simply on violation of some first-order duty. The view should also

enable us to account for *compositional second-order duties*, those resulting
from a determination of which of two or more conflicting first-order duties
is overriding. How might we extend Rossian intuitionism to achieve both
first- and second-order completeness and thereby overall normative completeness?[18]

A Kantian Approach to Conflicts of Duty

A broadly Kantian theory can help in this task by providing for some extension and unification of Rossian intuitionism without weakening it either
epistemically or normatively. I stress that I am speaking of a Kantian theory, not specifically Kant's, which can be captured only by extensive interpretation of his writings. The integration of a Kantian theory with a Rossian intuitionism may indeed produce a significant gain for Kantian ethics
as well. These points can be seen more clearly if we first consider the kind
of deliberation appropriate to deciding which of two conflicting duties is
overriding. Consider a case in which I realize that my sick daughter could
have a serious setback and that only I can keep watch; I see that if I break
the promise to meet my friend for lunch, the friend will only have to make
a needless trip to the restaurant and, not finding me, phone to see what is
wrong. Now suppose that, appealing to Kant's categorical imperative—
though not his own interpretation of it[19]—I consider both universality and
intrinsic end formulations of it.[20]

Kant's universality formulation (in one translation) is "*Act as if the
maxim of your action* [roughly the first-person principle underlying it] *were
to become through your will a universal law of nature.*[21] As I understand
this, its explicit use requires asking whether we can (rationally) universalize our maxim, which in my example may be plausibly taken to be 'If the
only way to keep my sick child safe is to break a promise to a friend at the
cost of inconvenience, but in a way the friend would not (at least on careful reflection about the facts of the case) resent, then I will break it'.[22] One
need not, however, do *everything* that passes this universalizability test;
what one is (overall) obligated to do is deeds whose *non-performance* con-
forms to *no* maxim that passes the test.

Kant's intrinsic end formulation (also commonly called the formula of
humanity) is "*Act in such a way that you always treat humanity, whether
in your own person or in the person of any other, never simply as a means,
but always at the same time as an end.*"[23] Kant apparently took these formulations to be equivalent, though not necessarily identical in content.[24]

Even if we accept the equivalence claim (which I cannot assess here), we can see a difference in function. The universality formulation is highly appropriate to *testing* acts for permissibility, particularly where we have an appropriate list of maxims to consider in relation to them, but not readily usable in *discovering* what to do where we have no promising options to consider, since it is at best difficult to arrive at relevant maxims to universalize if one does not have a definite or at least limited range of acts—or, more realistically, acts paired with circumstances—for which to formulate them. The intrinsic end formulation is appropriate to both tasks: it articulates a constraint on maxims and deeds, and it thereby provides a test for them; and it sets a twofold aim for action and thereby indicates, if not specific options, at least the directions in which to seek guidance of our conduct. Let us consider how these formulations might bear on conflicts of duties.

Would universalizing my maxim permitting breaking the promise to meet my friend undermine the practice of promising? No. We regularly accept promises fully aware that illnesses prevent their fulfillment in cases where non-fulfillment is not very serious. Would my breaking my promise in such a case offend a reasonable promisee?[25] I believe not.

A problem that remains is how we should formulate maxims. This is a difficult matter in interpreting Kant, and the problem cannot be discussed in detail here.[26] The theory I am developing, however, will not depend on the use of maxims as a basis for singular moral judgment and in that respect is less problematic than Kant's account. Indeed, since the theory focuses on understanding the categorical imperative in relation to selection, formulation, unification, and justification of Rossian principles and subsidiary rules, we may often bypass the problem of formulating maxims—at least of the specific kind Kant had in mind.

In any case, I suggest that whether we are framing maxims or testing principles already articulated, we might take Kant's intrinsic end formulation of the categorical imperative to be essential (at least for any Kantian theory) in determining what principles can be *rationally* universalized (at least from the moral point of view). Suppose my aim is to treat humanity never merely as a means but at the same time as an end. These notions may not be taken for granted. Two brief clarifications may help, each having some connection with Kant's uses of the notions but—more important here—both useful in guiding moral judgment. First, to treat someone as an end is above all for the relevant acts toward the person (the "treatment") to be motivated by a concern with the good, say the physical

or psychological well-being, of the person for its own sake. Second, to treat
someone merely as a means is for the relevant acts toward the person
to be motivated only by instrumental concerns and accompanied by an
indisposition to acquire any non-instrumental motivation toward the person (some such clause is needed to capture the callousness or exploitation
suggested by 'merely').[27]

With these points in mind, suppose I risked my daughter's health to
keep a promise of the kind in question, I would apparently fail to treat her
as an end in the relevant sense. I would be putting her in serious danger
for a less than weighty reason; treating her as an end, in the sense I take
to be most pertinent, requires caring about her good both to a significant
degree and for its own sake. The point is not that if I kept the promise, I
could not still care about the child at all; it is that the treatment is not
appropriate to the level of care that goes with treating persons as ends or
with my relationship to her. By contrast, in staying with her, I not only
express my valuing her well-being for its own sake; I am also acting in a
way that, from the point of view of the universality formulation, a rational
person in the friend's situation, could accept. Moreover, in breaking the
promise I would not be treating or using my friend merely as a means. I
would not *use* the friend at all, as I would by lying to get the friend's car
for a trip to the liquor store. Treating others merely as means in the Kantian
sense is at least typically a case of using them and seems to require their
being one's means to some end (or at least an attempted means that one
in some sense uses).

Perhaps more important, since my explanation of breaking the promise
would be accepted by any reasonable person in the situation, it seems a
mistake to say that the friend is treated objectionably. The intuitive idea—
certainly one intuitive idea—underlying the prohibition of treating people
merely as means is roughly that we may not use them *exploitively*. Kant
perhaps thought, and in any case we may plausibly claim, that his view
does not depend on any prior *moral* notion of exploitation.[28] The notion
of exploitation we need has as one anchor the idea of using something
merely as an instrument: it matters only in getting the job done; it may be
damaged in the process and trashed thereafter. Again, my aim is not to
preserve Kant's theory as he stated it but to draw on elements of it in
constructing an intuitionism that has advantages over both Ross's view and
Kantian ethics as commonly understood.

Ross might think that we have no theory of conflict resolution here,
only rules of thumb to facilitate the use of practical wisdom. It is true that

practical wisdom is required to apply the categorical imperative, particularly given that there can be conflicts between duties to avoid treating people merely as means and duties to treat them as ends. Such conflicts are most likely regarding people in different categories, say family members and unknown sufferers, and I assume that at least when other things are equal the avoidance of treating one group merely as a means takes priority over treating another group as an end. Still, I cannot see that we do not gain some help from the imperative beyond what we derive from just gathering the facts in conflict cases and trying to make a wise decision apart from reliance on this principle or a similar one.

Indeed, Ross himself would agree that if what we do is morally obligatory, it should in principle be describable in a way that is generalizable. For he regards moral properties as consequential upon natural ones, such as those involving the results of an action for pleasure and pain, approval and resentment. If it is natural facts, ultimately, that ground and justify our true (singular) moral judgments, it is plausible to hold that—in principle—one could describe these facts in a way that yields, for each sound moral judgment, a non-trivial general description of its grounds.[29] If they justify our judgment, then (on plausible assumptions) we can become aware of them through suitable reflection and, given sufficient conceptual clarity, formulate a description of them that expresses our justification.[30] We may then formulate a general principle. It may or may not be Rossian, in the sense implying that it is at least a candidate for self-evidence. Whether it is Rossian or not, it should be both readily applicable in the way Rossian principles are and in some sense subsumable under the categorical imperative. It may thereby clarify both the overall normative content of that principle and the broadly Rossian framework with which we are integrating the principle.

If we further assume that in order to make a justified moral decision to act, one needs a sense of the identity and bearing of the relevant facts, then we cannot reasonably deny that the categorical imperative provides a *test* even for judgments reached without its help. Ross might reasonably insist that we can be *guided* by facts without being able (at least apart from Socratic prodding) to *articulate* how they bear. Granted. This is indeed a place where moral emotions and moral intuitions may guide moral judgment. But his view implies no reason to deny that the effort to articulate the bearing of facts is appropriate and often successful; and he would surely grant that in a similar way the categorical imperative may at least be intelligibly invoked where duties conflict. Appeal to it will not always be conclusive; but given the vagueness of moral terms, one would expect some recalcitrant borderline cases, and the Kantian intuitionism we can construct by integrating a Rossian framework with the categorical imperative may do as well on this score as any alternative theory. Moreover, if, as may perhaps be the case, bringing this two-tiered theory to bear can always yield a minimally satisfactory answer as to which of two (sets of) conflicting duties is final, the theory has second-order normative completeness.

The Beneficence Problem

We can see further reason for integrating a Rossian intuitionism with a Kantian view if we consider one of the most serious challenges confronting any Rossian theory, and probably any plausible ethical pluralism: how to deal with conflicts between the duty of beneficence and other duties. This duty poses serious problems for any plausible ethical view that takes the value of the welfare of persons to imply weighty obligations to better their lives. It is not clear that any theory provides—or should be expected to provide—a solution to it that resolves all of the associated theoretical worries or cuts through all the "knotty points" Mill noted, those hard cases where even the wisest may be uncertain. Why is it that my duty of beneficence does not virtually always outweigh my ordinary fiduciary duties to, say, my family, as well as nearly all my duties of self-improvement whose fulfillment will not conduce to my doing more for humanity? This should suggest the more general question of how a Kantian intuitionism can at once admit a general duty of beneficence and avoid treating as obligatory many acts that are only supererogatory.

Ross heightened the beneficence problem by describing the duty of beneficence as resting "on the mere fact that there are other beings in the world whose condition we can make better in respect of virtue, or of intelligence, or of pleasure."[31] To be sure, the duty of beneficence would still be only one among other duties, whereas the maximization idea, say in the case of utilitarianism, posits just one basic duty. But the pull of the duty of beneficence in a world with as much suffering as ours seems incalculably strong. Ross also stressed, however, "the highly personal character of duty" and maintained that, other things equal, the duty of fidelity outweighs that of beneficence.[32] A Rossian intuitionism can thus take it as clear on reflection that even a large contribution to the welfare of humanity does not *necessarily* outweigh all duties of (say) fidelity or of self-improvement, and that there is no quantitative criterion—such as maximization of welfare—that we can appeal to in deciding each case.

There are at least three respects in which the Kantian approach outlined here can help both to clarify and to rationalize this point. The first concerns the conditions under which we *have* a duty of beneficence. The second concerns its *stringency* in relation to conflicting duties to avoid treating anyone merely as a means—i.e., to meet the first demand of the intrinsic end formulation. The third concerns what it is to treat others as ends, the second demand of the intrinsic end formulation, and how understanding that demand may clarify the duty of beneficence. Let us take these in turn.

A Kantian Intuitionist Approach to the Beneficence Problem

It is instructive to view the beneficence problem—the problem of the grounds, scope, and stringency of the duty of beneficence—in the light of the Kantian idea that autonomy is central in understanding moral obligation.[33] Suppose for the sake of argument that moral agents have a kind of radical autonomy. This claim is not implicit in the categorical imperative, but something at least close to it is in the spirit of Kant's ethics. I begin by speculating with a notion of autonomy that might be considered broadly Kantian insofar as we regard agents as fundamentally legislative and in that way authors of their own standards of obligation, but also might be viewed as Rossian insofar as it takes duties to others to arise in specific relationships. Even if this notion does not solve the beneficence problem, it provides a useful background for applying the categorical imperative.

On the radical autonomy view, we do not have a duty of beneficence unless we autonomously incur it. We often do incur it, of course, and in at least two ways: *explicitly*, say by promising to do good deeds, and *implicitly*, by some other free undertaking or commitment. Communal living with others may create obligations of beneficence in several ways, for instance by raising expectations of good deeds and allowing those expectations to continue, or by accepting help in a way that, without amounting to a tacit promise to do good deeds toward our benefactors, would make them assume our reciprocity in such conduct. And there is something subtler. We may want beneficent conduct from others while quite aware of their similar desires for such conduct in us. We may accordingly criticize departures from such conduct. Such criticism may give rise to a duty to live up to the standards implicit in it.

How far can the autonomy thesis about the duty of beneficence go? Could there be a society in which no duty of beneficence arises other than by autonomous deeds? Might there be a society in which children are prevented from coming to believe they owe anyone anything (e.g., where food is put in the right place, but children do not get help from anyone in a way they know is an effort—perhaps automated servers deliver it, to prevent any person's getting much credit)? Suppose no one promises children anything positive, or expects them to promise anything positive, in part because the conditions of life do not make people needy in the way they are in our world. Moreover, although children are taught that others are also vulnerable, that harming others is morally wrong, and also learn whatever moral standards might be taught without teaching a duty of beneficence, no one exhibits any needs before children, say for medical help.

There are practical limits to what can be done in such a peculiar kind of upbringing, but one can perhaps conceive a society in which children have sufficient experience and understanding to develop, say, a duty not to kill and not to lie or be unjust, but (initially, at least) no duty of beneficence. To be sure, such a person could readily acquire *altruistic reasons for action*; but this is a different point. Even assuming that having such reasons entails a prima facie duty of beneficence, the autonomy line questions whether that duty is a "natural" one that we have simply as moral agents.

Suppose that, as Ross apparently thought, a (prima facie) duty of beneficence is entailed, at least in normal agents, by the possibility of contributing to the good of others. It might still be true that how *weighty* a duty of beneficence we have depends largely on our autonomous deeds, say on how many or how demanding promises or tacit commitments we make. One might also argue that the moral importance of autonomy can give us overriding reason not to help others (unless we want to) by efforts so demanding that we impair our autonomous determination of our own lives. Autonomy might be a basis for explaining why the duty of beneficence is so often overridden, even if it does not provide a basis for showing that the way in which this duty is incurred enables us to explain that apparent fact.

In the light of these points about the wide scope of autonomously undertaken duties of beneficence, one might argue that although Ross was deeply right about "the highly personal character of duty," he did not adequately bring out the diversity of the relevant relationships and was positively mistaken in suggesting that, by themselves, opportunities for improvement in well-being make someone an object of our duty. We all *do* incur duties to certain people and, by being constructively participating citizens, to others in our nation and, if we embrace certain moral or religious ideals, to the wider world. But on the autonomy view in question, duties of beneficence do not arise "from the mere fact that there are others in the world whose condition we can make better."[34]

To be sure, duties of beneficence seem to be a necessary feature of a truly *social* human existence, one in which cooperative practices and social institutions play a central role. Still, a defender of the autonomy line might contend that their necessity relative to our inevitable situation is quite different from their being basic natural duties like those of non-injury and fidelity; and if they are autonomously undertaken in the suggested ways, there is little plausibility in supposing that they are so stringent that they override other duties, such as those of fidelity and self-improvement, in the way they might appear to do in certain utilitarian frameworks. Normally, at least, rational agents would not autonomously undertake duties whose fulfillment would so substantially disadvantage themselves and those close to them.

Whatever may be said for the radical autonomy line, it raises more problems than I can address here, and I think it wisest to assume that it is too strong and that, as is consistent with a moderate conception of our autonomy, all of us normal adults do have weighty natural duties of beneficence which do not depend on our autonomously undertaking them. Must we all become full-time philanthropists, at least until human life on earth is far better? The question brings us to a second way in which an integration between a Rossian intuitionism and a Kantian theory—particularly with the categorical imperative—helps with the beneficence problem.

To put the problem starkly, suppose that, as on certain consequentialist views, one must, on pain of immorality, devote one's life chiefly to maximizing, or in any case take as one's overriding aim to maximize, the good of persons (or sentient beings—I leave open whether only persons, and indeed only actual beings, are in question). Consider submitting to this duty as obligatory on all of us—as opposed to pursuing the required good deeds out of a voluntary benevolent ideal (or to keep certain promises one has made). I have in mind bowing to a sense of duty, not embracing a high standard as expressing one's ideals. The latter would be an exercise of autonomy and might be supererogatory. The former undertaking—a life of beneficent servitude—is, if not a way of treating oneself merely as a means, at least a way of subjecting oneself to a liability to treating oneself so. For instance, if the duty of beneficence is supreme in this way, one's personal commitments and talents might not matter at all if maintaining them were in conflict with contributing to the general good of persons.

To be sure, on the kind of maximizing consequentialism in question, this overall good includes one's own, but only as a tiny and sometimes perhaps negligible part. The smaller one's own good in proportion to this overall good, the closer one would come to being obligated to treat oneself merely as a means to serving the latter. The notion of merely instrumental treatment expresses a negative ideal. Treatment of persons that instantiates it is prima facie wrong and commonly repugnant; but even conduct that approaches it is, if not wrong, then criticizable to the extent that it approximates merely instrumental treatment.

Moreover, although your potential good matters as much as anyone else's, this *can* be not at all if, say, you are incapable of pleasure (or of realizing whatever intrinsic value, such as virtue, is in question in defining beneficence). Persons are not, after all, ends in themselves. In any case, there is an extreme subordination of one's own good to the overall good of persons. That is not a kind of treatment we can expect rational persons to agree to, at least if they are guided by the categorical imperative.[35] A rational appraisal of moral status, conceived in the light of the intrinsic end formulation, seems to require, and certainly to permit, more self-concern.

Suppose, by contrast, that we reduce the distance from Rossian intuitionism (and similarly from Kant) by considering not a maximizing consequentialism but an a priori hierarchism on which the duty of beneficence has priority over any other single duty.[36] Consider a case in which my overriding duty is to maximize the good of persons. If two options enabled me to contribute equally to overall goodness and were otherwise alike except that in pursuing one I could also develop my talents and in pursuing the other I could not, then although I might rationally prefer the former for personal reasons, the development of my talents could not be a decisive element in determining what, morally, I ought to do. Choosing to develop them would be inferior to the other option. This intuitively objectionable result supports the idea that when the duty of beneficence automatically overrides any other single duty, I would at least approach using myself merely as a means: my interests matter only insofar as they do not conflict with my contributing to the overall good of persons conceived collectively. In a world like this, the maximization ideal *invites* a predominantly instrumental conception of oneself. Even if we did not try to *maximize* the overall good of persons, but always preferred making large contributions to it over maintaining our personal commitments and talents, we would, in a world like this, be liable at almost any point to approach using ourselves merely as a means.

Even if this last point cannot be sustained, a plausible application of the intrinsic end formulation would at least block an indiscriminate large-scale preponderance of the duty of beneficence over competing duties. Giving it such high and virtually invariable priority ill-befits our dignity as persons, a status partly captured by the idea—even taken in the ordinary sense of the terms apart from Kant—that we are to be treated as ends and never merely as means. Our own interests as rational beings have considerable moral importance. This is particularly evident where someone *harms* another person for the sake of the overall good of persons, as in taking organs from a salvageable accident victim (without consent).

The universality formulation of the categorical imperative is also pertinent here. Even if it is not irrational to universalize maxims requiring the beneficent servitude I have described, it is certainly rational to reject these in favor of maxims that substantially limit the duty of beneficence in relation to other duties. Since a kind of action is obligatory only if no rationally universalizable maxim allows omitting it, the extreme beneficence in question is not in general obligatory.

I can imagine a defender of autonomy noting here that one has a *right* to commit oneself to the maximizing standard in question. True, but the right would be voluntarily exercisable in a way that implies that the associated duty of extreme beneficence is not a universal moral obligation, as beneficence is on either Ross's or Kant's understanding, but self-imposed. This point is confirmed by the fact that no one else would have a right to demand or even receive such beneficence from one. Indeed, the perspective of rights (to be discussed further in Chapter 5) seems inimical to taking the duty of beneficence even to approach the strength it would apparently have for a maximizing consequentialism or even an a priori hierarchism with beneficence as the strongest duty.

Consonantly with these points, one might argue that—to use terms important for both Ross and Kant—there is a prima facie duty not to use oneself even *mainly* as a means; but I shall not pursue that line now. It is enough if the strong beneficence thesis, which implies that we each matter only secondarily to our role in maximizing the overall good of persons, is justifiably rejectable by a Kantian intuitionism.

One might wonder whether this suggested use of the categorical imperative cuts the other way as well. Might the omission of beneficent deeds, at least in a world like this, also in some way use others merely (or in some intuitively inadmissible way) as a means? Consider deciding not to do any charitable deeds toward the poor, with the resulting benefit of retaining one's resources. In many cases this seems morally reprehensible. Suppose it is. Still, one need not be *using* them. (It is different, of course, if they are one's employees.)

Moreover, suppose that—in the right spirit—a person does *some* charitable deeds toward the poor. Even though these fall short of what one would do if one sought to maximize the well-being of persons, this level of beneficence is still one way of treating *as ends* those for whom one does such deeds. To be sure, the strategy I have outlined for applying the categorical imperative does not provide a clearly successful procedure for deciding each case (as opposed to implying—what is of great importance in confirming or disconfirming moral judgments—that once a case is correctly decided and adequately described, there is a universalizable principle extractable from it).[37] But intuitionism is not committed to the availability, in advance of reflection on actual cases of conflicts of duties, of precise rules for deciding such conflicts.

Another respect in which the intrinsic end formulation of the categorical imperative can help us in understanding the duty of beneficence comes to light if we distinguish two interpretations of treating persons as ends. This can be given an impersonal reading, on which to treat people as ends is simply to promote their good for its own sake, something possible when one has no relationship with them and no notion of how this will occur, as where one contributes to a charity that one simply knows, through assurances from a friend, is philanthropic. It can also be given a personal reading, on which it applies only to people to whom one has some personal relationship. On this reading, you cannot fail to treat people as ends if there is no way you "treat them," since you do not have any personal relationship to them. The latter reading fits Kant's main illustrations of the imperative better. In applying the imperative to beneficence, for instance, he says that the agent "*sees* others who have to struggle with great hardships (and whom he *could easily help*)."[38] If, however, the imperative is to account adequately for moral obligation regarding people who do not now exist but may be expected to ("future generations"), treating humanity as an end must be taken to apply in some way to them.

Let us suppose that a Kantian theory countenances indirect relationships, say where one has a definite description adequate to provide a sense of who is in question, for instance poor children in one's own city. Suppose further that these relationships are such that we can fail to treat the persons in question as ends. Still, doing or giving *something* to help may suffice to prevent failure to treat them as ends. If one helps in the right way, one expresses a recognition of their humanity and of one's obligation to address it. Doing this—like many other ways of treating someone as an end—is compatible with failing to do the best thing one can. But on a Kantian theory, as for any Rossian intuitionism, there need be no final duty always to do the best thing one can to promote the well-being of others.[39] This is supported by the intuitive point that one cannot be said to fail to treat such children as ends simply because one does not do as much for them as one would if one were maximizing the overall good of persons.

A similar point holds if the intrinsic end formulation is applied to the suffering of poor children we see on television, who certainly can give us a *sense* of personal involvement. But there is an additional point. The personal-relationship reading of the duty to treat others as ends narrows, and may clarify, the field in which the duty of beneficence conflicts with other duties. This reading goes only partway toward solving the beneficence problem. But by distinguishing the two readings we can at least see that the issue is in part the extent to which moral obligation is personal and the extent to which it may arise from the mere opportunity to do good. Kantian intuitionism takes it to be predominantly personal and, on principle, does not quantitatively define the degree of predominance, nor require a maximizing standard of beneficence.

Quite apart from the radical autonomy interpretation of the grounds of duties of beneficence, then, at least two points about the application of the categorical imperative have emerged. First, if we regard duties of general beneficence, in the ways that are intuitively objectionable, as prevailing over other duties, such as those of fidelity or self-improvement, then in acting accordingly we are not only liable to use, or approach using, *ourselves* merely as means, but will also often fail to treat certain others, such as a promisee or our friends, as ends. For the pull of beneficence will often override their justified claims on us. Second, where fulfilling a duty of beneficence would result in either or (especially) both of these deficiencies under the intrinsic end formulation, one is justified in giving a very high degree of preference—though not automatic or a priori preference— to duties of self-improvement or, especially, fidelity over the duty of beneficence (and much the same would hold for other duties that might conflict with beneficence).

Kantian Intuitionism as Providing a Plausible Grounding of Rossian Duties

There is at least one further and more general consideration suggesting that a Kantian intuitionism is a good extension of a Rossian version. It concerns the moral principles we would choose to live by in the first place if the categorical imperative is our basic, or at least widest, ethical principle.

Rossian principles of duty (though perhaps not exactly Ross's list of them) may be argued to be just the general moral principles one would derive—even if not strictly deduce—from a careful application of the categorical imperative to everyday life. For instance, if one is to avoid treating people merely as means—and so to realize the negative standard expressed by the categorical imperative—one must recognize (prima facie) duties of non-injury (including avoidance of murder, brutality, and theft), of reparation, and of fidelity and veracity; and if one is to treat people positively as ends—and so to realize the positive standard it expresses—one must recognize duties of beneficence, gratitude, self-improvement, and justice (meaning, as Ross intended in this context,[40] rectification of injustice one discovers, as opposed to avoidance of injustice, which is at least typically a kind of injury).[41]

The kind of reference we find in Sidgwick and others to axioms and theorems ("middle axioms") invites expectation of strict deduction and is to that extent misleading as regards Kantian intuitionism. Not every derivation is a strict deduction, as opposed to, for instance, the provision of a rationale. If one wants a strict deduction here, one might have to do some regimentation on the Kantian side. We might, for instance, take the duty not to treat people merely as means as absolute, rather than suppose (more reasonably) that the only absolute duty under the categorical imperative in this formulation is to do deeds that are optimal with respect to *jointly* treating people as ends and avoiding treating them merely as means. Suppose, however, that the Kantian prohibitional clause does express absolute obligation. Then, with the added premise (which is not without some plausibility) that breaking promises tends to treat people merely as a means, it follows (given the assumption that treating persons merely as a means is absolutely wrong) that it *tends* to be wrong, which, for the relevant, non-statistical kind of tendency, is roughly equivalent to its being prima facie wrong. Similar points hold for the other Rossian duties.

The derivability claim here is not, then, that *every* violation of a Rossian (final) duty either treats someone merely as a means or fails to treat someone as an end; it is roughly that the violations of these duties tend to do that and that those that do not have close affinities to those that do. Perhaps, with sufficient modification of the crucial Kantian and Rossian notions, the former claim could be established; but from the categorical imperative taken without any artificial regimentation, we may be able to achieve only a weaker derivation of Rossian duties: a justificatory rationale for them rather than a strict deduction of them.

If we take a step beyond understanding the categorical imperative in terms of means and ends, we find a further reason to view Rossian duties as derivable from it. Suppose that, consistently with plausible interpretations of both its universality and intrinsic end formulations, we take the categorical imperative to imply a duty to avoid treating people in a way that is *disrespectful*. We rationally dislike being so treated, nor is such treatment consonant with treating us as ends on any plausible understanding of that notion. The kind of derivation I suggest—provision of a justificatory rationale—is now still more plausible. For there are cases in which one is not treating others merely as means but *also* not simply failing to treat them as ends. If I thoughtlessly talk during your presentation, I act disrespectfully; but I would not be either using you or treating you as a means. Still, this is quite different from my culpably failing to give to any charity that helps the poor in my city.

Ross would perhaps call such disrespectful conduct a kind of injury and its deliberate commission a case of injury or maleficence. A Kantian might call it conduct that not only fails to treat others as ends but is in *opposition* to that end. Thus, a Kantian partial explanation of why it violates the duty of non-injury and not merely the duty of beneficence—and of why there is a duty of non-injury covering this and many similar cases—is that someone who does such things may be expected, when there is significant gain and no threat of punishment, both to treat others merely as means and, minimally, to be disposed toward maleficent or disrespectful conduct. Here, as in understanding the beneficence problem, it is fruitful to conceive the prohibitional clause as expressing a negative ideal and the exhortatory (intrinsic end) clause as expressing a positive ideal.

The derivational strategy I am sketching gives the categorical imperative a double role—particularly on the assumption that disrespectful conduct is, as I propose, included in the Kantian prohibition as prima facie worse than simply failing to treat others as ends, though it is not necessarily treating anyone as a means. First, the imperative in some sense yields, at least in providing an inferential pathway to, Ross's prima facie duties— and possibly some further, independent ones (something I leave open). Second, as illustrated in the case of the sick child, it provides an account (a non-quantitative account, to be sure) of how to weight the factors associated with those duties in cases of moral conflict. It does this not by assigning an absolute weight to those factors, but by telling us what sorts of variables to consider and helping us to determine which of the alternative actions we then identify is morally acceptable.

Granted, one could perhaps justify the same first-order principles by appeal to utility, as is suggested by Sidgwick's appeal to his utilitarian principle as a basis for (or in some cases a corrective to) the principles endorsed by dogmatic intuitionists. But one could achieve such a justification only by invoking auxiliary assumptions that are both contingent and quantitative, whereas no parallel contingent assumptions are required in the derivation of Rossian principles from the categorical imperative.[42] (I leave aside the question whether, even if one could justify the principles in this second way, one could also explain their apparent self-evidence.)

Does Kantian intuitionism undermine the plausible ethical pluralism that is attractive in Rossian intuitionism? Does it imply that (pace Ross) there is some "general character that makes right acts right?" It does not. This ontological thesis about rightness is left open. Kantian intuitionism does not deny that there is a plurality of moral reasons for action, say distinct reasons for avoiding injury, rectifying injustices, and keeping promises. These reasons may even be considered *basic* in the sense that they meet the following important and closely related conditions. (1) Any of them can be known to be morally relevant to action without being derived from more fundamental considerations. For instance, that one has injured a person (say, in rushing to make a train) can be non-inferentially known to be a moral reason to make reparation. (2) Their normative force, conceived as sufficient to justify action, does not consist wholly in their indicating some *other* factor, such as enhancement of pleasure. In the injury case, for example, neither relieving pain nor any other non-moral consideration is needed as a basis for the prima facie duty of reparation. (3) Our justified level of confidence in the principles of prima facie duty can be higher, especially pretheoretically, than our justified level of confidence in the categorical imperative.

If Rossian prima facie duties are basic in this threefold sense, they are in a certain way irreducible, yet it does not follow from this Rossian point that there can be no significant general characteristic possessed by all duties (this is not equivalent to a property that "makes right acts right," since it need not be a *grounding* property). There might still be some general characteristic, perhaps something like expressing respect for persons or — to take a related notion embodying a recurring intuitionist idea — "befitting" the dignity of persons, such that, first, the moral reasons can be known to be morally relevant in the light of their connection with it and, second, they derive from it normative force sufficient to justify the kinds of action for which they are reasons.[43] The mode of this derivation of

Rossian duties is in part explained, by Kantian intuitionism, on the hypothesis that the categorical imperative is the central principle—though not necessarily the only principle—capturing in very general terms what sort of action expresses respect for, or befits the dignity of, persons.

So viewed, the Kantian imperative also helps us to see a difference between positive and negative duties as well as associated differences in stringency often attributed to perfect as opposed to imperfect duties: roughly, the perfect duties (often intuitively negative) may be viewed as those whose violation either treats someone merely as a means (roughly, in an exploitive way) *or* shows a similar disregard (or disrespect) for them, and the imperfect duties (often intuitively positive) may be viewed as those whose violation does not necessarily do this but does fail to treat someone as an end (that is, with adequate concern for the person's good for its own sake).[44]

If I have been correct so far, there is a plausible understanding of the categorical imperative on which it provides a measure of clarification, of explanation, and of (additional) justification for Rossian principles. None of these points is highly restrictive regarding the ontology of ethics. The epistemological, conceptual, and normative points essential for Kantian intuitionism can probably be accommodated to a plausible version of constructivism or even to noncognitivism. In any case, surely any ontology of ethics adequate to the categorical imperative should be adequate to the Rossian principles, and conversely. I cannot see that any plausible moral ontology precludes the moderate commitments in moral epistemology needed for Kantian intuitionism.[45]

3. KANTIAN INTUITIONISM AS A DEVELOPMENT OF KANTIAN ETHICS

The Kantian intuitionist approach has a further merit. It helps us to understand Kantian ethics—or at least Kant's major ethical writings—where they are quite abstract, for instance concerning the notions of universalizability and treating persons as ends. There are at least three points at which Kantian intuitionism can help to clarify and extend Kantian ethics conceived as a system of moral principles unified by, and in an epistemic sense groundable in, the categorical imperative.

First, we can think of Rossian principles as part of that system and indeed as formulating at least the main standards for treating people with the kind of respect appropriate to their dignity. The principles are constraints on the use of the imperative: interpretations of it that do not yield them, and applications of it that are inconsistent with them, are prima facie defeated by that fact.

Second, we can conceive the basis of the appropriate respect as the dignity of persons, understood concretely as in good part a status protected by adherence to Rossian duties and as typically undermined more by violation of a perfect duty like that of non-injury than by violation of an imperfect one like that of beneficence. Dignity is not the only candidate—autonomy and the capacity for rational thought are also morally important statuses—but dignity is a deep and comprehensive notion.

Third, if we take dignity to be a fundamental element in a Kantian view, we can conceive it as part of what underlies rights of autonomy, and we can take the proper sphere of personal autonomy to be that in which the Rossian duties, particularly the negative ones, are observed.[46] In outline, the idea is that each of us properly exercises autonomy up to that border whose crossing entails failure in our duties to others. This border is not always clearly marked and is often undefended.

One might think that if the categorical imperative can serve as a basis from which Rossian principles can be seen to follow (or to be implied in some weaker sense), then they can hardly be said to clarify it, as opposed to being part of what it implicitly says. But for one thing, what is implicitly said in *this* sense may be unnoticed even by those capable of seeing the implication and, where the implication is by way of unobvious or numerous intermediate steps, even denied by some who affirm the principle in question. Furthermore, some implications of a principle, far from being part of what a principle in any intuitive sense *says*, may never be discovered. That there is a reliable, or even deductively valid, inferential path from one proposition to another does not entail that anyone who considers or even reflects on the first proposition will ever traverse that path to the second. Theorems need not be discovered by reflection on axioms from which they follow, and sometimes axioms are not discovered unless someone seeks grounds, or explanations, or a unifying rationale, for theorems that follow from those axioms. We can reason backward to axioms, as well as forward from them.

These points about the possible relations between the categorical imperative and Rossian principles are easily missed in contexts where, as in the present case, we are considering *both* the categorical imperative and normative consequences of it that are clearly before us. Granted, any thoughtful moral agent reflecting on the categorical imperative in the light of wide experience is likely to think of many Rossian principles as implicit in it. But that may be so even if—and perhaps in part because—in the natural order of discovery, Rossian principles precede such general standards as the categorical imperative. It appears, in fact, that they do. Whatever the case for the categorical imperative from general principles of practical reason or the theory of value, it is not clear that the principle would have been articulated on the basis of those alone.[47] In any event, the order of discovery is neutral with respect to both the logical and epistemic relations. The first discovered may be derivable from what we discover through it; yet our justification for what turns out to be derivable may be no less strong, or even stronger, than our justification for the set of propositions from which we find we can derive it.

From the point of view of a Rossian intuitionism, it is natural to distinguish two kinds of relation that Rossian principles of duty can bear to the categorical imperative or to any other candidate to provide a ground for them. One is a *specification relation*, the other a *derivation relation*—not mere logical derivability, but an illuminating kind of derivability having some justificatory or explanatory power. If Ross agreed that his principles could be inferred from a version of Kantian theory, then, he might say that his principles specify what the categorical imperative comes to, rather than being derivable from it in a way that gives it any justificatory or explanatory power toward them. Far from its telling us why they hold, it is they that tell us what it says. A steadfast Rossian might claim that Kantianism is clarified by intuitionism, but deny that the latter gains much from integration with the former. A steadfast Kantian might make the converse claim.

There is a truth close to the specification view, but it does not undermine the point that the categorical imperative framework provides both support and unification for Rossian duties—or, in principle, for any intuitively acceptable set of prima facie duties. There is a sense in which any non-trivial derivation of consequences from a proposition specifies (at least in part) what it comes to. Still, the categorical imperative has meaning independently of the Rossian duties, however much they may clarify it. For instance, from our understanding of instrumental relations among both animate and inanimate things, we have a sense of what it is to treat someone merely as a means. We regularly use tools, and far too often some people similarly use others. Here, getting the job done is all that matters: what happens to the tool is of no concern—unless we may need it for another job or happen to like it for its own sake. We also have a sense of what it is to treat someone as an end. To be sure, the notion of a person as an end is somewhat technical, since ends in the ordinary sense are *realizable*; but from Kant's—and Ross's—writings we can acquire a sense of what it is to treat someone as an end. It is also fruitful to consider love as a source of such understanding. We do things for those we love with no further end than some aspect of their good.

It may seem that since Rossian principles express prima facie duties, and since the duties we have under the categorical imperative are final, the former principles cannot be groundable in the latter. Indeed, some of what Kant himself said may support this charge, since in places he apparently took perfect duties, such as promissory ones, to be absolute.[48] I have already suggested that if the categorical imperative itself—apart from any inferences from it such as might yield Rossian principles as "theorems"— expresses any absolute duties, they are highly abstract. Suppose there is an absolute duty always to act harmoniously with some rationally universalizable maxim or other, and an absolute duty never to treat people merely as means. To *fulfill* or even be guided by these duties one must interpret such directives; and for reasons evident above, the plausible interpretations will not yield only principles of final duty. They may indeed yield no such principles except where very general or quite open-ended language is used, for instance where we say that the only absolute duty under the categorical imperative is to do deeds that are optimal with respect to *jointly* treating people as ends and avoiding treating them merely as means.[49] We saw that the categorical imperative is not plausibly thought to prohibit all promise-breaking; and it is not clear that it would license, any more than Rossian intuitionism would, formulating an exceptionless rule requiring specific deeds (whether promissory or, say, beneficent) without something like an other-things-equal clause. Again, seeing the categorical imperative in the light of its interpretation as guided by the project of systematizing Rossian duties can significantly help us to understand Kantian ethics.

The categorical imperative, on the other hand, can also serve both to connect the Rossian duties with one another and (as already suggested) to provide a kind of rationale for them. Notice, for instance, how culpable failures to fulfill duties of gratitude, beneficence, and self-improvement seem (to some degree) to be or to imply cases of failure to treat one or more persons (or perhaps other sentient beings) as ends; and (with a few exceptions that will be considered in Chapter 5) culpable failures to fulfill duties of fidelity, reparation, justice, and non-injury seem (to some degree) to instantiate or at least approach treating someone merely as a means. These points interconnect the Rossian duties as constituting standards enjoined on us if we are to live up to the imperative's required treatment of persons; and the points provide a rationale for the duties by exhibiting their fulfillment as obeying its double-barreled injunction.[50]

Mutual Clarification between the Categorical Imperative and Rossian Duties

It should now be clear that just as application of Rossian principles and resolution of conflicts among them may be affected by how we interpret the categorical imperative, our understanding of the categorical imperative may be affected by what we learn from using it to systematize such normative principles as those expressing Rossian duties. All the principles in question embody vague elements that provide, as it were, open spaces to be filled by one or more of the others. Rossian principles add determinacy to the notion of treating as an end; the notion of treating merely as a means, so important in the categorical imperative, can make it clear to someone guided by Rossian duties that what looks like beneficence in negotiating a contract is really exploitive because it treats someone merely as a means.

Rossian principles are also open-ended: indefinitely many kinds of acts can instantiate them. Beneficent conduct, for example, includes multifarious ways of helping someone improve in knowledge. This, in turn, is a case of treating someone as an end. Here, too, understanding of the categorical imperative may be enhanced by reflection on Rossian principles, and conversely. Take another everyday example. Suppose a friend uses 'the reason is because' instead of 'the reason is that'. To promote knowledge, as the Rossian duty of beneficence calls for, should I find a polite way to note the infelicity, or would this be patronizing toward an adult who is not my student? It might be felt to be; but doesn't treating others as ends require helping them avoid mistakes? And wouldn't a rational person want to learn here? It turns out that *how* I can point out the mistake is crucial for *whether* I should, and that this bears on both what counts as treating someone as an end and on when the duty to enhance knowledge is, in the context, overriding. The manner in which we do something or can do it is (in ways Chapter 5 will bring out) often of great moral importance. There may still be no clearly right choice; but reflection on the Kantian notion of treating persons as ends can bring insight to the determination of Rossian duties, and the habitual adherence to those can set us in the right general direction to understand and realize the standards abstractly expressed in the categorical imperative.

These points are largely conceptual, concerning moral concepts and their application. There is a related epistemological point: our justification for accepting the categorical imperative can be enhanced by our justification for accepting the principles of duty it systematizes; and our justification for accepting them may be enhanced by our awareness of the support they receive from "above"—from the imperative—as well as by our awareness of their being intuitively confirmed from "below"—in application to concrete moral cases about which we have clear convictions.

The systematization in question can have many dimensions. One has been stressed: derivation of the target (systematized) propositions from the grounding proposition(s). The derivation may be by strict deduction or by plausibility argument, as where the categorical imperative makes plausible, but does not entail, a restriction of conversational interruptions. Another dimension of the systematization in question is interconnection of moral principles under a concept that figures in the grounding proposition, such as the concept of the dignity of persons. Dignity is central in the status of persons as ends in themselves; it is also broad enough to constitute a main basis of Rossian duties.

Still another dimension of the unification of Rossian principles under the categorical imperative is an explanatory connection: the categorical imperative, interpreted as I propose, partially explains why Ross's principles hold. This is not just a matter of an inferential connection. In part, the explanation consists in presenting dignity (or some other basis of the moral status of persons), which is central in grounding the obligation to treat persons as ends, as a basis on which people are owed the duties. (As this strategy indicates, I take Kantian ethics, conceived in a general way, to include an ideal of human dignity that goes beyond commitment to the categorical imperative.) And there may be further elements, such as a grounding principle's playing a role in resolving borderline cases. For instance, where it is not clear whether an assurance of support to a friend amounts to a promise—or at least generates a duty of fidelity—it is pertinent to ask whether if, without an overriding duty, one did not do the deed in question, one would be treating the friend merely as a means or, at any rate, disrespectfully.

One way in which the bi-directional justification I am describing can occur is this. The categorical imperative can figure as at least part of our best explanation of why Rossian principles of duty hold; hence, so far as we have independent justification for them, we may gain justification for it (and if they are self-evident, there of course *is* independent, non-inferential justification for them). Similarly, so far as we have independent justification for accepting the categorical imperative, we gain justification for the Rossian principles as derivable from it (they can receive additional justification from such a derivation even if they are self-evident). Moreover, insofar as the moral importance of respect for persons—or a principle expressing this value, such as that we must treat persons with respect—can explain *both* the categorical imperative and the Rossian duties, both are unified and receive some justification from their connection to this common ground.

Adequately interpreted, then, the categorical imperative and the set of Rossian principles may each help in clarifying the content of the other, in applying the other to concrete moral decisions, and, in different ways, in providing evidence for the other. We may, then, reasonably seek to bring our interpretation of the categorical imperative broadly understood and the set of Rossian principles into reflective equilibrium. Strictly conceived, reflective equilibrium is a relation among propositional attitudes, particularly beliefs; but we achieve it largely by adjusting them—especially by refinement, elimination, and addition—in a way that results in a set of them with contents that are mutually coherent, complementary in explanatory power, and reciprocally clarifying. If the method seems to foist a coherentist reading on intuitionism or on Kantian theories, it should be stressed that on both approaches, and certainly for Kantian intuitionism, reflective equilibrium is not taken to be confirmatory unless the cognitions placed in it have some intuitive plausibility independently of it.[51]

This procedure for achieving reflective equilibrium may seem impossible in a territory where successful formulations often capture self-evident principles. It is not. First, in the matter of content, the vagueness and open-endedness of the principles makes room for the procedure. Second, regarding justification, the defeasibility of our justification for both kinds of principles makes room for rational substitution of revised formulations for those cast in doubt by disequilibrium. And third, regarding explanation, the complexity and partial conceptual independence of the two sets of principles make it possible for explanatory connections to be made in both directions.

Once we free ourselves from a narrow theory of self-evidence and from the confinement of objects of intuition to self-evident propositions, our overarching moral principle and the set of specific prima facie duty principles it generates can each admit of clarification, justification, and explanation from the other. This is why there can be justification of Rossian principles both from above—in terms of support from the categorical imperative—and from below, in terms of the deeper or more comprehensive understanding we achieve of them through reflection on their applications to the kinds of cases they govern.[52]

To be sure, we may not have any comprehensive moral principle more basic than the categorical imperative, but (as I will argue in Chapter 4) this does not preclude every kind of grounding of such a principle in normative standards. We may at least consider it a reasonable principle to hold if respect for persons is the overarching moral standard that, above all, it is to express and if the dignity of persons is the primary value that the institution of morality is to serve.

It may now seem that I have in effect suggested not just a Kantian intuitionism but an intuitionist Kantianism. There is a measure of truth in that. I do not see how a Kantian theory can be plausible without both a high degree of epistemic dependence on intuition and a normative dependence on secondary principles: roughly, categorical imperatives with a small 'c'.[53] But although I do not see that anything important in Kantian ethics is falsified by the suggested account of how Kantian considerations can yield a more comprehensive intuitionism,[54] the position I am proposing is intuitionist. It says, in bare outline, that we have a plurality of moral obligations expressible in Rossian principles of prima facie duty, and that although these are non-inferentially and intuitively justifiable, they are systematizable by, and stand in a mutually clarifying relation to, the categorical imperative. The normative counterpart of this theory (to be partially developed in Chapter 5) fills out and extends both the Rossian principles and subsidiary normative standards. It thereby clarifies the normative demands of the categorical imperative.

Respect for Persons as a Partially Independent Moral Notion

In closing this section, I want to indicate one further reason to think that Kantian notions can help to develop an intuitionism more systematic than Ross's. I have already stressed that the notion of respect is central for understanding Kantian intuitionism, whose widest injunction is that we must show respect for persons. In addition to being partially explicable by appeal to the concepts of the dignity and autonomy of persons—which are essential in its normative basis—the notion of respect (and doubtless other notions important in Kantian theory) can be clarified to some extent from a virtue-theoretic point of view. Surely respect for persons, as a trait of character and not just an attitude, is a moral virtue. We can thus clarify it using our best theory of virtue.

The psychological basis of respect reflects the normative basis of the corresponding moral attitude. That psychological basis includes other-regarding desires whose objects are one or another kind of good, such as the desires to preserve the liberty and safety of others and to help them in freely realizing their constructive capacities.

As this suggests, the trait of respect is not psychologically basic; it is constituted by a constellation of suitably long-standing attitudes and behavioral tendencies ('respectfulness' may be a more accurate term). But a trait can be basic in the order of virtues even if it is not a psychologically fundamental property, or even basic in the order of elements of character.

The idea that respect may be a basic virtue does not preclude its being partly constituted by less comprehensive virtues such as restraint, tolerance, and civility. But it is surely not just an equivalent of any of these, including the virtue of justice, with which it shares some elements. Even if it is equivalent to some integrated group of virtues, our understanding of them can contribute to our understanding the notion of respect and thereby to our understanding of the Rossian principles of duty which that notion helps to systematize.

These points about respect do not entail that (as a strong form of virtue ethics might imply) the relevant virtues can be entirely understood apart from some independent normative notions, such as some concept of the intrinsically good and the moral notion of fair treatment. But Ross had no good reason to deny that our moral intuitions and moral sensibility can clarify virtue notions, including those, such as the notion of respect, to which practical wisdom may fruitfully appeal in understanding both the requirements of our prima facie duties and the resolution of conflicts among them. Even supposing Kant had theoretical reason to resist a virtue conception of respect as a comprehensive moral notion, countenancing such a conception in some significant role is nonetheless consistent with affirming a central role for the categorical imperative in normative ethics.[55]

4. BETWEEN THE MIDDLE AXIOMS AND MORAL DECISION: THE MULTIPLE GROUNDS OF OBLIGATION

If a Kantian intuitionism is viable, and if principles of the kind Ross proposed can serve as middle axioms, we have made a theoretical advance. Kant famously said that one could not do morality a worse disservice than to derive it from examples,[56] and this pronouncement, taken together with his formulations and explanations of the categorical imperative, has led some critics to regard him as too abstract. Ross, by contrast, is an epistemological particularist who accords cases of duty epistemic priority over principles of duty, and this view has led some of his critics to consider him insufficiently systematic, or even dogmatically limited to deliverances of intuition.[57] Quite apart from how well-founded these criticisms may be, one might conceive Kant's approach as *top-down* and Ross's as *bottom-up*. Kantian intuitionism incorporates both approaches, in part by making space for the search for reflective equilibrium to proceed in both directions—from principle to case and from case to principle—and to yield adjustments or clarifications at either end or anywhere in between.

A Kantian intuitionism, then, can also endorse a third strategy, consonant with Sidgwick's call for middle axioms: *up and down from the middle*, or indeed from any point between the "top" and the "bottom." This strategy is unlike Sidgwick's and Moore's in not subordinating Rossian principles to an overarching master principle. The systematization achievable by the categorical imperative may depend on, or lead to, reinterpreting (or even modifying) our interpretation of it in the light of what we derive from it, as well as to reinterpreting (or even modifying) Rossian principles as groundable in it.[58]

Indeed, as argued above, Kantian intuitionism is compatible with the plausible view that our justified confidence level is higher for Rossian principles than for the categorical imperative and, in some cases, higher for singular moral judgments than for any Rossian principles that subsume them. Commitment to the integration called for by Kantian intuitionism is neutral with respect to epistemic priority.

Purists in the Kantian and Rossian traditions may divide here, the former giving epistemic priority to the "top," the latter to the "bottom." I cannot see that either level must have hegemony. Kantian intuitionism allows that justified confidence can not only change with new or lost evidence, but also differ between levels, such as those of singular moral judgments and Rossian principles. There is no one place we must start in ethical reflection; there are many directions we may take once we begin; and no one level has unqualified priority over any other. Much remains to be said, however, to fill out the Kantian intuitionism I am developing. The most important remaining question is perhaps how this framework can aid us in practical ethics: in the kind of moral decision-making and appraisal that are essential in day-to-day life.[59]

The Problem of Identifying Factual Grounds of Duty

To see how Kantian intuitionism applies in practical ethics, we must view moral obligation not only from the top down, as is natural in applying principles, but also from the bottom up. It is useful to begin with a question

Ross did not adequately address, if indeed it occurred to him. To what extent can we "factually" specify the grounds of duty—the bases of our moral obligations—that are central in the principles of duty? Can we say in (non-normative) factual terms what it is to *promise*, or for someone to be *injured*, or to *need* our help? Such questions are crucial for the problem of the epistemic completeness of Kantian intuitionism, and they are important for a number of reasons.

First, if any set of principles is to be an independently good guide in moral conduct, we need a way of applying them that does not require an appeal to an independent basis of moral judgment, say an independent standard of justice as a ground for identifying a Rossian duty of justice. If, moreover, we seek a theory that approaches epistemic completeness, we need a way to proceed from relevant facts to overall obligation (or to its absence, as in cases—if any—in which we are utterly free of obligation).

Second, in addition to requiring the guidance of (non-moral) facts in applying moral principles, we need at least a rough account of the sorts of facts that *call* for moral decision or moral action. This point is easy to ignore or take too lightly because the literature of ethics is dominated by problems already awaiting judgment. It pays too little attention to conditions under which moral decision or action is called for in the first place. But not everything we do is morally significant. In what sorts of cases is moral decision needed, and when may we simply pursue non-moral ends?

Third, we must teach moral principles initially by pointing to such facts as one person's physically hurting another. Children, for instance, need experience of these objective grounds for judgment before they can develop moral concepts. How may these morally significant facts be fruitfully conceived from the point of view of ethical theory?

Fourth, in practice, at least, we must sometimes ultimately explain or justify a moral judgment by appeal to facts, as opposed to simply explaining its content or adducing some other moral judgment. This point is a constraint on normatively complete theories. Our judgments of overall obligation cannot be adequately explained or justified without appeal to facts, particularly when these judgments result from our resolution of a conflict of duties. The point does not imply reducibility of moral judgments to factual ones, but the former can and often should be shown to be grounded in the latter.[60] What sorts of facts have the basic (or at least special) moral significance that this explanation and epistemic grounding require?

Ross's list of grounds of duty is far from being entirely factual, but this did not seem to him to pose a serious problem (nor has the matter received much attention in the literature on Ross). He seemed unaware of it in setting out his list of duties: the duties of reparation "rest on a previous *wrongful* act"; the duties of justice concern distributions "not in accord with the *merit* of the persons concerned"; and the duties of both benefi-cence and self-improvement require making someone "better in respect of *virtue*."[61] How are we to understand the normative terms without going *outside* the Rossian framework, or indeed outside the framework provided by integrating Rossian principles with the categorical imperative? An ade-quate ethical theory should provide a way to understand and use its princi-ples without presupposing reliance on moral standards it cannot supply. This is in part why epistemic completeness, or a status approaching it, is important.

Here is the beginning of a solution (more will be said in Chapter 5). If the relevant normative terms (e.g., 'virtue') are understandable by appeal to the factual grounds Ross cites in setting out the whole list of duties— or that might be cited in clarifying a different but well-selected group of Rossian duties—then each Rossian duty has a roughly factual base, in the sense of a set of factually specifiable grounds sufficient to yield it: to render prima facie obligatory some action of the kind it calls for. Still, in some cases this factual specifiability of the grounds of Rossian duties may be in practice unattainable, even though it does not require either analyzability or even a full indication of the grounds of the duty in question, as opposed to an adequate basis for ascribing that duty.

I suspect that Ross, steeped as he was in Aristotle, took it that without begging any questions, we may assume that both virtue concepts and such concepts as those of injury, lying, and malice (which have been called "thick" moral concepts) may be presupposed by mature moral agents.[62] This may be a safe assumption in a certain kind of community, and I am not suggesting that Ross begged questions in presenting his account of morality. But surely we should try to advance intuitionism in ways that he and later intuitionists did not. In this, as in other ways, Kantian intuition-ism provides additional resources for dealing with the factual specification problem. For instance, insofar as we can understand, in factual (hence non-normative) terms, what it is to treat persons merely as means, that notion provides a basis for understanding, in factual terms, the grounds of certain Rossian duties.[63]

Self-Realization, Beneficence, and the Grounds of Virtue

Our difficulty may be seen in part in relation to the beneficence problem. Any plausible ethic faces the question of the extent to which we may concentrate on making our own lives good—on a kind of self-realization—without failing in our moral responsibilities to others. Moreover, there is no reason to think that an ethical theory should supply a precise answer to this question: it is a fact of moral life that it is often unclear whether even those who take the duty of beneficence very much to heart are doing for others all that they should. This question is an aspect of the dualism of practical reason that so deeply concerned Sidgwick: the normative power of both self-regarding reasons and (from the moral point of view) of other-regarding reasons.[64] Assuming those responsibilities include beneficence toward others, this problem substantially overlaps the beneficence problem. I have indicated how a Kantian intuitionism helps us to deal with that problem at the theoretical level. But in practice the problem requires us to tie beneficence to factual matters as closely as we can. I want to address an aspect of this problem that Ross does not.

Suppose Ross is right in taking virtue to be good in itself and thus an appropriate characteristic to honor and promote both in our self-realization and in our beneficent deeds. Can a Rossian—or Kantian—intuitionism, without begging moral questions, take promotion of virtue as a ground for duty, notably for the apparent duties of self-improvement and beneficence, each of which requires promoting virtue as essential to the good of the person(s) in question? How does such a theory *identify* virtue without countenancing a moral category independent of its basic concepts? If a theory cannot do this, it is epistemically incomplete. Then, even if it is normatively complete, it cannot do all it should in taking us from facts to duties.

Here is one approach open to any plausible intuitionism. Suppose that moral virtues are roughly the sorts of traits of character one would have if, guided by practical wisdom, one internalized the Rossian principles of duty understood in the light of the categorical imperative but *apart* from their appeal to moral virtue. Roughly, the idea is that the duty to make people better in respect of virtue might be interpreted as requiring us to help them improve in the direction of internalizing the Rossian principles, taken in the context of the injunction to treat people as ends and never merely as means, and with this proviso: any principle that essentially appeals to virtue is understood with that appeal replaced by appropriate reference to all the *other* principles so far as they are intelligible without reliance on that concept. (For this purpose, the other duties of beneficence—to contribute to enhancing the intelligence and pleasure of others—can be considered to yield separate principles.) How much of what is required of us by moral virtue could be accounted for by this strategy?

Surely one could identify at least many of the important moral virtues in this way, even if it does not provide a route to an *analysis* of virtue concepts, and even if, as suggested above, some aspects of virtue concepts are not capturable in terms of rules. If we habitually observe—in the way appropriate to practical wisdom—Ross's principles of fidelity, justice, noninjury, reparation, gratitude, and beneficence, each principle being understood in relation to all the others and to the ideal of the material and intellectual improvement of persons as ends and as beings never to be treated merely as means, we are likely to have a good number of important virtues. (The possibility of factual grounds for understanding the notion of justice and other notions crucial here is considered in Chapter 5.) If, in addition, we can bring to bear an account of the categorical imperative as systematizing Rossian duties, then any factual considerations drawn from that account may also be used to give a factual specification of the grounds of those duties.

If we view virtues in this light, then some of the points about how Kantian intuitionism can accommodate the moral importance of virtues become clearer. First, a moral virtue may be seen as at least largely constituted by an internalization of one or more basic moral principles together with an appropriate, though not necessarily articulate, second-order understanding—such as Kantian intuitionism would provide—of how to deal with conflicting moral considerations. This is not a formula for the *genesis* of a virtue; nor need the second-order understanding be articulate. Take the duty of beneficence. Above all, one may have a suitably deep, long-standing desire to promote the good of others, an understanding of how and when to do it, a tendency to do it on that basis, and a sense of what duties, under various conditions, override this goal. Second, none of these points requires that in the context of acting beneficently one must rehearse a moral principle. Internalized principles can guide us without our calling them to mind. This applies even to using the categorical imperative framework: we can work appropriately with the ideas of universalizability and of means and ends without reciting, or even being readily able to formulate, the imperative that guides us. Thus, a Kantian intuitionism does not require agents to be self-conscious rule-followers. Internalized rules may yield moral conduct much as virtues do, and both can allow spontaneous moral conduct. Neither here nor elsewhere does the theory imply an implausible moral psychology.

There is much more one could say about the shape and implications of Kantian intuitionism. But if we take this theory as a basis for further reflection on moral obligation, we can see the implications of the position more clearly. So far, at least this much should be clear. The categorical imperative, conceived in the light of respect for persons as a guiding moral standard, and with its intrinsic end formulation taken as primary, can systematize Rossian principles of duty, which can be brought to bear more directly than the imperative itself in formulating, understanding, and applying still more specific principles. The entire framework may be espoused with an eye toward interpreting elements at any level in it in the light of their interactions with elements at any other level. The framework has a good claim to normative completeness, and it may be argued to approach epistemic completeness as nearly as one should demand in a moral theory. The use of it that I suggest we make in understanding duties of beneficence and self-improvement can be clarified considerably by employing its own resources. These include conceiving respect for persons as a moral virtue. The theory does not depend on virtue ethics. It remains "deontological," but it does demand virtue *in* ethics. Virtue is important in ethical theory and indispensable in moral practice.

Kantian intuitionism does not claim to supply a monolithic or reductive account of moral obligation, nor a "general character" in virtue of which all morally right acts are right. But the theory may perhaps be seen as construing the property—if we may call it that—of befitting the dignity of persons as belonging to morally obligatory actions in general. This idea needs clarification, but can receive significant elucidation from the Rossian duties conceived as I have suggested. Some of the grounds of the property, such as the capacity for rational thought and for autonomous conduct, are directly connected with the grounds of the Rossian duties. Our understanding of those duties, in turn, can be clarified by connecting them with the categorical imperative, particularly but not exclusively its intrinsic end formulation. We can also clarify them from below: by framing more specific practical principles that address common problems in the professions or ordinary affairs. Kant and other philosophers who have done moral philosophy in the grand style have had too little faith in intuitive singular moral judgment; Ross and other intuitionists have had too little faith in comprehensive moral theory. Kantian intuitionism seeks to accommodate both kinds of approach.

There is still no bypassing practical wisdom, either in theoretical or in practical ethics. Ross was certainly right about that, and rule ethics in the grand top-down style epitomized in Kant does not easily do it justice. But that will hold for any approach in ethics. This one has, among other merits I hope, the advantage of countenancing many different interacting levels of reflection from which to understand practical affairs and guide conduct in everyday life. What it does not provide is an adequate account of how the institution of morality is related to human flourishing. We must still explore connections between duty and value, and particularly between obligation and goodness.

4

Rightness and Goodness

INTUITIONISM HAS BEEN STANDARDLY conceived as an uncompromisingly deontological theory. The concept of duty has been regarded as its central normative notion; and although Ross and other intuitionists have recognized the relevance of non-moral intrinsic values to determining our duties, Ross, at least, apparently viewed their bearing on moral conduct as derivative from their role in determining the content of some of our moral duties. Take, for instance, the duty of non-injury. This reflects the negative value of pain, in the sense that a constitutive "aim" of the duty and of the actions that fulfill it is roughly to avoid causing pain in others. Ross may have thought that since it is self-evident and unprovable that we have a prima facie duty not to injure people, neither considerations of value nor any other candidates for a status that is in some way more basic than that of this duty can ground the duty.

Whether Ross was committed to precisely this inference or not, I want to explore how Rossian principles might be groundable in considerations of value even if they are self-evident. In doing this I assume, with Ross, both the plurality of basic moral duties and the possibility of non-inferential knowledge of principles expressing them. On both counts he differs from Moore, who (in much of his work) takes our specific duties to be grounded in promotion of goodness and our knowledge of principles of duty to derive from considerations regarding the relation between human conduct and the realization of intrinsic value. On the first count, at least, Ross also differs from Sidgwick.[1]

Even apart from its integration with the broadly Kantian moral theory described in Chapter 3, Rossian intuitionism has significant advantages over consequentialism. For one thing, it *directly* affirms our basic prima facie duties, as opposed to taking them to depend on contingent causal relations between our available options and whatever good we are to maximize. For another, it avoids apparent commitment to using people, in unacceptable ways, as means to that end. Kantian intuitionism retains these advantages while gaining others. Sidgwick and Moore, however, though consequentialists, are also intuitionists, at least in countenancing non-inferential knowledge of many normative truths; and in one major respect their views have a strength that is missing from Ross's theory and even from Kantian intuitionism. I refer to their grounding of principles of conduct in a theory of value.

An axiological grounding of moral principles is a strength because a good ethical theory should account for how morality contributes to human flourishing. It should also provide a basis for explaining the role of each of our major moral duties in making this contribution and, more generally, clarify the connection between the right and the good. My main question in this chapter is whether, if we take a Kantian intuitionism as our model of intuitionism in ethics—hence retain the core of a Rossian pluralistic theory of moral obligation—we can preserve what is best in this intuitionism, and perhaps strengthen it, by incorporating it in a still wider theory that exhibits its basic, non-inferentially knowable principles of duty as grounded, or at least *groundable*, in considerations of value. The considerations in question concern what is intrinsically good or intrinsically bad, such as pleasure or pain, in a sense implying the provision of a reason for action: a broadly positive reason in the case of something intrinsically good and a broadly negative reason in the case of something intrinsically bad.[2] Let us begin with some fundamental points about intrinsic value in relation to reasons for action.

1. INTRINSIC VALUE AND THE GROUNDING OF REASONS FOR ACTION

The topic of intrinsic value deserves a great deal more discussion than is possible here, but I can outline a conception of it that will facilitate discerning its relation to moral obligation and thereby connecting it with the project of this chapter.[3] I begin with a characterization of the bearers of intrinsic value, the sorts of things that possess it.

The Experiential Bearers of Intrinsic Value

To achieve clarity about intrinsic goodness, we might first ask how abstract the good can be. Among the things commonly considered intrinsically good is beauty. But suppose there were no instances of beauty—no beautiful things. It may seem that beautiful things, including beautiful aspects of things that are not beautiful overall, are in some way more basically good than the property of beauty, if that property in the abstract is intrinsically good at all. This idea may be in part what leads some philosophers to take the primary bearers of intrinsic value to be concrete: specifically, instantiations of states of affairs. The beauty of a painting, on this view, is an instantiation of a state of affairs that did not obtain until the artist did the painting, thereby *realizing* the state of affairs that might earlier have been only imagined. In some terminologies, such as one suggested by Ross, this instantiation of beauty is an aesthetic fact.[4] Elsewhere, however, Ross said something quite different: that intrinsic goodness "is essentially a quality of states of mind."[5]

Perhaps we can capture the best intuitions underlying the value-as-instantiation view if we say that the primary bearers of intrinsic value are, in the most general terms, instances, conceived as concrete realizations, of certain kinds of states of affairs, and that these concrete elements are intrinsically good in virtue of their intrinsic (roughly, non-relational) properties.[6] A pleasurable experience, then, might be good in virtue of its felt qualities; a poem in virtue of its aesthetic properties, such as delicacy and musicality; a person's will in virtue of its (i.e., the agent's) intentions. The first is an instance of the state of affairs, someone's having a pleasurable experience, the second of the state of affairs, a poem's being delicate and musical, and the third of the state of affairs, someone's having good will.[7]

It is true that the category of instances of states of affairs is very broad; still, despite the wide diversity of things plausibly said to have intrinsic value, it is natural to look for a certain kind of unity and, in that light, to economize.[8] A plausible idea in this spirit is that (as Aristotle might have said) what is significant about intrinsic value is that its presence in our lives is what makes living them worthwhile (choiceworthy, to use a term employed by some translators of Aristotle), and that the only basic bearers of it occur where it is truly realized: in our experience. It is our experience that constitutes our *life* in the most intimate sense. Without experiences one is merely alive; even empty consciousness, a completely "blank" mind, is experiential in some way. Someone merely alive, however, can retain the potential to live well, but is not *doing* well. On this view of intrinsic value, if there could be no experience of beauty, it could not be true that beauty has intrinsic value. And, we might ask, what is intrinsically good about art or truth or even virtue, apart from contemplation or some other kind of experience of them, in ourselves or others?

Another way to see the appropriateness of taking the bearers of intrinsic value to be experiential is to consider the different "directions of fit" of the practical and theoretical attitudes. Whereas beliefs, which are paradigms of theoretical attitudes, are in a sense fulfilled when they reflect the world, and on this basis are said to have a mind-to-world direction of fit, practical attitudes, such as desire and intention, properly "aim" at changing the world to reflect them, and hence may be said to have a world-to-mind direction of fit and to be fulfilled by the occurrence of the action or (in the widest sense) state of affairs represented in their content. Now experiences, unlike substances, properties, and presumably facts, can be brought about: realizing experiences, say in enjoying a meal or relieving a friend's pain, can thus be a favorable change in the world, and they can figure as the objects of practical attitudes such as desire and intention. This objectual role is one the intrinsically good should be able to play.

Conceived as experiential, moreover, the intrinsically valuable can have two properties crucial for normative reasons for action. Since it can constitute the object of desires and intentions, it has a kind of *motivational potential*: the experience of hearing a sonata can be precisely what I want and hence, in prospect, can motivate me to act. Second, since experiences figure in consciousness, they have the internal accessibility appropriate to reasons and their normative contents. A contemporaneous experience, such as reciting a poem to oneself, is an episode in consciousness; experiences do not figure in consciousness in this same episodic way when we seek them or recall them, but these prospective and retrospective occurrences are still experiential in a way that enables them to appear in consciousness and to have intrinsic value. The pleasure of contemplating an experience one can bring about provides a prima facie reason to have that experience, much as the recollection of the painfulness of a past experience can provide a prima facie reason to avoid repeating it. At least normally, we can be aware of our reasons for doing the things that we actually do in responding to those reasons; and normally, when actions are in prospect as objects of desire, we can bring at least some of our reasons for them to mind.[9]

If these points are correct, one would naturally think that ascriptions of intrinsic value to non-experiences are always explicable in terms of properties of experience. The suggested view might be called (axiological) *experientialism*. On this view, the bearers of intrinsic value (and intrinsic disvalue) are experiences, including experiential states and processes, where these experiential elements are construed purely psychologically, roughly as qualitative mental states or processes.[10] I want to explore experientialism and indeed the general question of what has intrinsic value, by posing the kind of problem for it that would be raised by Moore's view that mind-independent entities also have intrinsic value.

Intrinsic and Inherent Value

Experientialism may seem too narrow. Does it not make sense to say, as Moore would, that the world could continue to contain beautiful things—hence things (aesthetically) good in themselves—even if there were no one to experience them? Moreover, could my wanting that it continue to have them not be rational even if I believed there were no one to experience them? And would it not be directed toward something of intrinsic value, namely the beautiful things in question?[11] A natural reply is that anyone who reflectively believes these things is conceiving the beautiful entities as valuable because experiencing them *would* be valuable—and clearly one cannot mount this objection at all without in some way thinking of such things, and thereby experiencing them "representationally" in thought. This reaction to the Moorean view confronts it with what we might call an *empty world problem*. Why would beautiful things be good in a world with no living beings to experience them?

It is true that a beautiful painting may be "good in itself." But this expression is too coarse to capture the notion of intrinsic value. I propose to call such things as beautiful artworks *inherently valuable*, in the sense that appropriately experiencing them—in this case, properly contemplating them—for their own sake (hence non-instrumentally) would have intrinsic value owing to their intrinsic qualities experienced therein.[12] Inherent value is distinct both from intrinsic value and from instrumental value, the value of a thing as a means.

Thus, an inherently good thing such as a beautiful painting is good "in itself": it has intrinsic properties (which can include internal relations) that reward us when we appropriately experience it as having those properties, and it is not a means (in any ordinary sense) to the value of experiencing them, since it is partly *constitutive* of that experience.[13] But inherently good things are also not good independently of their possible relation to contemplation (or some other kind of experience), hence not intrinsically good, at least where what is intrinsically good is conceived (as it usually is and will be in what follows) as providing basic reasons for action and, accordingly, as the kind of thing in one's life that makes it choiceworthy.

Inherent goods are, in Aristotle's terminology, less "final" than the intrinsic goods they enable us to realize.[14]

It turns out, then, that the idea of what is valuable "in itself" is too broad to capture the basic kind of value central for ethical theory, and this familiar term is misleading. The idea does reflect the important contrast between what is only instrumentally good and what is good in itself; but within the latter category are two kinds of valuable elements: the inherent, which are in a sense *dependent* goods, and the intrinsic, which, as the proper end of the former, are "more final."

There is one way, however, in which intrinsic goods are also dependent. They are *mind-dependent* or, if it turns out that the relevant kinds of experience do not require mentality, *life-dependent*. Since the realization of the value of what is inherently valuable consists in intrinsically valuable experiences, inherent value shares this dependence. But both kinds of non-instrumental value are objective, at least in being intersubjective: any appropriately sensitive person can have the kind of experience in question.

Furthermore, inherently valuable things are by their nature *necessarily* capable of being an essential component in something intrinsically valuable: they are essential to any experience that is *of them*. They are also necessarily experienceable: their inherent value consists in a certain kind of experienceability. In an important way, then, they are unlike things of instrumental value: they necessarily provide possible occasions for the realization of intrinsic value. Something of intrinsic value can have inherent value as well, on the assumption that there can be second-order experiences, such as experiencing with pleasure a child's delight (a good experience) in learning a new dance. But intrinsically good or bad experiences need not have inherent value, since the relevant experiences of them, say contemplating them, may have no intrinsic value.[15]

If experientialism is to be plausible, it must do more than solve the empty world problem. It must accommodate the point that there are inappropriate objects even of experiences that embody an intrinsic good, such as pleasure. There is, for example, something intrinsically bad in enjoying contemplating another's pain. In the terminology of Broad (among others), pleasure is unfitting to contemplation of another's pain. An experientialist might thus say that a sadist's pleasure in contemplating another person's pain—though good in itself and possibly greater in positive value than the pain is in negative value, might, owing to its being pleasure in something intrinsically bad, fail to yield an experience that, *overall*, is intrinsically good.

To see how, even if pleasure is intrinsically good, an experience of pleasure in the bad can be intrinsically bad overall, consider the dual use of 'pleasure'. In one use, which we might call *episodic*, it designates an experience that is (overall) a pleasure, say enjoying a tennis game. In another use, which we might call *aspectual*, it designates a hedonic aspect or element of an experience, such as the pleasure one has in playing a sonata where one is also pained by soreness in one hand. Here we might speak of some pleasure in the playing even if we cannot properly call the playing *a pleasure*. The proposed experientialist view should be understood not just as taking experiences (conscious episodes) as bearers of intrinsic value but also as taking them to have the intrinsic value they do in virtue of their properties, including hedonic aspects as one important kind of property. The idea that pleasure is intrinsically good should be understood not as implying that *every* pleasurable experiential episode is good overall—which is false—but as roughly the view that the property of being pleasurable is *good-making*, in the way promising is *obligation-making*. Just as a promissory obligation can be defeated and yield no final obligation, the good-making element intrinsic to pleasure can be defeated and fail to yield an experience that is intrinsically good overall.[16]

Intrinsic goodness, then, may be ineliminable without being indomitable: assuming that pleasure is intrinsically good, it still may be quite insufficient to render good the whole experience to which it belongs.[17] Goodness *in* an experience does not entail the overall goodness *of* it. We thus have an explanation of how *Schadenfreude* may generally be condemned on an experientialist view.[18] Because of its content—what it is pleasure *in*—the pleasurable aspect cannot be expected to contribute as much to the value of the whole experience as it would if it were pleasure in something good. That experience may be—partly on grounds of its moral character and the associated unfittingness of the pleasure to the pain that is its object—intrinsically as well as inherently bad, overall.

How can the proposed view of pleasure meet the Kantian objection that pleasure can be bad even when taken in something innocent, hence cannot be an intrinsically good kind of experience? For Kant, "a rational and impartial spectator can never feel approval in contemplating the uninterrupted prosperity of a being graced by no touch of a pure and good will . . . good will seems to constitute the indispensable condition of our very worthiness to be happy."[19] This point is consistent with construing pleasure (clearly a central element in prosperity and happiness) as, taken in the abstract apart from any particular object of pleasure, intrinsically good.

Indeed, if pleasure is not so conceived, what is so objectionable about its uninterrupted possession by people who lack good will? One might say that it is simply good *for* them;[20] but if 'good for' indicates instrumental value, it would include too much, for instance antibiotics. The kind of good in question is best conceived as intrinsic, or at least inherent; it is analogous to the liberty and other goods that (on even a much less rigoristic retributive account of punishment than Kant's) such people should, for at least a time, forgo.

The main point here is that such people can ill-deserve the good their lives contain. I have in mind (as I imagine Kant did) people who are malicious or at least thoroughly self-serving in a way that prevents their treating others as ends. If inherent and intrinsic value are organic rather than additive, the complex state of affairs, uninterrupted prosperity (or happiness or pleasure) on the part of someone without good will, can be considered inherently bad, *overall*, and the (higher-order) experience of it, such as we would have in contemplating it, should be expected to be correspondingly bad intrinsically.[21] Here, however, it is not pleasure as such, but its unfittingness to the character of its possessor, that makes the overall experience of contemplating the person's having it intrinsically bad: the experience will be, if not one of revulsion, at least morally disturbing.

The proposed experientialist treatment of pleasure is analogous to a Rossian treatment of the grounds of duty. For Ross, a basic deontic ground, such as injuring someone, is, a priori and necessarily, a moral consideration and, though it may be outweighed, it has a constant valence and yields an overall moral duty if it is not in conflict with any other deontic consideration. Similarly, pleasure and pain, as aspects of experience, and other basic axiological elements may be plausibly taken to be, a priori and necessarily, considerations having a constant valence and yielding an overall intrinsically or inherently good or bad experience if there is no outweighing factor, such as the (internal) unfittingness of a pleasure to its object or the (external) unfittingness of a pleasure to the person who has it.[22] The content of a pleasure is one of the conditions important for determining whether its presence adds to or subtracts from the overall intrinsic value of an experience of which it is an element.

Even a kind of thing having intrinsic value may make a varying contribution to the value of different wholes of which it is a part or aspect. We might thus speak of its variable *contributory value*. This property of bearers of contributory value—a property they may have whether they have intrinsic value or not—presupposes a relation between them and the whole in question and so is not a kind of intrinsic value. Moreover, the magnitude of contributory value is relative to context, as just illustrated by pleasure in the bad. Something having no intrinsic value, moreover, such as the experience of a certain silence between movements of a musical composition, can still play a positive contributory role in the value of the whole experience.

Since what lacks value does not literally contribute it, we might better use 'contextual value' for such cases as well as for those in which something having positive (or negative) intrinsic value positively (or negatively) contributes to the value of the whole of which it is a part or aspect. We might then distinguish *contextual contribution*, which is possible for things having no intrinsic value, from *transmissional contribution*, which is not. Transmissional contribution of value is in one way like monetary contribution: contributing money requires having it. But not all contributions by intrinsically good elements are like the monetary kind: pleasure in something intrinsically bad may contribute non-additively and even negatively—both reducing the overall value of an experience and doing so by more than its own "quantity."

To be sure, in order to appreciate the positive intrinsic value of pleasure in the bad, one must abstract from the (intentional) content of the pleasure.[23] This abstraction may seem impossible since pleasure must have a content. But since an experience of, say, someone's suffering can be either pleasurable or not, we can view the pleasure as an aspect of this experience that it might not have had and that, taken in itself, is a positive element in the life of the person in question. Consider an aesthetic analogy. If we know that a dramatic film is (visually) sharply focused, we may take it to have what, for this kind of medium, is a good thing in itself even if we do not know the content that is in sharp focus. This is compatible with there being a scene, such as one of ugly violence, in which slightly blurred focus would yield a better film. Here again we have the possibility of negative contextual value combined with positive intrinsic value, much as we may have this overall result in the case of pleasure in the bad. What such cases show is that something can be *overall* intrinsically good (or bad) without being *entirely* intrinsically good (or bad). In Moore's terminology, it would not be "ultimately good."[24]

For my purposes, there is no need to make a final determination in favor of experientialism regarding intrinsic value. My main points about intrinsic value—concerning, for instance, its plurality and its connection with reasons for action—could survive a different account of its bearers, say a mixed account maintaining that experiences, objects such as beautiful artworks, and certain relationships have such value, for instance the relationships that are *experienced*, as in the case of the actual relation (the two-place relation of *playing*) that one has to a piano one is enjoyably playing. The broad idea would be that intrinsic value is simply value things have "in themselves." I believe, however, that the experientialist account, which distinguishes intrinsic from inherent value, is preferable.

A further, related point about the importance of inherent value as a guiding standard in human life will help to dispel the impression that experientialism is too narrow. If things that experientialism takes to have inherent but not intrinsic value are not basic sources of reasons for action, they are very close to that: since they can be objects of intrinsically valuable experiences, they are *necessarily* sources of *non-instrumental* reasons for correspondingly strong action, even if not also of basic reasons for it. Arguably, there is as much non-basic reason to preserve or promote inherently valuable things as there is basic reason to preserve or promote the intrinsically valuable experience of them. In regard to reasons for action, then, an experientialism that countenances inherent value can posit as wide a variety of non-instrumental reasons for action as there are kinds of states of affairs worth contemplating or otherwise experiencing for their own sake. Despite initial appearances, experientialism is not a narrow theory of value.

Reasons for Action

The notion of the intrinsically good should now be clear enough for its role here. The most important single point is that *whatever* one may consider intrinsically good or intrinsically bad,[25] one is committed to taking it to provide a reason for action, specifically, some positive consideration that is normative at least in the wide sense that it counts toward the rationality of the action in question. For instance, if we believe that pain is intrinsically bad, we are committed to taking it to provide (negative) reasons for action, thus to regarding the fact that doing something causes pain as a reason to avoid doing it. Moral considerations are also reasons in this sense. If I believe that an action would be unjust, I am committed to recognizing this fact as a reason to avoid it; if you believe that an action would fulfill a promise you made, you are committed to recognizing that fact as a reason to perform the action. (I am not speaking of motivational reasons; I leave open whether the kind of normative cognition in question is necessarily motivating.) In this terminology, the intrinsic value of an experience provides, though it need not constitute, a basic reason for action.

As to what constitutes a basic reason for action—a basic "practical reason"—whatever else it is, it is something expressible by the kinds of infinitives that indicate the content of intentions and of in-order-to explanations, as where, in answering 'What is your reason for taking off three entire days?' one says, 'I'm doing it (in order) to attend a funeral and support a bereaved cousin'. One thing we might say to capture part of the notion of a basic practical reason is that such a reason is *a projection of something of value*. This does not entail an *act* of projecting. The reason is a *projection* because one sees the state of affairs in question, such as eliminating pain, as realizable in the future by the relevant action. It is a projection of *value* not because the agent must exercise the concept of value (which need not be done), but because—given that we are speaking of objective reasons—the projected state of affairs would actually be good: hedonically, morally, aesthetically, or in some other way.

If the projected state of affairs only appears good *to* the agent—so that the action would not yield anything actually good (including a reduction of something objectively bad)—then there is not a basic practical reason but only a kind of subjective reason, though it would remain a projection of value and could certainly be supported by grounds adequate to make it rational for the agent to act. Compatibly with this idea, we can also speak of (at least many) basic reasons for action as constituted by facts, such as the fact that doing something would be aesthetically rewarding.[26]

It is important to see that *moral* values are among those that can be projected and that when we act to realize a moral value, its fulfillment does *not* always depend on the consequences of the action. I may say something simply in order to tell the truth or may do something simply to keep a promise. Here the performance of the act constitutes the fulfillment of the value that guides me; I need have no future-directed goal. One way to put the general point here is to say—as a deontologist like Ross might wish to—that reasons for action, though intrinsically *purposive*, are not intrinsically *teleological* (roughly, consequentialist). Reasons for action are directed to bringing something about and may often be conceived as aimed at realizing some value; but they need not always be directed toward bringing about something *further* than what, in the circumstances, is entailed in the action itself. This is one way to express the contrast between deontological and consequentialist ethical theories.

The overall view of reasons I am presenting comports well with the intuitionist view that there is a plurality of grounds of duty. Some of these grounds, such as unjust states of affairs and, on the positive side, promises one has made, clearly provide *moral* reasons for action. Others, such as the possibility of improving people in respect of happiness or knowledge (a possibility crucial for understanding the duty of beneficence) do not obviously provide moral reasons; but they nonetheless can give rise to duties we naturally call moral, in a sense implying that the degree of a person's attentiveness to such considerations is a major factor in determining how moral the person is. Perhaps it is the associated *facts* that are the grounds of duty, for instance the fact that doing an extra seminar would help one's students. This fact-based interpretation of the Rossian position would accommodate the naturalness of saying such things as that the fact that one has injured somebody gives one (or indeed constitutes) a reason to make reparation, that the fact that one can prevent an injustice gives one a reason to do it, and so forth. In any event, these Rossian grounds are surely considerations of value. Ross himself says that pleasure and knowledge are among the things having intrinsic value. If they are, then (other things equal) we are to promote them.

However anti-consequentialist Ross's overall view is, then, his theory apparently presupposes that considerations of intrinsic value play a role as, if not partially grounding duty, then at least as providing a way to see performance of duty as respecting or promoting something intrinsically good. His view is not, to be sure, that our duties are determined by facts about what kinds of deeds have the best overall consequences, even the best consequences for promoting the *plurality* of intrinsic values he recognizes.[27] But one can deny that view and still hold that facts about the promotion of goodness (e.g., production or maintenance of what is intrinsically good) and facts about the avoidance of evil (e.g., abstention from producing, or prevention of, what is intrinsically bad) are among the grounds of our duties. Sometimes these valuational facts indicate a good that can be realized in the performance of the action itself, independently of what it brings about. Bringing *it* about can have moral value, regardless of what it *brings* about.

Moral Worth and Moral Creditworthiness

This is another point on which the moral theory I am proposing differs from Ross's. Speaking of a representative moral agent, he maintained that "if we contemplate a right act alone, it is seen to have no intrinsic *value* . . . If he does it [pays a debt] from a good motive, *that* adds to the sum of values in the universe."[28] By contrast, "Four things" are "intrinsically good—virtue, pleasure, the allocation of pleasure to the virtuous, and knowledge (and in a less degree, right opinion)."[29] Given the diversity of goods Ross countenances, and given that some of these are not experiential, one may wonder why he should hold this restrictive axiology.

It is true that we think of what is intrinsically good as an "end" of action and as capable of being brought about by it. But actions themselves— including allocating pleasure to the virtuous—are among our ends. Some of them, such as making a just distribution, apparently have moral value. I take these to have inherent value. If we distinguish inherent from intrinsic value, there is no good reason to resist this ascription, and I do not see why Ross's position would have committed him to resisting it if he observed the distinction. We need not, however, take such actions as just distributions to be *intrinsically* good; for action, even if it entails having an experience, is not reducible to having an experience. But the kinds of actions in question are experienceable, and their relevant moral qualities are intrinsic to them. The contemplation of them as inherently good can be one kind of intrinsic good.

Perhaps Ross was influenced by Kant's idea that an act not done from duty has no moral worth. It is by no means clear that Kant meant to imply that those acts can have *no* kind of moral value in themselves.[30] In any case, that view (which Ross and many others have accepted) seems false. We should distinguish the moral worth of an act from its *creditworthiness*, in the sense of its counting as a positive indication (a "credit") regarding the agent's moral character. It is true that even a courageous performance of duty does not count toward, or even manifest, good moral character if its motivation is entirely selfish. In suggesting, however, that Ross's conception of moral value was apparently too narrow, I am *not* implying that rightness is a kind of goodness. I am simply extending pluralism about the good to include inherent moral goodness in actions as well as in character and motives.

A further dimension of the relation between the good and the right concerns me in this chapter. Consider the place of moral norms in human life as a whole. This in turn requires exploring the role of moral reasons for action in relation to other kinds of reasons for action. It is surely plausible to take moral norms and rules as properly functioning to serve human flourishing or, if one prefers some other term in the same family, human welfare, human good, or the well-being of human persons.[31] It is probably uncontroversial that moral agents are persons; it is certainly uncontroversial that the paradigms of morally right conduct consist in treating persons in certain ways (for instance, the ways that clearly accord with Ross's principles) and that the paradigms of immoral conduct consist in doing the opposite.[32] Suppose we try to view a broadly Rossian intuitionism in the context of this conception of moral norms, and assume we have a satisfactory way to determine our final duties given our prima facie ones. We can then begin to see how conduct adhering to the framework of prima facie duties might conduce to—even if it need not "maximize"—human flourishing. In doing the right, we are also doing at least one kind of good.

In explicating the determination of final duty, however, Ross left us with less than he might have. He said that it is practical wisdom that enables us to see what, finally, we ought to do. Even leaving aside non-moral conduct, such as the prudential or aesthetic, is this as far as ethical theory can take us? I want to explore how far we might go beyond this or, alternatively (and in terms Ross might prefer), to what extent we might specify how practical wisdom is to be applied, if we take values as a basis for duties.

2. INTRINSIC VALUE AND PRIMA FACIE DUTY

If, with Mill and the predominant strand in the empiricist tradition, one thought that there are no *moral* intrinsic values, one would find it easy to see how the deontologist in Ross might recoil from viewing our prima facie duties as groundable in values, or even being in any theoretical or, especially, practical need of grounding in values. For if intuitionist deontology represents anything above all else, it is a rejection of the idea that morality does not stand on its own feet. A number of convictions belong with this metaphor. Among the most important (found in the work of Ross, Prichard, and others) is that moral judgments, even if their warrant requires a basis in facts, need not themselves be grounded in non-moral normative judgments. Ross emphatically rejected the idea that duty is grounded in the contribution of actions to the good. But this rejection is perhaps not as far-reaching as it seems. Consider virtue. Ross regarded it as an intrinsic good and presumably took our justification for considering it so to be intuitive. Correspondingly, he took promoting virtue as part of what the duties of beneficence and self-improvement require.[33] Here we have a category of duties that apparently have at least a partial value base.

Even aside from Ross's own theory of value, if we countenance moral inherent value, we should count actions among its bearers. Is there any reason to deny that doing an injustice is a paradigm of an inherent moral evil and that adhering to sound standards of honesty is a paradigm of an inherent moral good, at least in the sense that there is a non-instrumental axiological reason to avoid the former and to achieve the latter?[34]

One could maintain that there is nothing of inherent (or intrinsic) value here, but only the fact that we take deeds of the kind (the act-types) in question to indicate basic reasons for action: that an act would be an injustice we consider a basic reason to avoid it; that another act would be honest we regard as a basic reason favoring it; and so forth. For intuitionism as commonly conceived, and certainly for Prichard and probably Ross as well, justification simply comes to an end here. If this terminal status is explained at all, it is not by appeal to our reaching a justifying ground in something that has inherent or intrinsic value, but rather by appeal to our reaching something that is self-evidently a ground of duty, whether or not it has such value.

I see no necessity for justification to come to an end in this way, with the specification of an appropriate obligatory act-type or a Rossian ground of duty (if, in such matters, it ever must end at any particular place). May we not sometimes say that one reason to tell the truth in an embarrassing matter is that it is good to do so? There is goodness in this kind of right conduct; being truthful with people constitutes one way of according them a certain kind of respect. Moreover, although in calling a veracious action a (morally) good kind of conduct we commit ourselves to there *being* a reason to perform it, this is not all we express. We leave open, indeed we perhaps even presuppose, that such deeds have admirable qualities and play a certain kind of role in human life.[35] Although Ross's overall intuitionist ethics may not require his denying that there is a kind of moral goodness simply in the doing of the right thing, in various places he takes only virtue as morally good; and (perhaps following his reading of Kant) he maintains that actions are morally good only if grounded in character, hence never simply in virtue of their type, say as just distributions of profits in joint ventures.[36]

Moral Experience

Many who tend, as empiricists do, to conceive intrinsic value as belonging to experiences (as Mill did) will also tend (like Mill) to be hedonists. Perhaps the clearest cases of positive and negative intrinsic value are pleasure and pain, but we can be experientialists about the bearers of intrinsic value without being hedonists about its nature. There are not only experiences of pleasure and pain but also *moral* experiences, and some of these seem to have intrinsic value. Think of indignation that arises upon witnessing one person's abusing another, or the sense one can have of acting, against temptation, to fulfill a promise, or the experience of suffering an injustice when unfairly excluded from voting on something that lies within one's competence.

One could try to reduce these moral experiences to hedonic ones accompanied by a moral belief, such as the belief that the painful action in question is wrong; but I doubt that in general moral experiences will yield to such a strategy.[37] Furthermore, at least some of the kinds of moral experiences in question seem to have intrinsic value. An experience of rectifying the situation which causes the pain of being unjustly treated has one kind of moral value; an experience of reinforcing virtuous conduct has another kind. Surely experiences like these are, depending on their specific properties, among the sorts of things in life that are intrinsically good. The experience of being a victim of injustice, by contrast, is (as such) intrinsically bad. The experience of one's moral self-determination prevailing over temptation is intrinsically good.

A single experience can have both intrinsically good and intrinsically bad aspects. Indignation can be intrinsically good in an overall sense as a moral experience, though the displeasure, often in the form of a felt resentment, that sometimes goes with it, is intrinsically bad in its hedonic aspects (and perhaps the relevant kind of displeasure is itself intrinsically bad). Indignation can also be a kind of moral distress that is properly relieved by an appropriate act, such as issuing a reprimand. It can thus provide a basic moral reason to reprimand someone. Here the reason might be to express one's indignation, where one may also presuppose that this could change the wrongful conduct. Indignation may, however, be intrinsically bad overall. It may be misplaced, as where a malicious tyrant is indignant over an underling's taking pity on an innocent prisoner who was to be tortured. Here it provides no moral reason for the agent to act.[38]

The Organic Character of Intrinsic Value and Moral Obligation

In my view, then, a plurality of experiences have intrinsic moral value. Some of those experiences, moreover, such as indignation, illustrate the possibility that what is intrinsically good overall may have an intrinsically bad aspect or part.[39] Similarly, an intrinsic good (as noted earlier) can be a constituent in an experience that is overall intrinsically bad. To take another example, consider witnessing a sadistic man's enjoying brutally bullying a female employee. In itself, the pleasure, *as* the kind of thing that "makes his day" and is naturally and rationally sought for its own sake, is good (a good aspect of his experience); but because of what it is pleasure in, he ought not to have it, and his pleasurable experience, construed overall, is an intrinsically bad state of affairs.[40]

Granted, pleasure cannot occur without a determinate object whose nature is relevant to the overall value of the concrete pleasurable experience in question. But just as, in the abstract, one can take the fact that an act is of a certain kind, such as a promise-keeping, to have a moral weight even if the reason for action it provides may be overridden, we can take the fact that an experience is of a certain kind, such as being pleasurable or painful, to have an axiological weight even if the experiential state of affairs of which they are aspects has elements of greater opposing weight and the reason for action it provides is also overridden. Thus, the overall intrinsic value of an enjoyable sadistic experience can be negative; and because the sadist enjoys causing pain in others, we view him more negatively on account of his doing this, and we consider him, as a person, morally the worse for enjoying such a thing. He is, on this score at least, inherently bad.

Inherent, as opposed to intrinsic, badness may also apply to states of affairs. Suppose a malicious and unrepentant murderer is living in hiding. His going unpunished is (morally) bad. But imagine that he begins to enjoy life (through pleasures of food and drink with no redeeming value). The overall state of affairs, his going unpunished *and* enjoying his life, is inherently worse than his simply going unpunished, and our contemplating it should be morally distressing and in that respect intrinsically bad.

The best way to explain these facts is to suppose that although there are some things, such as pleasure, that are intrinsically good—hence (taken in the abstract apart from their particular content) good wherever they occur—nonetheless, overall value, for instance that of a complex state of affairs like going unpunished and enjoying oneself, is not just the "sum" of the intrinsic or inherent goods and evils of the elements or aspects of that state of affairs. If it were, then the addition of pleasure to the murderer's life would produce a better, not a worse, state of affairs. This is not the normal effect of adding pleasure to a state of affairs, though there might be an exception for such cases as the murderer's taking pleasure in the thought of sincerely and apologetically making amends to the victim's family. *That* pleasure seems to improve the state of affairs.

The point of calling overall intrinsic (and inherent) value organic is largely that certain relations among elements, and not just the values intrinsic to elements or aspects standing in those relations, are essential to determining overall intrinsic (or inherent) value. Moore and others have construed intrinsic goodness as organic in this way, and perhaps Kant takes a similar view in relation to his example of undeserved prosperity. I find this view plausible: intrinsic and inherent values seem non-additive in the way illustrated by the case of sadistic pleasure and, in a different way, a malicious murderer's coming to enjoy life.[41]

It is natural to take reasons for action to be grounded in elements having intrinsic value, including moral value. (I am not ruling out their being simultaneously grounded in another way, but I here leave aside the possibility of such overdetermination.) If they are so grounded, we should expect that in a concrete case of action, what counts as an overall reason for acting is an organic matter relative to the constituent reasons for or against the action. Now suppose we restrict attention to reasons of the kind that constitute (or at least generate) moral duty. We might now say that our overall duty is not just a matter of the number of reasons we have, nor of just the quantity of good we can produce—assuming that goodness can be quantified adequately—but of how all the relevant considerations fit together. This point is crucial for understanding such "deontological constraints" as strong prohibitions of sacrificing one person for the sake of the general happiness. To be sure, there can still be pure deontological reasons, such as the act's being a killing of an innocent person; that this kind of sacrifice is inherently bad in the organic way in question need not be the only kind of negative reason there is for it.[42]

Ross would not deny this organicity of overall duty, but he apparently thought that there is no general theory of value or of morality that adds significantly to the procedure of simply using practical wisdom to determine what one's final duty is. He seemed to be convinced of the unprovability of his principles of duty and would probably also have denied that we can in any other way establish them, or even justify them, on the basis of anything else. There are, however, many kinds and degrees of justificatory support that one set of propositions can give another. Ross apparently did not consider this epistemological complexity raised by his position. Let us first explore the notion of proof.

Proof and Other Modes of Justification

Proof admits of weaker and stronger interpretations. Suppose we take as a rough necessary and sufficient condition for the kind of proving possible for moral principles that (a) one non-circularly infers the true proposition in question from one or more premises that one either knows or truly and, with strong justification, believes, and (b) one's premise set provides a cogent reason for the conclusion. This is *proof as sound justification*. This characterization—which corresponds to what seems the main everyday, non-technical notion of proof—leaves open whether such an inference must be (logically) valid, as it must be on a second, strong notion of proof that we obtain by adding a validity requirement to the one just sketched. This is *proof as sound deductive justification*. There is, however, a third notion of proof. In a somewhat loose use, one might prove a (true) proposition by showing, through sound reasoning, that it is the only, or at least the best (and a good), explanation of some true proposition. Here we have *proof as sound abductive justification*. (I assume that a false proposition cannot be proved, though it is true that in logic and mathematics one may speak of a "proof" that fails and thus may have a false conclusion.)

If we think of Ross in relation to Kant, we may then suppose that some version of the categorical imperative might, in the way Chapter 3 outlines, sustain a derivation of the kinds of moral principles Ross plausibly defended, or indeed of Ross's own principles. We can leave open (as does Chapter 3) whether such a derivation need be a proof, but a case can be made for the possibility of such a proof of the first of the three kinds just sketched. Kantian intuitionism can at least provide for some extension and unification of Rossian intuitionism. Let us consider a further reason to think this.

Ross himself would agree on one point that supports the applicability of the categorical imperative: if what we do is morally obligatory, it should in principle be describable in a way that is generalizable. For he regards moral properties ("attributes") as consequential upon natural ones, such as those involving the results of an action for pleasure and pain, approval and resentment. As noted in Chapter 3, if natural facts are ultimately the grounds of the justification and indeed of the truth of our moral judgments, it is plausible to hold that—in principle—one could describe these facts in a way that yields, for each sound moral judgment, a non-trivial general description of its grounds. If it is these grounds that justify our judgment—even if non-inferentially—then (on plausible epistemological assumptions) we can become aware of them through reflection and, if we achieve sufficient conceptual clarity, formulate a description of them that expresses our justification for the judgment in question.[43]

One might think this claim unrealistic. But for one thing, moral judgments are properly made subject to a *principle of discriminative threshold*: only factors we can discriminate can be justificatory grounds of our moral judgment. I need not be able to articulate what it is that leads me to judge that a man has ill-treated his wife (it may be a subtle domination perceptible only in tone of voice and body language); but if it grounds my intuitive judgment, I must have discerned it. If an influence on moral judgment is below this threshold, it is at most a causal basis of the judgment, not a justificatory ground.

Moral discrimination need not be conscious. This is why we can properly disapprove of domineering conduct on the basis of how it treats the person it is directed toward, and on the same basis can justifiably judge that the conduct is wrong, even if, without special efforts, we cannot say what it is about the conduct that is objectionable, much less why it is domineering. But I take it that if a ground of moral judgment is discriminable in the relevant way, then, at least through reflection guided by questions, whether raised by ourselves or someone else, we can describe the ground and bring it to bear in supporting the judgment. If this were not so, moral judgments could be grounded in elements that are in a fairly strong sense inaccessible to the subject—something appropriate for a mere cause but not for a (justifying) element.[44] A ground of judgment, like a ground of action, should be one the agent is able to bring forward in explanation or justification. If we do something for which we can find no such element, we feel alienated from the action in a way we do not where we are acting as moral agents.

If grounds of moral judgment are accessible to the agent in the way I have suggested, then with suitable efforts one can produce some kind of account of why one holds an adequately grounded moral judgment (as opposed to one based on, e.g., prejudice or wishful thinking). If, in addition, we understand the relevant categories of moral appraisal—as we will if we have some command of the basic principles of prima facie duty—then we will by and large be able to produce a generalization to justify our judgment by appeal to one or more of those duties. The generalization may be rough-and-ready, say that it is wrong to talk down to other people.

Even a broad generalization like this, moreover, may be difficult to evoke from an ordinary person apart from Socratic prodding. Nonetheless, to make a moral judgment on a morally relevant ground is in part to be disposed to adduce the ground in a way that lends itself to at least rough generalization.

An Axiological Integration of Rossian Principles

Given what I have so far proposed, we can see how Rossian principles of duty can be clarified, rationalized, and to some extent unified both by values and by wider moral principles. Might we not be able to retain Ross's principles of duty even if we take them to be grounded in certain values, as well as to be clarified by, and perhaps even derivable from, a version of the categorical imperative, as proposed by Kantian intuitionism? It will help us in answering this if we distinguish several kinds of grounding of principles.

In speaking of Rossian principles as possibly grounded in (or based on, in a roughly equivalent terminology) certain values, I have in mind a kind of ontic grounding. To say that a (moral) principle is (at least in part) *ontically grounded* in a value is roughly to say that it is *true* at least in part because action in accord with the principle is at least a partial realization of that value. Ontic grounding must be distinguished from two other kinds. To say that a principle is *epistemically grounded* in a value (or in some other principle) is roughly to say that *knowledge* of, or *justification* for believing, the principle depends on knowledge of, or justification regarding, the grounding principle or value. The third kind of grounding applies not to principles but to cognitions. To say that a cognition, such as a judgment or a belief of a moral principle, is *inferentially grounded* in another cognition is roughly to say that the first is *held* on the basis of the second (or cannot be properly held by the person in question apart from such an inferential connection). Overdetermination is possible both across the categories and within each of them. One element can be grounded in more than one of these ways, and in either case it can be grounded on more than one supporting element or grounded more on one supporting element than on another.[45]

In any of its forms, actual grounding should be distinguished from *groundability*. It may be in part because Ross and other intuitionists saw that intuitively known moral principles are not (as such) epistemically grounded in other propositions—as they properly might be if the principles are epistemically dependent on other propositions—that they denied their epistemic groundability in any sense (their "provability").[46] But the epistemic independence they insisted on is compatible both with inferential and epistemic groundability and with ontic grounding.

Suppose we can take Rossian principles to be groundable in certain values and that these values provide basic reasons for action. It may still be unclear what the relevant values are. It is of some help to recall Kant's view that persons are ends in themselves and, at least in that sense, have intrinsic worth.[47] Kant rightly took their value to be essential to a full understanding of the basis of the categorical imperative. It is noteworthy that in introducing its intrinsic end formulation he spoke as if he regarded the imperative as grounded, and certainly groundable, in value: "Suppose . . . there were something whose *existence* has *in itself* an absolute value . . . then in it, and in it alone, would there be the ground of a possible categorical imperative—that is, of a practical law."[48]

We may still wonder what it is about persons in virtue of which, for Kant, they must be treated as ends. Kant employs a number of notions. Consider just one: dignity. This may in turn be taken to be based on autonomy, rationality, or other characteristics of persons. The most important point here is that dignity is a moral value. This is in part to say that it is essential to it that beings possessing it have moral rights. In part, to call the dignity of persons a moral value is to say that in virtue of it there are *moral* reasons to act in a certain way toward them and that certain other ways of acting toward them are wrong.

A second important point about dignity, or indeed any comparably broad moral value that might ground the categorical imperative (such as "worth"), is that there is a far-reaching moral attitude that goes with it: respect for persons. If this is so, we might take both dignity and respect for persons as fundamental elements in a value-based intuitionism. On one conception of the basis of the categorical imperative, dignity is the underlying central value, and indeed its inherent goodness is intuitively knowable; respect is the central attitude.[49] May we not think of Rossian principles of duty (perhaps including some Ross did not formulate) as expressing prima facie requirements on respecting the dignity of persons? And is there not a notion of respect for persons—epitomized in always treating them as ends and never merely as means—that properly goes with carrying out these duties?

One dimension of respect for persons is, in Kantian terminology, acting from duty in (at least some of) our relations with them. But there is a second dimension easily assimilated to the first but not reducible to it: doing one's duty, whether Rossian or of some other moral kind, does not have moral value (or at least suffers in moral value) unless the deed is performed *with respect*.

Despite the naturalness of putting this second point in Kantian language, it goes beyond the prominent Kantian requirement that actions must be performed from duty if they are to have moral worth. Even when an action is performed from duty, it may not be performed respectfully. The latter mode of conduct is not, for instance, equivalent to being performed *from* respect, where that is an attitude yielding a motive of, say, reverence for persons, or an intrinsic concern with their well-being. What motives underlie an action is determined by its ground; the *manner* of an action is largely determined by one's attitudes in performing it.

Manner and motive are, to be sure, connected. There are ways of performing acts that tend to undermine any claim that they are done from duty. But in general the motive of an action does not foreclose the mode of its execution. The idea is that even if an action is performed from duty—or from some other appropriate moral motive—if it is to have maximal moral value, it must also be performed respectfully, i.e., with an attitude, in a spirit, that is part of or adequately exhibits respect for persons, particularly including any who are the object of the act or directly affected by it. This is not to say that respect for persons is to be manifested in the same way in every action having moral value. Nor is it to say that such an action must be performed with the *maximal* respect possible in the context; that might be only supererogatory. But it is morally insufficient, for instance, to keep a promise out of a sense of obligation if one does it in a mean spirit, with a patronizing attitude, or with visible resentment that the promisee should expect it. Doing something respectfully toward another person must be such as to create a basis for understanding the action as intended in a certain way and not in other ways (Chapter 5 will treat this in more detail).

I do not find this requirement on action—call it *the respectfulness requirement*—explicitly expressed either by Kant in the *Groundwork* or by Ross in *The Right and the Good*. To see its importance we must distinguish the psychological side of moral theory—concerning moral requirements on the motivation and manner of obligatory conduct (or otherwise morally appropriate action)—from the more prominent normative problem of what act-types are obligatory or appropriate in the first place. Moral philosophers have tended to concentrate on the latter—the problem of *what* we must do—far more than on the former: on *why* and *how* we should do it. Aristotle and some virtue ethicists influenced by him are exceptions, and in practical ethics we often consider, in assessing people, their motives and their manner of discharging their duties as well as the extent to which they fulfill them. Kant and Ross stand out in contrast to many moral philosophers in sensitivity to the problem of determining precisely what our duties are, and Ross is quite illuminating on the differences between assessments of action in these two dimensions. But on the problem of determining why and how we should do our duties, both are more illuminating on motive than on manner. It is fully in the spirit of both positions, however, to adopt the respectfulness requirement, and doing so helps to bring out the scope of the kind of grounding of moral conduct which a value base makes possible.

The notions of human dignity and respect for persons are to a certain extent open-ended. Their application is limited, however, in that they operate together and (so far as we are working within broadly Kantian constraints) both are fruitfully understood in reflective equilibrium with the categorical imperative, which in turn must be understood in reflective equilibrium with Rossian duties, even if not exactly the set of duties Ross formulated.

As I understand human dignity, a necessary condition for our possessing it is our moral agency; but its basis is not solely our moral agency and our capacity for the experience of moral value. It is also our rational capacities and our distinctive kind of sentience—both of which are explicable in non-moral terms and hence provide an anchor for dignity that does not depend on any moral notion. These capacities are normally present at birth.[50] That human persons can reason, that we can pursue complicated projects, and that we can enjoy some things and suffer from others, are among the capacities essential to our dignity. We can be delighted by poetry, music, and conversation; we can smart from embarrassment and suffer moral anguish. In these and other capacities, we have elements of dignity that even the higher (non-human) animals lack.

Supposing I have been right in thinking that Rossian principles can be integrated axiologically as well as deontologically, it still does not follow that one can deduce or even strongly justify Ross's principles from the categorical imperative itself or from any particular well-developed theory of value. I cannot show this in detail, but perhaps I have said enough to establish that in the light of a plausibly developed interpretation of that imperative and of human dignity and respect for persons, such a unifying, grounding derivation is at least a reasonable project. This kind of derivation (as suggested earlier) need not be strict proof, but does provide a connection strong enough for the grounding elements to supply both a justification and a partial explication of the principles grounded in them.

There are at least two possibilities here. First, understanding the values—both negative and positive—whose realization is central for human dignity helps us to justify and understand the categorical imperative; this, in turn, helps us to justify and understand Rossian duties. Second, one could proceed more directly to Rossian principles, from an account of the relevant values to a kind of derivation of them. An axiological grounding of Rossian principles of duty does not require their prior integration into a Kantian intuitionism; but I prefer the more comprehensive theoretical grounding in two partially independent domains. In both cases, moreover, the grounding in question allows that there be related justificatory and explanatory connections running the other way: our understanding of Rossian duties helps us to justify and understand any overall moral directive that can ground them, as well as the values that account (or at least can account) for the place of all our duties in human flourishing.

Value-Based Intuitionism versus Maximizing Consequentialism

Since Moore's normative ethics is value-based and his metaethics is, in at least one way, intuitionist, it may be useful to note some differences between his view and both the value-based intuitionist theory sketched here and Ross's intuitionism. First, Moore's intuitionism is value-dependent, in the consequentialist sense implying that knowledge of duty depends on knowledge of the goodness of consequences of the relevant acts. The right is epistemically dependent on the good. I reject this dependence view, as did Ross: groundability of duties in considerations of value is important, and I propose a way it may be achieved; but this grounding is not the only route to knowledge of moral principles or of individual duties. My view could be called an axiological or value-oriented intuitionism, but in the light of the distinction between value-dependence and axiological groundability, 'value-based' seems a preferable term.

Second, although Ross agreed with Moore in taking self-evident principles (or at least those Moore called "intuitions") to be unprovable, Moore was unlike Ross in not conceiving everyday moral principles as self-evident. He may have thought it self-evident that we are to maximize intrinsic value, but he also thought (plausibly) that applying this to everyday decisions requires determining (or in any case knowing) empirically the probable contribution of certain act-types to whatever has such value.

A more important contrast between Moore's theory and mine is this. His, like Sidgwick's, is apparently a maximizing consequentialism,[51] whereas on the value-based intuitionism I am constructing, in order to determine what is morally required we need not subordinate our conduct to any broadly quantitative standard, nor even, in general, ascertain the likely contribution of our options to the overall good. Even when we have occasion to conceive our options in the widest terms, we need at most to determine a way to respect the relevant intrinsic values. Some of these are moral and belong to actions as opposed to their consequences. Determining this kind of morally significant deed can be a matter of appraising the kind of options we have, conceived in relation to their appropriateness to human dignity, and in some cases it can be determined non-inferentially and intuitively. There is no requirement to realize as much overall intrinsic goodness as we can, though doing so may, for some of us, be our ideal. Often, we quite properly just do our salient Rossian duty, with no attention to the need to maximize. Thus, a problem that besets the maximizing consequentialist in attempting to distinguish the obligatory from the supererogatory is forestalled.[52]

To be sure, Moore's consequentialism is not monolithically quantitative, but organically so: producing maximal value in an overall, organic sense might require generating less sheer quantity of such goods as pleasures than would be achieved by some alternative action. As Moore put it,

> In order to shew that any action is a duty . . . we must know accurately the degree of value both of the action itself and of all these effects [its effects broadly conceived]; and must be able to determine how, in conjunction with the other things in the Universe, they will affect its value as an organic whole . . . Ethics, therefore, is quite unable to give us a list of duties . . . [though] there may be some possibility of shewing which among the alternatives, *likely to occur to anyone*, will produce the greatest sum of good.[53]

Moore might grant, then, that in practice Rossian principles can serve as rules of thumb, but he would insist that their moral authority derives wholly from considerations of overall goodness, on which he would take moral obligations to be consequential. These grounds would contrast with the non-consequentialist grounds Ross and other deontological intuitionists treat as self-evidently central for moral obligation. (It is true that one might be able to know that an act is a duty without being able to *show* that it is. But if Moore noticed this, he apparently did not think we could know our duties in this presumably non-inferential way; he would otherwise have spoken differently about the incapacity of ethics to give us a list of duties.)

Everyday problems of moral decision tend to be more tractable on a value-based intuitionism than on a Moorean (or other) maximizing consequentialism. On the former view, knowing one has a duty does not require that one even think of it or of duties of that kind as such that their fulfillment conduces to human flourishing. One certainly need not think of maximizing any value, though one may. Moreover, when one does something for an ordinary Rossian deontic reason, say replants a neighbor's flowerbed in reparation for driving over it in a hasty exit, one's reason may simply be to make amends, just as one's reason for doing something else can be simply that one promised to. That a reason can be grounded in further considerations does not bring those considerations into its *content* or, necessarily, into either the motivation or the reflection of an ordinary conscientious moral agent. These are among the points essential for a Rossian deontology. In these ways among others, morality stands on its own feet.

Our moral freedom from subordinating duty to maximizing the good does not license indifference to our contribution to the good. This can be seen by reflection on the duties of beneficence, among others. But there is a more general point easily missed if we one-sidedly emphasize rejection of maximizing consequentialism. Suppose we are making a choice between two otherwise equally acceptable options and it is plain that one of them conduces more to (say) human flourishing, as where one charity is more efficient than another in serving the same beneficiaries. We should choose the better one. That we need not always be maximizing does not permit us to ignore differences in opportunities to advance the good when those differences actually present themselves in the course of our everyday activity or our discharge of duties. But it would be a serious mistake to infer, from the defeating role of the perceptible inferiority of an option in conducing to flourishing (or any other value), that we are obligated always to maximize some value or even that we must always positively aim at maximizing some value.[54] A commitment to such a *preferential standard* in making concrete choices does not entail a commitment to adopt a maximizing standard as either a criterion of rightness or a general policy of deliberation. It is one thing to avoid choosing a perceptibly inferior alternative when one has options; it is quite another to take maximization as governing one's choices and deliberations at the outset.

Epistemologically, as well as in reflecting normative grounds, Rossian duties have an appropriate independence of moral theory. On the value-based conception of such duties, both Rossian principles of duty and our specific duties under them can be known non-inferentially and in the intuitive, deontological fashion Ross described. Indeed, derivability of the principles from a wider one, such as the categorical imperative, or from a set of axiological standards, does not in the least imply that our justified confidence in the wider one is any greater than in the derivable principles. It need not be as great. Even among self-evident propositions, there is room for considerable variation in one's justification for confidence in them. There is also variation in the related factor of the ease of their knowability.

A further contrast can be drawn on the plausible assumption that, for Moore, as apparently for Sidgwick and for utilitarianism generally, an overall moral obligation to do something is a special case of having overriding practical reason ("best reason") to do it. A value-based intuitionism, as I conceive it, recognizing as it does distinctively moral values, and taking certain everyday moral duties as in an important sense basic, construes moral reasons more narrowly. Final moral duty may coincide with what one has best reason, overall, to do, but on an intuitionist view it is understood primarily in terms of grounds for moral action; and as Ross wisely noted in describing the scope of our duties, some intrinsic values, such as enhancement of one's own pleasure, apparently do not figure among the values central for moral duty.[55]

Here Ross (and certainly a value-based intuitionism of the kind I am sketching) is closer to Aristotle. We are, in ways appropriate to fulfilling our ordinary moral duties, to *realize* the good, for instance by developing virtues of character and doing beneficent deeds. Goodness can be realized not only in our character but in right actions (and activities); it is not just something to be sought among their consequences. Nor is the good something we must maximize, say by producing as much of it as we can by becoming selfless philanthropists at great cost in our personal fulfillment.

The value-based intuitionism I have outlined preserves not only the major elements in Rossian intuitionism but also other points central for a plausible intuitionist ethics: that intrinsically good and intrinsically bad kinds of things are intuitively knowable as such; that there are irreducibly moral values; that final moral obligation need not be a case of what one has overall best reason (including non-moral reason) to do; that it need not be determined either by quantitative weighting or by inference from an overarching principle like the categorical imperative; and that there may be not only types of moral obligations that can be known a priori to be binding on us, but an irreducible plurality of these. The most attractive and most distinctive features of Ross's ethics may be preserved by its integration with the wider framework introduced in this book.

3. THE AUTONOMY OF ETHICS

We can now see the main lines of a Kantian intuitionism integrated with a pluralistic axiology that includes moral values. The best way to clarify this integrated theory further may be to show how it can deal with some problems and objections. In some cases, I will be defending a Rossian intuitionism and not specifically the value-based Kantian intuitionism now before us. But even that limited effort should be useful: Rossian intuitionism is a good theory, even if incomplete.

Groundability versus Epistemic Dependence

If it is important for intuitionism to claim the possibility of non-inferential knowledge of moral principles, do we not lose something by providing a value basis (axiological grounding) for the principles? Are they not at the mercy of the relevant derivations, so that, for instance, we cannot know what in general our duties are without considering the relation of our options to one or more basic values? Recall that inferential and epistemic groundability do not imply either inferential or epistemic dependence. Even if Rossian principles of duty are derivable from, and unifiable by appeal to, something more comprehensive, such as a theory of value or the categorical imperative, they can *also* be known non-inferentially and even self-evident. They are plausibly considered mediately self-evident (roughly, self-evident, but not knowable by us apart from reflection—possibly a great deal of reflection—on their content). I grant that their self-evidence does not entail the indefeasibility of our justification for believing them. I must also grant, then, that theorizing, or even careful but ordinary reflection, may defeat that justification. This, however, is a possibility compatible with any plausible ethical theory.

Moreover, if, as I maintain, Rossian principles can be known apart from inferential derivation from something else, then we may call them, on that score, *epistemically autonomous*. Epistemic autonomy is the only kind that Ross, as an ethical intuitionist, needed to claim for his principles. The epistemic autonomy of Rossian moral principles does not entail the *ontic autonomy* of the properties that figure in them. That would require that those properties' be undetermined by other properties. This ontic indepen-dence is not a status plausibly claimed for moral properties (or, deriva-tively, for propositions ascribing them), since, as Ross saw, they are conse-quential properties.[56]

Axiological Grounding and Rossian Particularism

If, given the epistemic autonomy of Rossian principles, we can have non-inferential knowledge of our *general* duties and, given this, well-grounded subsumptive (hence inferential) knowledge of some of our specific duties as instances of the general ones, can we also have non-inferential knowl-edge of our specific duties? We can, for reasons given in Chapter 2 in distinguishing conclusions of inference from conclusions of reflection. This question raises a second objection. If Rossian moral principles are self-evident, and especially if they are also derivable from something more comprehensive, can we account for the particularism of intuitionism as Ross presented it, i.e., for the view that it is through understanding a partic-ular case of duty that we come to see ("apprehend") that a *kind* of deed — presumably a kind it saliently illustrates — is a duty?

I take the apprehension in question to result from intuitive induction, not induction by simple enumeration or any other kind requiring infer-ence from premises that provide independent support for the moral propo-sition in question. The point is that through knowledge of a particular case one sees something general, not that one generalizes from properties of particular cases of a given kind to properties of that kind of case. The latter kind of generalization is possible, but not what Ross had in mind.[57] The intuitively *inductive particularism* he portrays is apparently a matter of grasping not contingent general patterns but necessary, a priori discernible relations between natural and normative properties.

Self-Evidence Revisited

A third objection to intuitionism in its rationalist forms concerns self-evi-dence. Self-evidence, at least in substantive, non-formal principles, has seemed to some to be mysterious and, to empiricists, impossible. Much has already been said on this issue in Chapter 2.[58] I shall confine my response to three points.

First, it is doubtful that we can account for knowledge of logic and pure mathematics without some notion of self-evidence (or at least a notion of the a priori that raises similar problems). I doubt that it can be shown that knowledge of pure mathematics is possible without reliance on substantive (as opposed to "analytic") propositions, and in any case there seems to be such knowledge outside mathematics and logic.[59] Second, it is worth stressing again that beliefs of self-evident propositions need not be justificationally indefeasible. As we know from studies in logic and mathematics, even what is a priori and necessary need not be such that one cannot lose one's justification for believing it. We may, for instance, discover errors in our crucial proof. Moreover, in part for reasons I have already suggested in noting how formulation of the moral principles in question should provide for reflective equilibrium to have a major role, we can see how certain kinds of disequilibrium can defeat justification even where the proposition is true and justification for believing it can be restored.

The third and perhaps most controversial point is that even on an empiricist epistemology, as indeed perhaps along noncognitivist lines, one could maintain a kind of intuitionism much like the one presented here. There would be difficulties in either case, including, for empiricism, that of explaining how we can have non-inferential *empirical* justification for moral principles. But for certain empiricist views, and even for certain noncognitivist positions, both non-inferential justification and a unification of a plurality of principles under a more comprehensive one would be possible. Noncognitivists cannot account for non-inferential justification in terms of relations between *beliefs*, since they do not construe moral judgments as expressing beliefs (or as otherwise "cognitive"); but—and this is a point Rossian intuitionists can also use to good purpose—moral attitudes can be based on other attitudes, or indeed on beliefs, in a way that may be plausibly considered broadly inferential. Some moral attitudes, however, might not have such inferential grounding and might, for some versions of noncognitivism, be plausibly considered both intuitively and non-empirically justified.

4. DEONTOLOGICAL CONSTRAINTS AND AGENT-RELATIVE REASONS

Can the proposed value-based Kantian intuitionism account for the need to countenance deontological constraints and agent-relative reasons? The former are sometimes invoked to rule out conduct that would maximize intrinsic value yet be wrong because it uses someone merely as a means.

The latter kinds of reasons are stressed to bring out that not all reasons are of the impersonal kind countenanced by a maximizing consequentialism. Anyone has a reason to save a child from drowning in a nearby swimming pool; you alone may have the reason that *you* promised to watch over that child. I want first to consider deontological constraints and, given what emerges from that examination, proceed to agent-relative reasons.

Suppose I could save one hundred innocent people from summary execution by terrorists if I executed one innocent person. Here the duty of non-injury conflicts with that of beneficence. The case is apparently also one in which I have reason to use someone, if not merely as a means, then impermissibly so. But persons are often said to be "inviolable," and such an execution seems a clear case of violation of the kind in question.[60]

I have already stressed that it is strongly prima facie wrong to treat people merely as means and indeed even to approach doing this, as by treating them disrespectfully. I have also said that this duty tends to be stronger than the duty to treat people as ends and that (as this priority would suggest) Ross was correct in suggesting that by and large the duty of non-injury outweighs that of beneficence.[61] But I have also argued that overall obligation is a holistic matter and cannot be determined by either adding the non-moral values of the consequences of the relevant alternative acts or in any precise or entirely quantitative way. The axiological deontologism I have been developing does not imply that we may make such a sacrifice, and it permits resisting it on moral grounds concerning the horrendous character of the action. The position does not, however, offer a precise method of deciding such a matter. To endorse a precise method would be like defining an intrinsically vague expression like 'democracy' in terms which, by their precision, resolve matters that its proper use leaves indeterminate. There *is* no precise number of years marking the maximal interval that a democracy must have between free elections, just as there is no precise number of deaths whose prevention may justify a serious violation of the duty of non-injury or of the injunction to avoid using people merely as means.

The possibility of resisting such a sacrifice can also be put in terms of values rather than duties. Once we countenance moral values, it is arguable that the negative moral value of using someone as a means in this way (perhaps merely as a means)[62] is greater than the overall positive (intrinsic) value produced. I think this may well be so, but it is not obvious that all of the relevant cases will exhibit such a difference in overall value. Suppose they do not. Nothing in the framework I am developing undermines the intuitionist idea that, regardless of the possibility of finding an axiological basis for reasons for action, there are deontological reasons for or against doing certain kinds of things just because of the *kinds* of acts they are, say instances of keeping a promise, of relieving distress, or, on the negative side, of lying or of doing an injustice. I have argued not that duties must be grounded wholly in values, but rather that they may be *groundable* in them, hence sufficiently justified by them. In any case, if moral value is a basic kind, considerations of value might still yield the intuitively right result.[63]

Suppose we change the example so that the innocent person I am asked to execute would otherwise be forced, through brain manipulation, to coerce one hundred people into using someone else merely as a means by killing that person to produce the amount of goodness I could produce in the first example. Might I still decline to step into this evil stream? Here it looks as though, in addition to saving lives by the execution, I could avoid multiple perversions of the value I would serve in abstaining from the act. There is plausibility in this claim; but it does not change the non-additivity of the values in question, nor does it obviously create a moral permission to execute. A number of points must be made here.

One possibility is that I have an overriding or equally strong agent-relative reason to abstain. May I not decline on the agent-relative ground that *my* deepest standards forbid so using a person, even if I believe my doing so would add more to intrinsic value in the world? (I presuppose that my deepest standards are rational.) Perhaps the answer is not clear, at least apart from further details. Details make an enormous difference in such cases. But let us assume that I may decline to execute one innocent person to save one hundred. Might we also reach this answer by assessing the overall value of my options organically? In doing this, we must consider not just their consequences, in the sense of effects distinct from the act that would produce them, but the acts *themselves*, which, for a deontological theory, may be inherently good or bad and may have *moral* values or disvalues. We are not comparing two worlds that differ only in that, in the first, one person is sacrificed and, in the second, one hundred are sacrificed in the same way. Obviously the second is worse.

We must distinguish here between *reproductive additivity*, that of merely adding exactly similar independent elements, and *combinatory additivity*, that of adding differing elements (interconnected ones, in the most important cases). Even intrinsic and inherent values may perhaps be reproductively additive. Just as a world with only two exactly similar experiences of a beautiful painting might be twice as good as one with only one of them, a world with only two exactly similar wrongful killings might be twice as bad as a world with one of them. But the comparison in question is between different kinds of *acts*, each prima facie right in virtue of a different kind of ground. Perhaps bringing about a great good, or even preventing a great evil, by doing something that sacrifices a person in a certain way is, overall, inherently bad or at any rate morally wrong. I cannot see why this should not be so. A single blemish can spoil an entire painting.

The blemish in the sacrificial deed in question is one that would be exhibited in my appealing (as I would likely do) to something like the inviolability of persons (as reflected, e.g., in the prohibition of treating them merely as means) to justify a violation of that very principle. Executing a person just as a means to save innocent life might be seen as akin to spoiling part of a painting by abusing the technique whose application is designed to make the whole beautiful. This could ruin the painting. Neither our duties under Kantian intuitionism nor the values we serve under a pluralistic axiology that countenances moral value as a basic kind would clearly allow such a deed. But there is no way to be precise about how horrendous an evil might excuse a sacrifice. The larger the painting in relation to the size of the blemish, the less effect it has on the aesthetic value of the whole—other things equal.

Sound moral judgment depends on a pattern of considerations, however saliently some elements in the pattern point in one direction. Not every blemish on a painting spoils it, and the question of when a blemish does and when it does not is difficult. Only limited generalizations are possible in such matters. Here we see the kind of particularism that stresses the holistic character of final moral judgment: the overall value of a complex organic whole must be determined in relation to all its relevant aspects. What these are will differ depending on whether the evaluation is moral or aesthetic; and in the light of experience, useful generalizations may emerge. But the appraisal cannot always be made by subsuming the case under generalizations. These points do not rule out the possible truth of some unqualified generalizations, such as those that prohibit one people's enslaving another simply for its own aggrandizement. But in those cases we are speaking not of blemishes but of malignant tumors.[64]

The Basis of Agent-Relative Reasons

There is, however, a further question: is the force of agent-relative reasons ultimately derivative from, or at least explainable in terms of, the results of an appraisal (actual or hypothetical) of one's overall reason for action in the context? This appraisal would be understood in relation to one's contribution to enhancing intrinsic value organically conceived—including agent-relative moral values, such as that of my keeping a promise to a friend. It is not clear that the answer is negative. Agent-relative reasons are properly opposed to value-based reasons *if* the latter do not reflect the moral values served by fulfilling duties of the kind intuitionism stresses. These include duties of fidelity, reparation, and gratitude, which arise in personal relationships and generate agent-relative reasons. If there is (inherent) moral value in doing a just deed, in truth-telling, in promise-keeping, and in other actions conceived apart from their consequences— if there is goodness in doing the morally right thing—then the opposition between agent-relative and value-based reasons may be avoidable.[65]

There is another way the term 'agent-relative' may mislead. It is true that the agent and the specific situation of action are crucial for the question what should be done. I may be obligated to give to a charity that you are not obligated to support, since I promised to do so, and you promised support to other charities. But my agent-relative reason applies to me only in a way that has identical moral significance for any exactly similar agent in exactly similar circumstances. In any case, it is certainly not obvious that the force of agent-relative reasons is not derivative from one's contribution to intrinsic value *together with* deontic considerations that are also organically conceived. If it is, the point would be explicable by the value-based Kantian intuitionism I have presented. But even if it is not, there is at least no good reason to expect a disparity between a sound moral judgment based on agent-relative reasons and a judgment properly made in the light of the same factual information and grounded in this value-based Kantian intuitionist theory.

Given what I have said in taking account of agent-relative reasons, one might raise a different objection. It is related to the worry that the notion of self-evidence is mysterious. The objection (posed by John Rawls among others) is that intuitionism posits brute facts where explanation should be possible.[66]

This objection is perhaps invited by Ross's claim that his principles are self-evident and unprovable, at least if one assumes that any proposition having this status must simply be accepted by anyone who understands it. But, in addition to noting that we need "mental maturity" in order to see the truth of his principles, Ross acknowledges the defeasibility of the justification of intuitions (or "convictions"), even when he conceived these as beliefs of something self-evident.[67] I think, then, that the brute

fact objection is invited by some of Ross's epistemological pronouncements, not by his actual application of his view of the epistemic or ontic
status of moral beliefs. If we move to the more systematic value-based
theory set out here, there is even less reason to call Rossian moral principles brute. Nothing in their nature prevents informatively deriving them
from, or integrating them in relation to, other propositions; and, even apart
from the explanation this can make possible, their conceptual complexity
makes them appropriate objects of explanations of other sorts.

One might think that even if moral principles are not brute, singular
moral judgments must be, at least for a particularistic intuitionism. But
despite appearances neither Ross's theory nor the wider theory developed
here is *acontextual*, in the sense that it implies that independently of circumstances, we "just see" what we ought to do.[68] Granted, some factors,
such as lying and promise-keeping, injury and relief of suffering, have a
moral *bearing* in any context in which they occur, though it may be slight.
But for Ross, as for a value-based intuitionism, final duty is a contextual
matter determined by the overall composition of moral forces.

Intuitionism and the Concept of a Person

A further objection posed by Rawls is that intuitionism offers too thin a
concept of the person.[69] There is some reason to say this about some versions of intuitionism. Both Ross (whom Rawls had in mind) and some
other intuitionists (such as Prichard) often write as if, quite apart from our
sense of what a person is, we should simply see that the prima facie duties
are incumbent on us. Ross took it as obvious that persons have such morally important characteristics as the capacity for joy and suffering and such
good qualities as virtue and intelligence, qualities of which, as an Aristotelian scholar, he surely had considerable understanding.

Whatever we say about the concept of a person that Ross brings to his
intuitionism, that position does not require or imply a thin concept of a
person. Indeed, by referring to grounds of duty under terms for virtues,
such as 'fidelity' and 'beneficence', he called attention to the importance
of the corresponding broad dimensions of character, those involving com-
munication and hence veracity and those in which promises are made and
good deeds are done for others. Perhaps even more important, on his view
of intrinsic goodness, virtue, broadly conceived, is pre-eminent. When he
speaks, moreover, of the highly personal character of duty, he seems to
have in mind a wide range of human interactions and not, for instance,

the notion of a person as simply a dutiful moral agent or, on the other hand, a contributor to the amount of goodness in the world. We are not merely moral agents, or even simply agents as opposed to patients—doers of deeds rather than subjects of experience—and our inherent value is not exhausted by either our actions in themselves or the goodness of their consequences.

On the theory I have sketched, the dignity of persons is multidimensional, involving at least rationality, the capacity for normative judgment and moral agency, a kind of sentience, and other values warranting respect for persons. These values are central in grounding moral obligation. They constitute a rich and open-ended array. If it turns out that Ross's intuitionism, taken as he intended it, does not do justice to the concept of a person, the fault can be eliminated by the wider theory I propose.

5. THE UNITY PROBLEM FOR INTUITIONIST ETHICS

It will be clear that I have sought to present an intuitionist theory that answers another criticism of Ross: the hodgepodge objection.[70] For if Rossian duties—possibly including some beyond those he formulated—are appropriately derivable from considerations of value and are unifiable in the light of a certain understanding of the categorical imperative, they are not a hodgepodge. This is not to imply that mere derivability implies unifiability; not all entailing premises can achieve that for what they entail. Nor does unifiability require strict derivability. Illuminating interconnections among principles can be made without deriving them from a common set of premises.

One might, however, grant that the theory I propose succeeds in overcoming the hodgepodge objection and indeed in unifying Rossian principles, but still wonder whether it implies something Ross plausibly denied: that there is really only one duty. In denying that there is just one, Ross was thinking of Moore and other maximizing consequentialists. But might it not be claimed that my theory is also deontically monistic, say in representing Rossian duties as each expressing ways to fulfill the duty to respect the dignity of persons?

I do not deny that Rossian duties can be seen in this light: fulfilling them, particularly in a respectful way, is largely constitutive of duly recognizing the dignity of persons. But it is not as if we had a conception of dignity as a one-dimensional quantity to be maximized. Dignity is an open-ended notion whose content is in part given by the duties that it demands we fulfill.[71] Rossian duties are central among these. There is, to be sure, an organic notion of well-being available to consequentialist theorists such as Moore, but for him, at least, maximization would still be the applicable goal.

In any case, suppose that the *property* of being a prima facie duty were equivalent to a "single" deontic property (something I certainly do not claim). One candidate would be the disjunctive property of being either a duty of fidelity or one of beneficence or . . . and so on for all the basic first-order prima facie duties. A more economical candidate, and one more in keeping with my theory, would be the property of being a reason for action whose observance constitutes a way of morally respecting the dignity of persons, as do being truthful, being beneficent, and the other obligatory act-types. Still, the *concept* of a prima facie duty need not be simply the disjunctive one in question, nor need the concepts of each of the duties in question be tied directly to that of respecting the dignity of persons. Let me explain how this can be so.

I take duties to be individuated quite finely, at least as finely as intentions, which are central among the psychological elements crucial for moral agents in their representations of the objects of their duties. The duty to A, then, is not the same duty as the duty to B, unless the act-concepts in question are equivalent. Thus, a beginning geometry student's duty to draw an equilateral triangle is not identical with a duty to draw an equiangular one (and a beginner may not even see the connection). Moreover, clearly the disjunctive property just specified (that of being a prima facie duty of fidelity or one of beneficence or . . . and so on for all the first-order prima facie duties) is intelligible only on the basis of an understanding of its several disjuncts. If this is a general property that makes right acts right, its generality is achieved by packaging together a diverse set of particulars whose independent intelligibility it presupposes.

The least deontologically pluralistic outcome we would have, then, would preserve conceptual independence of the first-order duties: for each of them, one could have a concept of it, and non-inferential knowledge that people are subject to it, without taking it to be an instance of respecting the dignity of persons, indeed probably without even having the relevant concept of dignity. This could hold even if there is either an ontological equivalence between being a prima facie duty and being a duty of respecting dignity, or, on the other hand, an ontological dependence of the former duty on the latter. Such theoretical equivalences and dependencies need not affect the ordinary morally sensitive agent, the kind whose reflec-

tive confidence in moral matters is an essential starting point for any particularistic intuitionism.

Clearly, there can be a multitude of distinct duties even if they can
all be integrated in the light of certain values, such as those essential in
explicating the dignity of persons, and can all be exhibited as consequences of more basic duties. Duties can be as multifarious as intentions.
In neither case is there any reason not to see some duties as grounded, in
one or another way, in others, or any bar to viewing their fulfillment as a
realization of various kinds of value.

If the main ideas suggested in this chapter are sound, we can retain the
attractive features of a Rossian intuitionism and still extend the theory to a
more comprehensive, better unified view. There can be a comprehensive
principle, which may or may not be non-inferentially knowable, that can
unify first-order principles of duty without undermining the point that they
are non-inferentially knowable and in that way epistemically independent.
Chapter 3 shows how the categorical imperative can play this role. This
chapter shows that there can also be one or more values associated with
such a principle which can both indicate how adhering to the principle
conduces to human flourishing and help us to resolve conflicts of prima
facie duty. The intrinsically good and intrinsically bad kinds of things in
question can be non-inferentially and intuitively known to be good or to
be bad, as some of the principles that reflect them can be non-inferentially
and intuitively known to be true. And, without the burden of having to
maximize any value, moral agents can see themselves as realizing the good
in fulfilling their moral obligations.

Overall duty, like overall reason for action, is commonly a matter of an
organic composition of basic prima facie reasons; and though the fulfillment of an overall duty can be seen to realize values, and its existence can
even be ontically grounded in considerations of overall value, it is not an
additive result even with respect to a plurality of values as components.
Despite this ontological complexity in the basis of moral obligation, it is
often obvious what one's final duty is. Even if there is a conflict of duties,
it may still be plain that we should, for instance, tell the truth or reach
out to a suffering friend. In many such cases (though not in all), we may
have a moral intuition that constitutes a kind of non-inferential knowledge
of final duty.

When, on the other hand, we encounter a conflict of duties that leaves it at least initially unclear what to do, the theory I have presented points to two avenues of resolution. First, as Ross saw, if we have practical wisdom, we can often determine our final duty without the help of theory. But, as he did not fully appreciate, theory is available to assist practical wisdom in recalcitrant or borderline cases. It can play this role even for a person of practical wisdom who is highly intuitive. This relationship between theory and, on the other hand, intuitions about particular cases is not a one-way street. The exercise of practical wisdom—which often leads to plausible and highly stable intuitions in moral matters—may also extend our theory. Intuitions about cases, like principles of general obligation, retain moral and epistemic authority; but intuitions about cases may also be corrected by a good theory, even though, without them, we could neither develop a good ethical theory nor adequately conduct our moral life.

5

Intuitionism in Normative Ethics

FOR ETHICAL INTUITIONISM of any plausible kind, there can be non-inferential knowledge of moral truths, including both singular moral judgments and certain general principles. For Kantian intuitionism, there can be both non-inferential and inferential knowledge of Rossian principles, and some of these, including some at least close to those Ross formulated in *The Right and the Good*, may be plausibly considered *both* self-evident and groundable in a version of the categorical imperative. For either a Kantian or a Rossian intuitionism, then, there are intuitively plausible principles of prima facie duty. These include most—and perhaps all—of the first-order everyday moral principles to which any sound normative ethics is committed, and a number of them appear, in differing formulations, not only in Kant's treatment of his examples and in Ross's principles of duty, but also among the Ten Commandments, in Aristotle, in Aquinas, in Hume, in Mill, and in such major international statements as the United Nations Declaration of Human Rights.[1]

These points do not imply that an intuitionist ethical theory must have a fixed normative content. There is no a priori limit to the number of self-evident principles one could discover, nor is there any bar to a given intuitionist's formulating plausible principles that, whether or not they are groundable in self-evident or Kantian principles, fall short of self-evidence. There is a role for non-self-evident moral principles in any plausible ethical theory. Indeed, on a fallibilist view, a theorist may in some cases be justified in holding a false principle, particularly if it approximates a true one.

The principles Ross formulated, whether or not we consider them candidates for self-evidence, are a good starting point for an exploration of intuitionism in normative ethics. Even though a position constituted by such a set of principles is not necessarily *theoretical*, in the sense in which this contrasts with being ordinary and non-technical, it may be considered a (normative) theory in the sense of a formulation of basic principles governing a domain of judgment. It may also be viewed as part of an ethical theory in the overall sense in which I am using the term: to designate a comprehensive account of the nature and basis of normative ethical principles and judgments, *together with* an affirmation of a set of such principles. The more comprehensive the theory, the wider its account of the principles and the closer the set of principles it affirms will be to normative and epistemic completeness. I have taken the value-based Kantian intuitionism of this book to be quite comprehensive: it aims at a wide, though by no means complete, epistemological and (to a lesser extent) ontological account of moral principles and, in part through it, at articulating a normative position that may approach normative and epistemic completeness. This chapter will extend and clarify the normative side of that theory.

1. FIVE METHODS IN NORMATIVE ETHICAL REFLECTION

From the point of view of a value-based Kantian intuitionism, we should distinguish at least five major ways to develop a normative ethical theory. All of them have been discussed in this book, and each may be developed in a "pure" form or—as is more common—combined with one or more of the others.

One approach is to work *from the top down*. This is natural for what might be called *master principle theories*. Chapter 3 illustrated it in relation to the categorical imperative, and also in relation to working from certain basic values to various Rossian principles, "middle axioms," in Sidgwick's terms. We can also proceed, even if not by strict deduction, further downward from those principles. A competing approach that is similarly top-down is Sidgwick's: working downward from a standard of maximization of goodness to a utilitarian principle, and proceeding further down from there to everyday moral principles. Moore's theory of moral obligation may also be conceived as top-down.

A second way to develop a normative ethical theory is *the case-based method*: working from the bottom up by examining specific cases of action, whether actual or (more likely) hypothetical, described in sufficient detail and then, where possible, generalizing from moral judgments intuitively plausible for those instances to moral principles about cases of the same kind. Much of what is commonly considered applied ethics proceeds by this method, and Rossian intuitionism has considerable affinity with it. I have called its practitioners "intuitivists," whether or not they are intuitionists. Indeed, this method also has an affinity with intuitive induction: although the case-based method need not have the same genetic role, it is highly similar in yielding general knowledge from a grasp of connections exhibited in concrete cases that support intuitive judgments.[2]

If certain Kantian and utilitarian modes of ethical theorizing are top-down strategies, and if the development of theory by intuitive induction or by generalization from specific cases represents a bottom-up strategy, virtue ethics may be conceived as proceeding *from the inside out*, in particular, from traits of character. In a pure form, it takes us from an understanding of moral virtues as traits of character to determinations of conduct: from the right kind of internal structure and dispositions in the agent to standards of moral conduct. Any rules of conduct we can formulate are not only not self-evident but also posterior to, and so not "above," our understanding of virtue. Here the basic moral appraisals concern traits; and, by contrast with rule theories or axiological accounts of morality, virtue ethics treats trait concepts as ethically more fundamental than action concepts. The intuitionism developed in this book provides a great deal of space for moral reasoning and moral judgment that are grounded in reflection on character, but it does not take traits of good moral character as morally basic. It seems nearer the truth (though by no means unqualifiedly true) to say that such traits are internalizations of moral principles than to say that the latter are summaries of conduct that expresses the former, or even established by generalizing on the basis of knowledge of these traits.[3]

A fourth way to construct a normative ethics is to work *from values to principles*. This approach might posit only non-moral values, such as pleasure and pain; but a wider pluralism is more plausible and provides a richer base. For instance, one might proceed particularly but not exclusively from moral values—for instance from an examination of justice, fidelity, or veracity—to principles of conduct appropriate to those values. This strategy is neither intrinsically top-down nor intrinsically bottom-up, though it may (with certain added assumptions) lead to a master principle, such as Mill's principle of utility, and, at that point, license a utilitarian top-down approach. It is an axiological pluralism; and although it treats the good and the bad as more basic than the right and the wrong and has strong affinities to consequentialism in giving great weight to the consequences of actions for the values in question, it may also be developed in a way that has affinities to deontology in according moral significance to act-types independently of their consequences. It is not, however, restricted to considering values and types of action only abstractly. It may also accord a special place to virtues. Since moral virtues correspond to the relevant moral values and other virtues correspond to the relevant non-moral ones, such as kindness, forgivingness, and generosity, this approach is quite compatible with an emphasis on the role of virtue in both moral conduct and ethical reflection.

A fifth approach (to be exemplified below) is *by reflection in the middle,* or at any rate between the highest-level principles or the basic values and, on the other hand, individual cases calling for moral judgment. Such reflection can be done with a focus wholly or mainly on principles; but it allows taking account of values, and it lends itself readily to attending to both the widest principles and the deepest values which bear on the justification or interpretation of the middle-level principles that are the main focus of attention. One way to work in the middle is by reflecting on Ross's proposed principles or other sets of moral standards meant to apply directly to action. A Rossian intuitionism would treat principles like his as, if not the most general we are justified in holding, then basic and hence in need of no grounding or rationalization. A value-based Kantian intuitionism, by contrast, permits working from this level as a good practical strategy even though the theory allows applying higher-level principles, or values conceived apart from principles, to concrete cases of moral judgment.

The approach of this book can account for the fruitfulness of any of the five methods. I have tried to provide a framework in which the merits of each can be appreciated. As stressed in Chapter 3, Kantian intuitionism makes room for the search for reflective equilibrium to proceed upward from Rossian principles, downward from them, or laterally, and to yield adjustments or clarifications at either the top or the bottom or anywhere in between. This is what one might expect if moral properties are, as they appear, both consequential on non-moral ones and discernible on the basis of those. Thus, even where we make a singular moral judgment in an intuitive way, we should be able to learn something general from proper reflection on the case.

The generalizability of singular moral judgments partly underlies the success of the case-based method. Thus, if a distribution is unjust, it will be because of something like a disproportion; and if we are warranted in judging it to be unjust, we should be able to describe our grounds in a way that may at least serve as a precedent, even if we are not able to frame a useful generalization. If, on the other hand, we adequately understand a general moral principle, we should be able to apply it to cases having the relevant properties, those that enable us to subsume those cases under it. If, for instance, rectification of harms done to others is a moral duty, we should be able to identify representative harms that call for rectification and to find at least a range of appropriate compensations. Neither the task of application nor, especially, that of generalization is automatic. In cases like this, seeking reflective equilibrium has great value, and the categorical imperative, understood in the context of moral and other values, can provide both unification and insight.

2. THE NEED FOR MIDDLE THEOREMS

In constructing an ethical theory, as opposed to making everyday moral decisions, we naturally want more than Rossian principles. If we are theoreticians, we want at least one moral principle that is more general; and even if we believe we have a principle that can unify and in some way ground Rossian principles, we may want to see how conforming to it serves basic values and thereby contributes to a life worth living.

Even in the conduct and guidance of everyday activities, however, and quite apart from theorizing, we may also want more than Rossian principles. We may seek *middle theorems*, roughly principles that are less general than Ross's and, whether or not they are in any sense self-evident (as Rossian principles are supposed to be), take us from facts to prima facie moral judgments that the facts warrant. Thus, if theoretical ethics tends to look above the middle axioms for something more general, practical ethics tends to look below them for something more specific.

Since I am developing an intuitionism that, provisionally, takes Rossian principles as the middle axioms and as normatively central, I will concentrate on sketching some principles whose application yields prima facie moral judgments of the kind one would make in accordance with such principles. In doing this, we can again address the problem of how to specify the grounds of duty in a broadly factual way, so that we approach as nearly as possible an overall normative ethical theory that is epistemically complete.

Rossian Principles as a Basis for Formulating Subsidiary Rules

Ross's principles of prima facie duty—stated in terms of grounds of duty—as he summarized them in *The Right and the Good*, are as follows:

(1) Some duties rest on previous acts of my own. (a) Those resting on a promise or what may fairly be called an implicit promise, such as the undertaking not to tell lies . . . (b) Those resting on a previous wrongful act. These may be called the duties of reparation. (2) Some rest on acts of other[s] . . . the duties of gratitude. (3) Some rest on the fact or possibility of a distribution of pleasure or happiness (or the means thereto) which is not in accordance with the merit of the persons concerned. In such cases there arises a duty to upset or prevent such a distribution. These are the duties of justice. (4) Some rest on the mere fact that there are others in the world whose condition we can make better in respect of virtue, or of intelligence, or of pleasure. These are the duties of beneficence. (5) Some rest on the fact that we can improve our own condition in respect of virtue or of intelligence. These are the duties of self-improvement. (6) I think that we should distinguish from (4) the duties that may summed up under the title of 'not injuring others'. (P. 21)

The Rossian duty of non-injury is a good point of departure. Many factual sufficient conditions for an injury are uncontroversial. I do not claim that we can adequately explicate the notion of injury in purely (non-normative, non-moral) factual terms—nor even that the notion of the factual is altogether clear. But some sufficient conditions for an injury are identifiable without begging moral questions. We surely have a long list of clear physical injuries to work from.

There is also psychological injury, for instance creating, by threats, a persisting fear for oneself or loved ones, or hurting the feelings of a person, or teasing someone to the point of tears; and there is social injury. This may be direct, as where someone is publicly humiliated, or indirect, as where a reputation is sullied without the person's being aware of it. If there are enough factually specifiable injuries to enable us to teach children the Rossian principle of non-injury, to appeal to it in justification, and to recognize cases in which moral judgment or moral action is called for by an injury, this may be as much as we should demand. We do not need a definition.[4]

The three middle theorems corresponding to the kinds of injury just cited—physical, psychological, and social—are principles positing a prima facie obligation to abstain from physically injuring people, from psychologically doing so, and from socially doing so. These latter two notions are probably less clear than that of physical injury; but in any of these cases, injuring someone in the relevant way constitutes sufficient ground for a prima facie judgment that one has violated the duty of non-injury.

For each kind of injury, then, we can formulate a principle subsidiary to the basic principle of non-injury. To the most salient of these, 'Do not kill', we can add numerous prima facie duties prohibiting physical injury, as well as 'Do not frighten', 'Do not hurt people's feelings', and the still subtler 'Do not embarrass'; and there are many other injunctions, each expressing a Rossian prima facie duty. Some of these duties may of course be stronger than others.

There is an important element of vagueness here. That is intrinsic to moral language. It is not, however, an unmitigated liability. Not only would we be unable to use moral language as we do in guiding and appraising conduct if we had to be precise; we would also have far less room to refine or heighten our moral demands and to expand our prohibitions and permissions. There is such a thing as moral development and moral discovery; and a good ethical theory must provide space for moral imagination as people, ideals, and social structures are evaluated. The value-based Kantian intuitionism set out here does this.

As the various prohibitions of injury may suggest, the notion of a *harm* may be more naturally used than that of injury for what Ross apparently had in mind. The former notion seems broader, yet the kinds of reasons there are to prohibit harm—the kind suggested by a value-based Kantian intuitionism, at least—seem of the same sort. There are various prohibitional principles which can serve as middle theorems that mediate between a quite general principle—an injunction against harming other people—and one closer to everyday action, such as the principle that one should not point a gun at people.

There is some disanalogy between the kinds of middle theorems we are exploring and Rossian principles. The middle theorems may not be, as Rossian principles are, good candidates for (mediate) self-evidence. Self-evidence is not, however, to be generally expected in a theorem (though it is not ruled out by theoremhood); and middle theorems may still be both intuitively plausible in their own right and systematizable in a way that supports and clarifies them in the light of more general principles. What is not self-evident may still be reachable by self-evident steps from what is; and even what is not self-evident can be intuitive. It may thus seem correct on reflection—"intuitively correct"—and admit of justifiedly non-inferential acceptance.

It should be clear that violations of the duty of non-injury are among the things that call for reparation. Surely, if one injures somebody without a reason, such as medical necessity, or an excuse, such as the need to dash into the water to save a drowning person, which requires rushing through a crowd blocking a pier, one has a prima facie duty to make reparations (one might have it even given an excuse). This illustrates one respect in which duties may be as it were counterparts of one another in such a way that if one of them is in part factually specifiable, the other is too. Reparation is owed for wrong-doing, but one kind of wrong is injury, and insofar as we can give a factual sufficient condition for that, we can also give one for the duty of reparation.

To be sure, the duty of reparation may not be *final* if there is an excuse for the injury, and even then there may be at least a final duty to apologize or explain, a duty grounded in the general moral obligation to treat people with respect, even if not in any Rossian duty. Can we, however, provide factual sufficient conditions for the absence of excuse? In some cases we can, but it must be granted that the concept of an excuse is normative in a way that may preclude giving conclusive (non-normative) factual grounds for its application. If, however, we have a normatively complete theory, such as (arguably) a value-based Kantian intuitionism, we at least know how to find the relevant kinds of facts, those that may constitute an excuse—or at least mitigation. These include such facts as that someone will die if a promise is kept, that someone will be set back a year in getting a university degree if a minor good deed is done which delays an exam, and that a spouse will suffer anxiety if affection is openly expressed to an old flame.

The duty of non-injury is important in another way to understanding intuitionism (or indeed any moral theory). It is widely believed, though by no means universally agreed, that duties of non-injury have priority over those of beneficence, other things equal. The law in many countries reflects this by imposing no penalty for not helping someone who is, say, drowning but, on the other hand, a severe penalty on anyone who causes a drowning. This priority is supported by our intuitions about individual cases, but it also comports well with the idea that the avoidance of treating people merely as a means—or, often approaching this, exploitively or disrespectfully —is (other things equal) more important than treating them as ends.[5] If that point in turn needs to be rationalized, we can note that various values support the same judgment: there is a lack of respect implicit in (wrongfully) injuring someone; there need be no lack of respect exhibited by not doing beneficent deeds. One may not only respect persons as ends but also respect someone in particular very much, yet still prefer pursuing one's own projects, even over doing something for the person that is not demanding. Similarly—and this is in part a point under-lying the one concerning respect—wrongful injury to persons tends to violate their dignity; but this does not hold for simply not doing beneficent deeds toward them.

It is important to see that treating people merely as a means is not the only way to act in a manner inappropriate to their dignity. There are kinds of violation of the dignity of persons that do not constitute treating them merely as means; there are also *affronts* to it that do not amount to viola-tions. Brutally but gratuitously trampling people on one's way to a destina-tion when by doing so one neither saves time nor fulfills any of one's ends is a case of non-instrumental violation; talking audibly during someone's lecture is an example of an affront that does not rise to a violation of dignity. Neither is an instance of treating someone merely as a means.

A violation of dignity can be an affront as well, but not every case of either is a case of the other. Both kinds of cases are, however, instances of harm (a notion crucial in Mill's *On Liberty*, and, as noted, a close relative of the notion of injury), though at least in the case of an affront the harm might be minor. Granting that anyone violating the dignity of others or affronting them would fail to treat the others in question as ends, this would be no mere violation of an "imperfect" duty. For Kantian intuitionism (and for any plausible view capturing the spirit of Kant's ethics), there are cer-tain deeds we have "strict" duties to avoid even though doing them would not have the special characteristic of treating someone merely as a means.

These and similar examples indicate some of the ways in which reflec-tion on dignity and the associated values is clarifying. Apart from such reflection, one might mistakenly think (as perhaps Kant himself did) that the perfect duties, or in any case the strongest ones, accounted for by the categorical imperative are equivalent to those whose violation entails treating someone merely as a means. To be sure, one can also discover the limitations of this view by reflecting on concrete cases as opposed to val-ues. But apart from an appeal to values, what one learns is not as well grounded, and one's understanding of it may be confined to a compara-tively narrow context.

Professional Ethics

The current age is notable for the extent to which the various professions are raising numerous ethical concerns and, partly as a result, producing codes of conduct. In the context of Kantian intuitionism—or even of a less ambitious Rossian intuitionism—one can think of professional ethics as partly concerned, especially in its negative, prohibitional aspect, to specify what counts as an injury in the relevant domain, and similarly for fidelity, gratitude, and the other duties central in professional practices. Each of these requires a different interpretation in the contexts of the various professions. This conception of professional ethics indeed explains why the field is considered a domain of *applied* ethics. The same broad moral principles that guide our ethical thinking in general are applied in different areas of professional activity. What counts as an injury will differ in, for instance, business, medicine, law, and journalism. There is likely to be a similar variability in what counts as an injustice or, especially, a rectification for an injury or injustice.

Another application of the ethical framework I am proposing is to codes of ethics. A good code of ethics, or at least some of the principles it should contain, may be viewed as, in part, a formulation of a subset of middle theorems appropriate to its domain. A code of general ethics abstracts from any particular profession; a code of professional ethics addresses one. It is fruitful to view codes of ethics—at least plausible full-scale ones—as both (in principle) more finely charting the overall territory covered by Rossian duties *and* systematizable, directly or indirectly, under the categorical imperative as I have been interpreting it.

A code of general ethics, such as might be formulated by a close-knit religious community or certain voluntary associations, might contain not only requirements expressing special aims but also many requirements that instantiate Rossian principles. An injunction to give something to the homeless, for instance, might be an application of the principle requiring beneficence. Such a principle is also groundable in the categorical imperative. Indeed, the universality formulation of the imperative would have us refine the injunction so that we can be more or less evenhanded given the number of homeless we are likely to encounter. One might, for instance, select efficient and otherwise appropriate charities, some local, some not. Similar points hold for certain codes of professional ethics, as where lawyers adopt principles expressing some degree of obligation to do pro bono work.

If we consider the value base possible for a Kantian intuitionism, we can understand another aspect of morality that may or may not figure in codes of ethics. I refer to ideals. Moral ideals may be named by the same terms as duties, for example 'beneficence' and 'fidelity'; but when they are, the ideal represents a level of actual commitment higher than that required by duty.[6] Simply meeting duties of beneficence and fidelity would not entail realizing ideals thereof. The latter (positively) exceeds what duty requires and is in that sense supererogatory. If we tried to erect a strictly deontological ethics, with duty as our only morally important normative category, we could not properly accommodate ideals. A value-based Kantian intuitionism, by contrast, can ground both duties and a wide range of ideals. Some of these concern the interconnected notions of merit and justice, to which I now turn.

The Notions of Merit and Justice

Understanding, in broadly factual terms, the notion of merit crucial to the Rossian duty of justice is perhaps even more difficult than achieving such an understanding of the notion of injury. Here we have a problem central not only for the professions, but also in employment, education, and other contexts. I have already suggested that we have a concept of exploitation— in the sense of treating someone merely as a means—that can be explicated at least largely in terms of psychological and other factual notions. This concept can be taken to provide, at least in many cases and, for a full-blooded Kantian ethics, in all cases, a sufficient condition for treating people in a way that does *not* accord with their merit. The concept also provides one element that is significant for understanding rights. One of our important rights is the right to be so treated.

If, however, avoiding exploitation is necessary for treating people in accordance with their merit, it is not sufficient. Consider ignoring someone to whom one owes the courtesy of a greeting. We might say that the person "deserves better." But even if there is a kind of desert, the action need not be in any way exploitive. If there is a right here, it is perhaps grounded in the general right not to suffer social injury. If, however, there is a kind of merit that does not entail a right, we can surely say that (in moral matters) merit is a matter of a kind of moral fittingness. This is not to deny that both merit and fittingness are multidimensional and apparently do not admit of any analysis that is both simple and illuminating.

One might be tempted to identify merit with desert, which is plainly a sufficient condition for it. But the notion of desert (which is also in need of explication) does not provide a necessary condition for merit. Two fellowship contestants can equally merit an award; but if there is only one award available for them, neither can be said to deserve it. What they deserve is equal and adequate consideration, and the judges may in the end quite fairly draw straws. The loser may not properly complain of being denied something deserved (though people do loosely speak this way). Suppose, on the other hand, that the judges go beyond the call of duty and by much effort secure funds for a second fellowship. Here they fulfill an ideal of rewarding merit, and what they do is morally praiseworthy.

We could say that each contestant is "equally *deserving*," but only if that does not entail that either is wronged if, by a fair random procedure, the other is selected. Strictly speaking, then, although it is fitting and even desirable that people receive what they merit, their not receiving it does not entail a prima facie wrong, whereas this is entailed by one's not receiving what one deserves. There may be an excuse for not giving someone something deserved, but there is also a wrong. Arguably, we have a right to what we deserve, but not to what we (simply) merit. We do have a related right—a right not to be denied what we merit except for adequate reason—but that is quite different.

The fittingness central in the notion of merit is a relation we intuitively understand quite well. It is closely connected with meeting certain standards understood to govern the activity in question, such as the rules of a fellowship competition. It is also closely connected with reciprocity in human relations and with what we think of as "equal treatment" of persons, a kind of treatment that can be properly universalized, to put the idea in Kantian terms. Moreover, we think of merit as a status to be *respected* and of a certain kind of respect as generally merited (perhaps even deserved) by persons as such. This is one reason why exploiting people contrasts with treating them in accord with their merit. It will help here to pursue the notion of exploitation further, in part to see what factual grounds of it can be identified.

Although the concept of exploitation is not necessarily tied to distribution, that is an important domain of its application. There we may cite *disparities* as prima facie indications of maldistribution, say where people of equally long experience and equal productivity receive different remuneration (there may or may not be a factual measure of productivity, but often there are at least some important factual criteria of it). Second, punishment for a crime one did not commit is a still clearer case of injustice as a failure to treat people in accordance with their merit under the relevant statutes; this is a *misattribution* of a ground for harmful action, and it can easily be part of an exploitive pattern of conduct, or facilitate or result from exploitation. A less clear case of such injustice is a governmental or other institutional distribution that exhibits a certain kind of *disproportion*, as where a tax increase falls on the poor in exactly the same proportion as on the rich.

To be sure, this kind of institutional disproportion could be due to an insistence on equal treatment in a quantitative sense, say a ten percent tax increase for all. That kind of equality may be far from just, owing to how it may greatly worsen the lives of some and affect others almost negligibly. But in some cases, equality of a quantitative kind is a factual criterion morally relevant to justice, as where equal allotments of food are given in a war-time rationing system.

An apparently more plausible notion of equal treatment, however, centers on providing equality in opportunities to pursue human flourishing and on making some basic contributions to its material elements, say public education. By that standard, proportionate equality in the tax case (or at least some weighted equalization) seems prima facie (morally) preferable to absolute equality, whereas absolute equality is prima facie preferable in determining voting rights and even in the rationing case—though even there one could argue for differential allotments in accordance with people's differing physical needs.

The problem of how to work out factual indications of injustice is a major challenge for practical ethics, but the question of appropriate criteria for justice and injustice is difficult on any moral theory and in any well-balanced casuistry. Suppose, however, one could take a theory of justice like that of Rawls as providing distributive principles groundable apart from substantive moral assumptions (and a case can be made for this, provided we distinguish between moral and other normative assumptions). One can adapt those principles, or similarly derived variants, to the understanding of the Rossian duty of justice.[7]

If our point of view is a value-based *Kantian* intuitionism, moreover, we can select factual grounds for injustice, or more generally for actions not in accord with the merit of the person(s) in question, with guidance from the categorical imperative. Insofar as we have a good psychological understanding of what it is to treat people as ends or merely as means, this is a promising approach. These notions are by no means uncommonsensical, and moral psychology has much to say about them.[8]

To the principles of professional ethics already cited in this section and the other subsidiary principles that a value-based Kantian intuitionism would tend to endorse, we could add many others. Each profession requires types of actions that call for moral regulation. Every major kind of human relationship can have dimensions, such as those of unignorable need, allowable intimacy, appropriate requests, and limits of tolerance, for which prima facie moral principles can be formulated. There is also the important domain of institutional ethics: institutions act through certain people occupying appropriate roles, and these institutional agents are morally constrained by standards for their institutional conduct that go beyond, though they never nullify, Rossian principles.

There is no need here to detail other middle theorems. Enough has been said to indicate how a value-based Kantian intuitionism can help us to formulate and appraise them. A more urgent need is to reexamine the beneficence problem in the light of the overall ethical theory that has now emerged.

3. SOME DIMENSIONS OF BENEFICENCE

So far in this chapter, I have developed the normative side of value-based intuitionism mainly by indicating how the view enables us to formulate principles below the Rossian level: general, yet less comprehensive than Rossian principles and, unlike them, not necessarily candidates for self-evidence. One might think that if these principles follow from self-evident principles by self-evident steps, then they must themselves be self-evident. But that is not so. To be sure, what follows by self-evident steps from something self-evident is *provable* and, in a broad sense, a priori. But the conditional linking the first, self-evident proposition to the last proposition in the relevant series need not itself be self-evident. One can, for instance, understand certain conditionals with the form of '*If A, then T*', where A is an axiom and T is a theorem provable from it by self-evident steps, without being able to see, even on reflection, that these conditionals are true. For another thing, the only proof(s) of T may require many steps.[9] A proof can be like a long path whose every segment is perfectly clear: one may still be quite unable to see its end from its beginning. Thus, even given that Rossian principles are self-evident, the discovery of subsidiary principles through reflection on them cannot be assumed to be a mere exercise in a priori inference or a matter of routine thinking.

This point applies to a Rossian principle of beneficence as well as to other comprehensive principles, and we have seen that the duty of beneficence is among the most important moral duties and the one that threatens to drive an intuitionist normative ethics too far in the direction of a maximizing consequentialism, a position that intuition will not endorse.[10] I have already described some of the ways in which a Kantian intuitionism can avoid letting this pressure push us too far. I have also clarified what beneficence comes to if we try to understand it independently of moral concepts. In both respects, we can see how integrating Rossian intuitionism with a Kantian theory is an advantage. But there is a further aspect of beneficence that must be brought out, and here the value elements that can ground both Rossian moral principles and perhaps even the categorical imperative are a good resource.

Consider, from an axiological point of view, the two sides of beneficence: contributing to the good of others by enhancing the positive values in their lives and doing so by reducing the negative values. Utilitarians have not in general held that, other things equal, the latter kind of beneficence has priority over the former (though in principle they might find a rationale for holding this); but that it does is quite intuitive and is related to the intuitively greater stringency of such "perfect" duties as the duty not to kill in comparison with such "imperfect" duties as the duty to save (a difference utilitarians tend to deny).

To see a difference between the two kinds of beneficence, consider that for most of us, at least, if we are pained by even a minor toothache, we feel that we need relief, and getting it is normally more important to us than it is to have something enjoyable to do when we are, say, bored. Granted, it is difficult to compare quantities here; but for most of us, even ten minutes of an acutely unpleasant toothache is commonly, and surely not unreasonably, felt to be worse (a more seriously bad thing) than twenty minutes of, say, an ordinary enjoyable chat is good. We also tend to be more motivated to avoid things like the former than to achieve things like the latter.

How might this difference in apparent value be explained? Insofar as we can regard pains and pleasures as roughly equal in quantity, why should we tend to prefer avoiding pain over achieving a comparable "quantity" of pleasure and also tend to prefer *reducing* pain over *increasing* pleasure by a comparable amount? Relative to a given period of time, say ten minutes, making an acute toothache bearable is generally preferable to making a merely satisfactory conversation delightful. Many would indeed give up such a conversation in favor of thus mitigating the ache. People differ in such matters; but differences in resolving cases like this do not imply differences in the assessment, as positive or negative, of the kinds of elements to be considered. Just as we can differ over final moral judgments while agreeing both on what kinds of elements are relevant and on their valences, we can differ on overall choices concerning our well-being while agreeing both on what elements are to be considered and on their having positive or negative intrinsic value.

One hypothesis suggested by the value framework of this book is that pain can and sometimes does interfere with our characteristic functioning in a way that threatens or obscures our very dignity or at least impairs its characteristic manifestations. Pain can make us acrid or listless, angry or bitter, even unable to focus on anything. We can even be reduced to an irresistible animalic writhing. Admittedly there are pains that serve a purpose, such as making us value accomplishments that require painful training, and our *bearing* some pains can be one kind of manifestation of human dignity; but even such "valuable" pains, sufficiently magnified, tend to have a detrimental effect. Pain, and indeed even the kind of suffering that involves little or no pain, can be so pervasive and intense as to make it rational, for at least some people, to prefer death to their lengthy continuation.

In addition to being intrinsically bad, pain tends to produce responses or incapacities that are, whether intrinsically or extrinsically or both, also bad in their impact on certain elements of our dignity or its characteristic manifestations, or destructive of the basis of our desire to live. I do not mean by 'dignity' the kind of bearing that earns such phrases as 'a dignified manner'. In speaking of elements of dignity I am referring mainly to the capacities on which, at least in part, human dignity as a morally important quality rests.[11] A point of special importance here is that pain tends to impair agency, and extreme pain drastically hinders it. Intense pleasures may also do so; but this effect is not comparable for two reasons: these pleasures tend to be short-lived; and, more important, we can normally stop them at will or, in any case, by readily accomplished shifts of attention or activity.

Another element of the importance of pain in comparison with pleasure is that, despite providing positive (defeasible) reasons for action, pleasure need not have a positive impact on, or even be appropriate to, elements of our dignity, though it does not, as such, tend to have a negative impact on these or to be *in*appropriate to them. If it does in certain kinds of cases tend to be so, as occasionally with some intense pleasures (say, some that are drug-induced), they can normally be prevented by ordinary means from having long-lasting or debilitating effects on us. Moreover, although pleasures do not in themselves (apart from their having inappropriate objects) negatively affect elements of our dignity or their manifestations, having pleasures need not enhance anything in virtue of which we possess dignity. They do not have a positive effect on our dignity or our function comparable to the negative effect that pain has on them.

There is still another respect in which pleasure has a relation to our dignity (and to other things we reasonably care about) different from that of pain. Merely lacking pleasures does not detract from any element of our dignity and, for non-hedonistic theories of value, need not prevent life from being amply worth living. These points may in part explain why we do not tend to consider being deprived of pleasure to be as bad as being caused comparable amounts of pain.

We cannot be rigorously quantitative here; and even if we could be, the matter becomes more complicated when we try to explain why avoiding non-hedonic evils is also more important morally than — and may be preferable in other respects to — promoting hedonic goods. Not cheating people is, for instance, more important than providing them with enjoyable conversation. Even here, however, dignity is a factor, as are associated values that are central in various virtue concepts. Veracity is the virtue plainly relevant in this context, whereas the traits most pertinent to the conversational pleasures are charm, wit, repartee, and the like. Life should have an abundance of all of these goods. But from the moral point of view veracity is more important than the others.[12] Let us explore how some of the values associated with dignity bear on the scope and strength of the duty of beneficence.

4. TOWARD A COMPREHENSIVE INTUITIONIST ETHICS

One reason why the beneficence problem is serious is that there are so many other people, and so many values which goodness toward others leads one to promote, that the total demands of beneficence are numerous and extremely wide. Ross probably meant to reflect this breadth in his reference to contributing to the virtue, intelligence, and pleasure of others. But even this description does not encompass all of our obligations to others not covered by the remaining duties on his list. This section indicates some values not adequately reflected by either this description or Ross's principles, yet specially relevant to morality. The result should be a framework for normative ethics that is more comprehensive than Ross's, richer in resources for dealing with the scope of the duty of beneficence, and, in some places, more specific.

Freedom Values: Liberty and Autonomy

We can quite rationally want to be free to do as we like; this holds even when we have no specific plan to use our freedom in a particular way. We can also enjoy exercising our freedom even when doing so yields no further pleasure. Even apart from this, we can find free activity rewarding in a way we value: there are times when just doing as one wants has positive rewards. It can hold such rewards even when the value of objects of the desires in question is not crucial: sometimes it is the sense of freedom in doing as one wants that is rewarding, rather than the satisfaction of getting any particular objects of desire. We can look forward to such times with anticipation; we often look back on them with pleasure.

The sense of exercising freedom, then, seems to be among the things having intrinsic value, and freedom itself has inherent value.[13] This is not to deny that exercising freedom tends to be enjoyable; and even apart from that, it is certainly required for the most enjoyable kind of life. But neither these facts nor, so far as I can see, any others justify concluding, as hedonists would, that exercising freedom is not among the things having value in themselves.

If the exercise of human freedom is valuable in itself, and if even its possession can have inherent value, we can see not only one reason why it is wrong to deny or reduce people's freedom without adequate reason, but also why promoting their good may involve contributing to their freedom, either by enhancing it or at least by protecting it. I believe, then, that an adequate normative ethics should take account of these values. If the Rossian duties of non-injury and beneficence are understood broadly enough (if perhaps with artificial breadth), they include these liberty values; but acknowledging the values separately provides a clearer account of our basic obligations.

The value of freedom is apparently not exhausted by its contribution to one's happiness or even to the other elements of one's well-being that Ross included in his characterization of beneficence. A person might rationally value exercising freedom even apart from its yielding any external rewards, including any of the kind uncontroversially thought to constitute part of one's good. Granted, there are people for whom it would be better, in relation to their good, not to enhance their freedom (or even autonomy, if they are governing themselves under corrupt values), but this is not the normal case. The clearest way to express liberty values in terms of moral obligation—even if they may in the end be subsumable under duties of beneficence and non-injury—is to formulate principles specifically directed to the ends in question. One principle is that there is a prima facie obligation not to restrict the freedom of others.[14] The second is that there is a prima facie obligation to contribute to preserving and enhancing others' freedom.

It is not just the exercise of freedom that is important to us; we also value autonomy in its exercise. Freedom implies doing as we like; autonomy implies governing our conduct. Whimsical behavior may be free without being autonomous; our autonomy is expressed by (among other things) our carrying out certain plans and realizing certain standards.[15] One could enhance people's overall freedom, then, without enhancing their autonomy. Both values are morally important, and both are important for understanding human dignity. A sufficiently enlightened beneficence will include a disposition to contribute to these values in others, but we achieve a clearer normative theory if we treat them as distinct values grounding duties that, in Ross's work and many other contexts, are not ordinarily considered duties of beneficence.

Duties of Matter and Duties of Manner

There are other duties that concern treating people well that may be at least partly grounded in the dignity of persons, but are not strictly duties of beneficence and are not adequately accounted for in Ross's intuitionism. To understand the kind of duty I have in mind, consider first how duties are typically conceived. We typically think of duties as *to do* something, to perform an act of a certain type. These are duties of matter: they are specified by the act-type whose performance fulfills them. But if we take respect for persons as a central moral attitude, and if we think of people as in general meriting a kind of respectful treatment, we may also speak of *duties of manner*: adverbial duties, we might say. I emphasized in Chapter 4 that in fulfilling a duty of matter, we may or may not do so respectfully. A painter could fulfill a duty to paint a portrait while making abusive complaints about how difficult the working conditions are; a teacher could announce a high grade to a student with a patronizing air of surprise that the student did well.

One reason we have duties of manner is that the *way* we do things is often morally important and broadly under voluntary control. We are properly judged morally, as in other ways, by *how* we do what we do, as well as by what acts we perform. This applies even to negative duties, such as the duties not to lie and not to injure. These are typically fulfilled by mere non-performance of the prohibited acts, but often they are not only fulfilled but *observed*. Observing them may require certain intentional acts, such as exercises of effort to conform to the relevant standard, that may be done in significantly varying ways. It is true that certain duties, say to hurry a task, can be viewed both ways: as either duties to do a deed of the appropriate kind, or as duties to do the thing in an appropriate way. But even where a duty of manner can be described non-adverbially, as with hurrying a task, there will still be various ways to carry it out, and some may be morally significant.

The distinction between duties of matter and duties of manner should not be assimilated to either of two related ones, which I take in turn.

Kant and other philosophers have rightly emphasized the importance of acting from the right motive, and it is plausible to maintain that a fulfillment of duty has at best a reduced moral creditworthiness if it is not performed from duty.[16] But I do not take acting from a motive to be a *manner* of acting: acting from a motive is a matter of *why*, not *how*, one does the deed. Moreover, whereas we can have a duty to act in a particular way, I do not think we can have a duty to act from a particular motive (as opposed to trying to dispose ourselves so that we do so). This is not in general an action at all: 'acting from gratitude', for instance, designates not an action but an action *and* a factor that explains it.

The second distinction we need here is between merely fulfilling a duty and *performing* it, or *executing* it, or *carrying it out* (notions that are roughly but not exactly equivalent). If I meet you at the library by accident at ten, having forgotten my promise to meet you there at ten, I fulfill my promise; but since I do it by accident, it does not count as treating you respectfully, and I am not *performing* my duty. This failure to act respectfully is not just a result of my lacking the right motivation, the kind appropriate to doing one's duty; and I could have carried out my promise, and executed my duty, for a merely prudential reason, which would be the wrong kind. Duties of manner are neither "duties" to act from duty nor duties to fulfill duties of matter in a way that counts as *performing* them. The former notion is not coherent, the latter not sufficient to specify what it is to have a duty of manner.

It is far easier to illustrate duties of manner than to define the notion. Furthermore, the notion is far more readily applicable to positive than to

negative duties, though even the latter can be carried out in a wide variety
of ways whose differences may be morally significant. But we do not need
a definition. What I can offer is a conception. It is unified by the notion
of how we treat people, and that notion in turn helps in understanding
what it is to treat persons as ends. There are at least two basic kinds of
such duties.

The first kind is constituted by standing, "natural" duties of manner.
These are to treat people with respect, in the sense of an attitude that befits
the dignity of persons. This attitude does not entail *respecting the person*
in the ordinary sense, something impossible toward, say, certain violent
criminals. It is more a matter of recognition of the status of the person in
question as a rational and moral agent with vulnerabilities and feelings (or
a potential rational and moral agent, as in the case of very young children,
or a former rational and moral agent, as with adults who have permanently
lost their moral faculties from diseases or injuries). The attitude implies
civility though not necessarily warmth, non-violence though not necessarily gentleness, and a disposition to accommodate basic needs, though not
necessarily provision of comforts.

The second category of duties of manner is constituted by special duties,
owed to particular people or people of a certain description: we can promise to be tactful to someone in particular or to be gentle to children. We
carry out *some* of these duties by doing specific deeds, such as giving a
gradual explanation of one's disapproval of a person to whom, as administrative superior, one must give a negative evaluation. Executing a duty of
manner can require fulfilling a duty of matter. But even the deeds specifically required by duties of manner may be done in varying ways, and
duties of manner cannot all be reduced to duties of matter. Even where
one of them may so reduce, as where one promises to break sad news
personally and with certain words (the relevant manner of conduct being
specified simply by the act-types fulfilling this description), there is still a
difference between the "primary," promised action and the manner of its
performance. Since doing something in a particular *way* presupposes
doing it, we must grant that doing something in a particular way—a manner of acting—is behaviorally dependent on action simpliciter (on doing
that thing). We can indeed give an action-name to any given way of doing
a deed; but there will remain possible differences in the way the newly
described behavior can be performed. Styles and manners of acting cannot
be buried by supplying substantival descriptions. These may not capture

them. There are significantly different ways even to utter the same words. Much of the day-to-day moral quality of our lives is determined by how well we and those we interact with carry out duties of manner.

Fulfilling duties of manner can constitute treating people well; violating them can constitute treating people badly. If doing the right thing can be a case of goodness in action, doing it the right *way* can be also: goodness of manner. Fulfillment of duties of manner can be both an element in treating persons as ends and an instance of the good in the right.

Moral Rights

If we think not only of respectful treatment, but particularly of freedom and autonomy, it should be apparent that these are not only something we ought not to deny or deprive people of, but also something to which people have a moral right. I am thinking of a right as (roughly) a defeasible normative protection from a certain kind of coercive conduct, such as suppression of free speech (and here I will for brevity concentrate on freedom).[17] To see what this characterization entails, consider how a right should be specified. Regardless of our theory of what it is to have a right, to specify what a given right amounts to we must indicate at least this: (1) its possessor—who has the right; (2) its addressee—the person(s) against whom it is held; (3) its content—the conduct it protects and concerning which the addressee (and possibly others) owe the possessor(s) non-interference; and (4) its domain, for instance moral or legal—the normative realm in which criticism or sanctions or both are (prima facie) in order for non-performance of the relevant conduct. These normative domains commonly overlap, as with the legal and the moral.

This conception of rights is highly akin to a Rossian conception of prima facie duties, which I have argued are ineradicable given their grounds, though they are still defeasible and their grounds are cancelable. For certain ascriptions of rights, say a right to freedom of speech, it is arguable, as it is for certain principles of prima facie duty, that these ascriptions are self-evident. As in the case of duties, this does not preclude rights' being grounded in something else, including principles.

If, however, we appeal to the notion of a right to clarify the framework of Rossian and other prima facie duties, we should not be content to clarify rights simply by saying that they are grounded in such principles. One thing we may say is that at least certain moral rights arise from the *same* grounds that yield prima facie obligations. Consider rights not to be harmed, not to be lied to or given insincere promises, and not to be treated unjustly. Insofar as these notions can be clarified in (non-normative) factual terms, we can use them to clarify the relevant rights, whether or not we conceive rights as grounded or groundable in principles.

There are many less general rights under these headings, particularly if we take the omission of reparations for harms and for certain other wrongs to constitute a kind of injustice or harm or both. There will then be as many kinds of rights as there are harms or wrongs calling for reparations. If the kinds of grounds in question do not provide for an overall account of the basis of rights, they at least suffice to anchor them in a way that gives us a handle on them independently of simply presupposing Rossian principles. My main concern with rights here is to clarify moral obligations and their interconnections, particularly the interconnections between obligations of beneficence and others; and the suggested factual grounding of a wide range of rights is a step in that direction.

If it turns out that rights cannot be properly characterized by a Rossian intuitionism, a proponent of that view might add them as irreducible moral elements. The perspective of this book, however, does not require that and indeed provides various resources for understanding rights. From the point of view of a value-based Kantian intuitionism, we can broadly conceive rights (of the basic, natural kind) as such that, first, having them is essential to having dignity in the sense in which it demands the attitude of respect for persons, and second, infringements of them without adequate justification tend to constitute violations of dignity. Justification here can be understood partly in terms of the categorical imperative; but there will also be a need for a theory of the forfeiture of rights.[18] In both matters, we can partially explicate rights using the notions essential for specifying the grounds of Rossian duties, as well as such notions as treating people merely as means—a kind of treatment we have a right to be spared—and treating them as ends, to which we have at least such conditional rights as the right to receive such treatment from others *given* certain kinds of familial or friendly relationships to them.

Using the notion of a moral right just sketched, we now have a further way to deal with the beneficence problem. We can say that one has a right not to do beneficent deeds unless one has a special obligation to do them, as one might through a promise or some other ground of a Rossian duty. This right would usually be considered an aspect of, or at least within the scope of, one's appropriate freedom and autonomy, in the sense that one may properly decide to exercise it or not to do so; but it should be emphasized that to say this does *not* commit one to the view, criticized in Chapter 3, that the prima facie duty to do beneficent deeds must be autonomously undertaken. Autonomy can extend to a right not to do something even if the moral reason(s) for doing it have another basis. I can have a right not to help a student who has never taken a course with me even if, as a member of the student's department, I have a prima facie obligation to help. I may be properly criticizable for exercising this right in certain cases; it might even be wrong for me to decline. But these are different points.[19]

A similar though not equivalent point about our rights is that others do not have a right against us to have us do beneficent deeds toward them. By contrast, they do have rights against us not to have their freedom or autonomy restricted or to be otherwise harmed. I have already suggested why this should be so: one way (though not the only way) to explain it is in relation to the value of dignity. That value in turn is connected with (and perhaps more basic than) the categorical imperative, understood as presupposing that the duty not to treat people merely as means is more stringent than the duty to treat them as ends. As I have argued, the former tends to be a violation of dignity; the latter does not.

If, however, there is a right not to do beneficent deeds, how can it be true that we have a duty, Rossian or other, to do them? Is doing them only a matter of living up to a moral ideal?[20] This is too weak a description. I must confess, however, that I also find Ross's word 'duty' slightly out of place, at least for some cases in which one ought to do a good deed but need not, so that one does not have what is strictly speaking a duty to do it. To see what kind of 'ought' this is, we should explore the notions of ideals and oughts in relation to that of a right.

Oughts, Ideals, and Virtuous Conduct

There are many kinds of ideals. Consider forgiveness. It can be both difficult to achieve and a very good thing on both sides. It need not be an ideal for everyone, though it is necessarily an ideal for some, say for Christians. The same holds for gentleness, which differs from forgiveness in being an ideal governing the manner of action more than its content. By contrast, sincerity and certainly honesty are ideals for moral agents in general.

The sense in which these positive elements in life constitute ideals does not entail that they are unobtainable, as is implied by some uses of 'ideal' (at least where complete attainment is in question). They are at once good things and difficult though not impossible to achieve at the highest levels or, even at a minimally acceptable level, throughout a lifetime. The sense in which they are ideals is partly captured by their goodness together with their difficulty of attainment. But there is something more: there is no general right on the part of others to our *complete* sincerity or even our complete honesty. If we are asked questions that ought not to be asked and that are highly intrusive, we may be indirect or, in some special cases, less than veracious, without violating the questioner's rights or going beyond ours. This is not to say that we *should* be less than completely sincere, only that our being so need not violate others' rights.

It would be a mistake, however, to treat the ideals of honesty and sincerity as just matters of discretion. They correspond to virtues of character that moral agents as such should have and should try to cultivate if they lack them. By contrast, the ideals of generosity and, even more, of conversational charm or athletic prowess, are, from the moral point of view, *voluntary ideals*. They might also be called *optional ideals*. We need not adopt them as goals. If we do adopt voluntary ideals, this may constitute supererogation, though that notion applies more naturally to doing more of the relevant kind of thing than is required by a Rossian prima facie duty such as beneficence or by an involuntary ideal such as sincerity.

To say that a voluntary ideal need not be adopted as a goal is not to countenance the opposite extreme. Generosity—in the sense that implies giving more than is due from one—is a voluntary ideal, but we have no right to be cheap to the point of not doing our share, and we should not be. The same holds for being boorish in conversation or physically clumsy when others depend on our competence in a team effort. But in matters of generosity and good manners we are not criticizable for simply falling short of the relevant ideals. We may not even be criticizable for not achieving a good approximation to them, as we are for falling short of, and particularly for not even approximating, ideals of sincerity and honesty. We need a justification for the latter kind of failure, such as we would have in those special cases where deceit is on balance appropriate. The better the justification, the less the inclination to say we have fallen short.

There are, then, things we ought to do that we have a right not to do and that, correspondingly, no one has a right to demand of us. We ought to be sincere and honest, and we are criticizable for failure to achieve these ideals at a rather high level even if this level of achievement cannot be demanded of us as moral agents, in the way non-injury can be. More specifically, there is a high level of sincerity and honesty—which may vary with circumstances—such that we *ought* to achieve it even though we have a right to fall short of it. The case of spouses talking to each other is one thing; that of defense attorneys speaking for their clients is another. There is, however, *also* a level of attainment of these and other ideals—a minimal level of moral acceptability—that we do not have a right to fall below.

There is an important contrast here with beneficence: if (as I doubt) there is no right not to do beneficent deeds, the level of beneficent conduct required of us is nonetheless intuitively lower than the required level of attainment for sincerity and honesty. Broadly speaking, we must have the *traits* of sincerity and honesty if we are to have morally acceptable character. We need not have the trait of beneficence, as opposed to a disposition to do *some* minimum of beneficent deeds, to meet that standard. Without the former traits, we may easily tend to treat people merely as a means or at least disrespectfully. This does not apply to lacking beneficence; but without even a disposition to do some beneficent deeds, we will often tend to fail to treat people as ends.

Correspondingly, the criticism appropriate to falling below the relevant level in avoiding treating people disrespectfully or merely as means is more severe than that appropriate to falling below it in merely failing to treat people as ends, as might be expected from the difference between the two cases in relation to respect for human dignity. This contrast is not, however, my point here. The overall point is that in the domains of virtues and ideals there are standards which, in certain contexts, we ought to realize even though we have a right not to do so. Rights do not exhaust oughts.

It is a short step from this point to the conclusion that duties *also* do not exhaust oughts, at least not if the duties are conceived as Rossian prima facie moral obligations. We can be morally criticized for failure to meet certain standards even if we had nothing naturally called a duty to do what is in question and indeed nothing naturally called a moral obligation if that notion is associated with conduct that may be demanded of us even in a way that does not rise to claiming we have violated a right. There is, then, a voluntary ideal of beneficence which we do not have a duty to try to realize. There are duties of beneficence which we have a right not to fulfill. And there are other duties, including those of non-injury, that we have no right not to fulfill and others have a right to demand we fulfill.

Another way to see the relative strengths of duties and other oughts is in relation to mitagatory and excusatory power. Other things equal, avoiding a killing excuses injuries, whereas doing beneficent deeds would not; and doing beneficent deeds may excuse breaking promises where providing someone with engaging conversation would not. There are also differences within a given category; other things equal, beneficence in reducing suffering has more mitagatory power than beneficence in enhancing the happiness of those already comfortable. Taking the time to bind a serious wound would at least mitigate a failure to appear to give a lecture; it would excuse a ten-minute delay at the doctor's office.

If this set of distinctions seems to expand moral categories beyond necessity, I would reiterate that the wide theory I am developing takes values and the virtues associated with them, as well as principles and rights, to be morally important. None of the associated views requires claiming anything counterintuitive, and each major concept, such as the concepts of prima facie duty, of dignity, and of a right, can be clarified in relation to the others. Indeed, my main normative views in this book are meant to be supported by intuitions at the level of concrete cases as well as by inferences or explanations proceeding from the top down or from one principle to another. Statements of basic rights, moreover, may well have the status appropriate to Rossian duties: they appear to be middle axioms, intuitively knowable on the basis of sufficiently mature reflection and without inference from premises even if not without support from an intuitive sense of their role in singular moral judgments.

Prima Facie Duties Central in a Value-Based Kantian Intuitionism

In this final section, it will be clarifying to reiterate a number of the middle-level principles—in a sense the "middle axioms"—we have explored. It should be obvious that with certain comments and corrections, I consider Ross's principles of prima facie duty to be good candidates for such axioms. Let me first set out a revised version of them that reflects our inquiry in this book. This will provide the normative part of a Rossian intuitionism that, even apart from integration with the Kantian and axiological elements of Chapters 3 and 4, is a good if limited theory.

To avoid the institutional flavor of 'duty', and also to avoid the suggestion of correlative rights in each case, I express the principles using 'should' ('ought' is also appropriate, but seems unduly strong for some cases, such as routine gratitude). I take the principles to apply to at least normal persons capable of acting for reasons (which I assume they can do in some cases even in early childhood, though perhaps the kinds of reasons one must comprehend in order to be subject to some of the principles, e.g. the justice principle, require considerable maturity). Moreover, where Ross used 'fidelity' I formulate three related principles that more explicitly express the conception he may have sought to reflect. *All of the obligations are prima facie,* and I omit that term. I retain some moral terms, as Ross did, but take them to be partially explicable in relation to the non-moral grounds of duty referred to and the kinds of considerations (e.g., about matters of value) explored in this chapter and Chapters 3–4. I offer supporting comments on each principle I formulate; but I take all the principles to be intuitively plausible, and although a great deal should be said in interpreting each one, the need here is simply to outline a set of normative commitments appropriate to the overall intuitionist theory developed in the book.

1. Prohibition of injury and harm. We should not injure or harm people.

Unless we stretch the notion of injury, we should add the concept of harm to the principle Ross formulated. Injury, at least when minor, does not entail harm. Consider a nasty scratch from picking blackberries. Nor does harm entail injury. A stranger who gives a misbehaving child a stiff spanking in a supermarket may do harm to the child without causing injury. One could call the humiliation I have in mind psychic injury, yet one could also say it does no harm. In any case, a measure of harm seems possible without injury.

Physical harms and many physical injuries are paradigms of harms, but psychological harms, deprivations of freedom, and social harms also deserve the name. Causing pain or suffering is usually prohibited under the non-injury principle; but even if intentional or foreseen, as in medical cases, it is not always a clear case of either harm or injury. Such acts may be said to cause *temporary* injury or minor harm ('no real harm' is a phrase commonly used for, say, well-intentioned but hurtful criticism). Exploiting people also typically counts as a harm. The notion of a harm has wider scope than that of an injury, but its breadth is appropriate given the prima facie wrongs that must be captured.

One further comment is needed: the ground of the duty is taken to be objective, in the sense that actual injuries and harms are what is primarily to be avoided, not, say, justifiably expected ones. There is of course a derivative obligation to avoid the latter; but the principle is objective in the sense that one violates it if, without an overriding (or at least excusing) consideration like self-defense, one harms someone, even if one had excellent reason for the false belief that one's action would do no harm.[21]

It must be immediately added that a full-scale moral theory will provide for *excuses*, as where a risky military decision based on a false report loses the unit sent forward against what turn out to be overwhelming odds. I cannot here construct a theory of excuses, but there is no reason to think that an adequate one cannot be built from the raw materials from which plausible moral theories are constructed in the first place. In the military case, for instance, the excusable officer has that status by virtue having no good reason to doubt the report and otherwise of fulfilling obligations of loyalty (to the army), justice (in assigning dangerous assignments fairly), and honesty (indicating uncertainties and dangers to the troops), and, more generally, of treating the troops as ends.

To be sure, *some* of the grounds of basic duties may be, in a certain way, subjective: loyalty, for instance, *is* — in part — a matter of standing by others in times of their need as determined by one's best judgment. But the notion of injury is not cognitively filtered in that way. Even the standard of adhering to one's best judgment is not subjective in allowing one simply to do anything one *believes* is called for or even the best thing to do: one might, for instance, arrive at a belief through inexcusably overhasty reasoning. One's *best judgment*, moreover, is not equivalent to one's *judgment of what is best*. Here, as with wrong-doing in the light of externally objective grounds, one might or might not have an excuse. A fully comprehensive ethics must account not only for basic obligations but also for defeaters and excuses. I have concentrated on accounting for the first, but it should now be evident along what lines the kind of theory I have set out can deal with the second two.

2. *Veracity.* We should not lie.

This principle is not equivalent to the closely related principle that (in speaking or responding to questions) we should "tell the truth." For one thing, by not addressing certain topics and by not answering certain questions, we can, without lying, avoid telling the truth. Doing this may or may not be wrong. One can certainly do wrong in not answering or in being misleading, though without even implicitly lying, i.e. (roughly) by implying something one believes is false. We need, and in the ways I have illustrated in this book, we can find, middle theorems for many sorts of such cases; but the basic principle in question is the affirmation of an obligation not to lie. Unlike Ross, I do not take this obligation to be a special case of the duty of fidelity; but on my view the obligation can be both self-evident and equally strong even if it is so conceived.

Much could be said about precisely what it is to lie. Here I will add just one point. The notion is not even nearly equivalent to that of deception: many lies do not deceive; and deception is often possible without lying, as where one simply withholds information and thereby causes a false belief. Deception can also be unintentional, in a way lying cannot be if it can be so at all. An affable manner, for instance, can deceive someone into confusing geniality with affection. Deception, then, when it is wrong, can be so either because it is a case of lying or because it is a kind of harm (if only in the way it is exploitive), or a failure to treat someone respectfully.

3. *Promissory fidelity*. We should keep our promises.

A promise is not merely an expression of intention, though some such expressions can count as making a promise; and when such an expression comes close to it, there is a similar, though weaker, prima facie obligation to do the thing in question. I should add that although I have generally construed promising as a kind of objective ground of obligation, I have not meant to take the notion to be easily defined. If, at gunpoint, I am forced to say, 'I promise to leave the money at the rail station', have I made a promise at all, or have I made one that I have an excuse to break? Whatever the answer, there is no final obligation generated by such an utterance, and the theory I have presented can account for that either in terms of excuses (as I think most plausible) or by appeal to various conditions on making a genuine promise.

4. *Justice*. We should not treat people unjustly and should contribute to rectifying injustice and to preventing future injustice.

It is important to add something not clearly implicit in what was said about justice earlier: that deprivations of liberty and certain deprivations of pleasure—all of which are factually specifiable—count as injustices. These are distinct from not providing for pleasure or freedom on the part of others, which may, however, count as failures to fulfill the duty of beneficence. These deprivations may of course injure or do harm, but they need not. Even when they do not, depriving a person of freedom is doing an injustice, and certain cases of depriving of pleasure, for instance by certain kinds of surgery on sexual organs, are unjust treatment (which is not to say they do not deserve other morally negative terms).[22]

We may surely add that, other things equal, the first demand expressed in the principle has priority over the second and over the third. Perhaps the second duty also has prima facie priority over the third; but this need not be specified. Such priority does not appear, in any case, to be a basic demand of morality, even if it represents a morally reasonable standard. A major thesis of any plausible intuitionism is that there need not always be an ordering of potentially conflicting obligations; but a plausible intuitionism can allow that in some cases there may be warrant for the kind of qualified ranking just suggested.

The intrinsic end formulation of the categorical imperative is pertinent here: doing injustice at least has affinities to treating persons merely as means; failing to contribute to rectifying injustice does not do that, but commonly does bespeak a failure to treat one or more persons as ends; and not acting to prevent future injustice is similar to the second case, but differs in applying to future or hypothetical persons rather than actual ones who are candidates to be "treated" in a definite way.

5. *Reparation.* We should make amends for our wrong-doing.

The more serious the wrong, such as a grievous bodily injury, the stronger the obligation to make amends, and the more extensive the amends should be, other things equal. Not to make them (when there is no adequate reason to justify it) fails to treat the wronged person as an end, and it would commonly show the kind of disrespect that goes beyond that failing and is characteristic of (though it does not entail) treating a person merely as a means.

6. *Beneficence.* We should contribute to the good (*roughly*, the well-being) of other people.

I take the good of persons to be more than a matter of how favorable a "ratio" of pleasure to pain their lives exhibit; but—with due account of the organicity of intrinsic value—this is one essential element.[23] Moreover, physical and psychological well-being, insofar as they are separable from having some pleasure and minimal pain, are among the initial criteria for well-being. I have indicated sympathy with Ross's view that contributing to a person's virtue or intelligence constitutes contributing to the person's good. But I would again stress that we need a way of partially explicating virtue without depending on a moral standard not available in the theory we are constructing, for instance, by characterizing such virtues as veracity, fidelity, and respectfulness to the greatest extent we can using (nonmoral) factual notions and by relying on the content of other duties so far as it can be factually understood.

We should note here that not every kind or degree of intelligence — or knowledge (which is included in Ross's wide use of 'intelligence') — is something whose promotion is a good for every person. There are inappropriate ways to promote knowledge and intelligence and even to promote virtue. Some people should not know certain things; enhancing intelligence in malicious people might either not conduce to their good or be (indirectly) prohibited by, say, the duty of justice; and operating on someone's brain to enhance fidelity might be a bad thing, even with the person's permission.

In the light of the values in which the duty of beneficence can be grounded, we can also take as a "theorem" that we should be beneficent toward animals and other beings capable of pain and pleasure. This is not a principle derivable from the categorical imperative, though it is consistent with that and supportable by other elements in Kant's overall view, as by Ross's. One merit of the experientialist axiological pluralism outlined in Chapter 4 is its enabling us to see the plausibility of this principle. For similar reasons, we should observe (and give prima facie priority to) a parallel principle of non-injury toward animate beings other than persons.

7. *Gratitude.* **We should express gratitude, in deed or at least in words of thanks, in a way that befits good things done for us by other people, where, other things equal, our obligation is stronger if what was done for us was not owed to us.**

The goods in question include forgiveness and mercy, as well as favors, advancements, and material gifts. As in the case of making amends, the agent should observe a presumption of proportionality, though here it may be subtler and less strong. For instance, the greater the benefit, and the further it is from being owed, and, especially, the more burdensome its conferral is to the benefactor, the more extensive the expression of gratitude should be.[24] Such expression should sometimes go beyond the verbal;

services and other deeds are often required. Moreover, although we can discharge the duty of gratitude by performing acts of the right type, here perhaps even more than with the previously specified duties, the manner in which we do these things can be crucial for our success in giving the benefactor the sense that gratitude is being expressed. A duty of gratitude can be fulfilled without the benefactor's awareness of the grateful conduct; but the richest fulfillments are *communicative* and are seen by the benefactor as responses to the action that calls for gratitude in the first place.

8. *Self-improvement.* **We should develop or at least sustain our distinctively human capacities.**

The capacities in question include our intellectual, social, and aesthetic capacities. The intuitive idea here is wider than Ross's corresponding one, but it certainly applies to virtue and (with certain qualifications) intelligence. By and large, we are to try to become better people, particularly in respect of the standards represented by the *other* principles of obligation.

This duty of self-improvement probably makes substantial demands on everyone; but the reference to *sustaining* our capacities allows for cases in which, perhaps late in life and for some people at other times, morality requires only maintaining the level reached already, and self-improvement beyond that is a voluntary ideal. It might be unwise for anyone to assume this level has been reached; but perhaps it can be.

Not only are moral and intellectual capacities prominently included in the scope of this duty; it may also be true that we should give priority, other things being equal, to those capacities over certain other kinds, such as our physical capacities beyond those needed for efficient living. But it is not clear that this prioritization or any similar one is a requirement of *morality*, even if Ross was right in considering virtue to be of greater value in itself than anything else he considered good in itself. It may be, however, that morality does require that, other things equal, we give priority to improving our intellectual and other "higher" capacities, including our social skills, over enhancing our capacity for pleasure, as with developing purely recreational skills. If so, the requirement is not stringent: we would have a right not to adhere to it, even though we might encounter some moral criticism if we do not.

These prima facie obligations are understood to be moral; they need not and perhaps should not be regarded as indications of what a rational person, as such, should do. I take it, however, that in general rational persons tend to recognize such duties.[25] Some of the duties, particularly those of self-improvement, can be carried out in different ways depending on one's rational assessment of one's capacities. An artist, for instance, could give priority to painting over intellectual development.

In addition to this revised Rossian list of duties, I have suggested other moral obligations. Let me simply summarize the most general of them.

> 9. *Enhancement and preservation of freedom.* We should contribute to increasing or at least preserving the freedom of persons, giving priority to removing restraints over enhancing opportunities.

Although *some* obligations to increase, and certainly to preserve, freedom may be requirements of justice (as where there is oppression), and others may be requirements of beneficence (as where children must be given opportunities to try out many activities), I take this liberty obligation to go beyond the obligations of justice and beneficence and to be grounded in part in the values that largely constitute the dignity of persons. One could certainly argue that in fact we enhance people's welfare by increasing their freedom. This is, however, a contingent matter. Clarity is in any case best served by construing enhancement of freedom as a distinct prima facie obligation and by stressing the special value of its autonomous exercise.

The obligation in question is partly explicable in terms of a plausible reading of the Kantian injunction to treat people as ends. The exercise of freedom, for instance, particularly its autonomous exercise, is appropriate to the dignity of persons, which constitutes a major source of support from that injunction, and this exercise requires freedom. Indeed, without our exercising autonomy, our dignity as persons is not well expressed. I prefer, however, to avoid bringing autonomy into the formulation of the principle itself. Considerations of autonomy do, however, express constraints on how the principle should be applied.

It is barely possible that there might be no occasions to enhance liberty because there is no deficiency in either its permissible level or its exercise. But this seems highly unlikely in much the way it seems unlikely that there be no occasions for beneficence because everyone is doing so well. There might still be cases in which liberty might be undermined, and in that light the principle would call for vigilance. If moral principles are good guides in life as we know it, it is hardly an objection that in ideal cases there might be no need to invoke them.

There is one further principle implicit in much of what I have said:

10. *Respectfulness.* **We should, in the manner of our relations with other people, treat them respectfully.**

Respectfulness as understood here is a duty of manner, and I have already explained how such duties are to be understood and why they are not plausibly reduced to any set of duties of matter—though there certainly are many duties of matter that we must fulfill in order to treat people with respect overall. Even if such a reduction could be carried out, it would still be more perspicuous to cite this duty separately.

If, moreover, there are other duties on the list that can be reduced, the same point would hold. Given the value-based Kantian framework of this book, I have no theoretical need to resist plausible reductions as efforts to achieve theoretical economy; but given my emphasis on the value of Rossian principles as everyday guides, I do want to avoid unnecessary substitution of more general moral principles for more specific ones in guiding moral decisions. Those highly comprehensive principles may always be used to aid moral decision, but they are not in general a good starting point for it.

Many subsidiary principles can be formulated on the basis of the ten intermediate-level principles just described. Professional ethics formulates some of them; moral agents do so in ethically justifying their actions; parents do so in morally educating their children. In particular, the duties of self-improvement on one side, and those of beneficence on the other, imply that one should adopt *ideals.* Doing this greatly facilitates fulfillment of these two sets of duties, even if it is not a strict requirement for achieving that. These ideals yield an unlimited range of prima facie *oughts* of varying strengths, some of them moral, others not, depending on the character of the grounding ideal. Here both moral and non-moral values may yield choices in everyday life. Both kinds of ideals, moreover, may reasonably guide one's execution of the duties of manner. In these choices that are left open by our strict moral obligations, virtue is often manifested.

Moral commitment to strict obligation can be an impetus to virtue, including non-moral virtue, as where that commitment leads us to improve our knowledge. Non-moral values can also be an impetus to moral virtue, as where they inspire us to become more sensitive to the needs and sensibilities of others; and ideals and virtues, quite apart from any grounding they may have in moral values, may be mutually reinforcing. The normative ethical framework presented in this chapter, then, provides both specific moral principles and, taken together with the value-based intuitionist theory of the book as a whole, the raw materials for informed reflection on moral problems. No ethical framework makes solving those problems easy, but this one at least provides diverse resources to formulate new principles, both general and specific, and to support sound judgments in moral practice.

Conclusion

Ethical intuitionism as developed in this book may be viewed in two ways: as an ethical theory and as a full-scale moral philosophy providing both an account of moral principles and judgments—a metaethical account—and a set of basic moral standards. As an ethical theory it is, in outline, the view that there is an irreducible plurality of moral principles that are non-inferentially and intuitively knowable. As a moral philosophy affirming a set of basic moral standards, it provides moral principles that directly apply to daily life: principles governing veracity, fidelity, justice, beneficence, reparation, and much more. Here intuitionism, on its normative side, has advantages over other major normative ("practical") ethical theories. Reflective people, including such professionals as teachers, journalists, lawyers, physicians, and executives, who want guidance from ethical theories have often noted that theories with a single overarching principle, particularly Kantianism and utilitarianism, give them quite limited help. Virtue ethics may provide some needed correctives to these master principle theories; but much as many morally reflective people find Kantian reflection and utilitarian calculations at best difficult and often unclear in upshot, many of them find that determining what conduct is virtuous requires going beyond virtue ethics and appealing to principles or standards not clearly implicit in any pure virtue ethics. The intuitionism developed in this book is intended to accommodate the Kantian, utilitarian, and virtue-ethical elements that are most needed in practical ethics. Let me briefly review the route we have taken in constructing this position.

Chapter 1 introduces intuitionism through a partial interpretation of its major early twentieth-century proponents, who developed it as a distinctive alternative to Kantianism, virtue ethics, and classical utilitarianism. Sidgwick saw himself as improving on the utilitarianism of Bentham and Mill, but he differs from both in—among other things—being a rationalist. Moore made intuitionism in some ways more precise than Sidgwick had, and he contributed distinctively to the theory of value. Ross adopted ideas of Moore's and some from Prichard, but his ethical theory is richer and more plausible than Prichard's and both more pluralistic and better developed than Moore's.

I have represented Ross as the leading twentieth-century intuitionist in normative ethics and an important contributor to ethical theory as well. He combines merits of Kant and Aristotle; he is a powerful critic of utilitarianism; and he goes beyond Moore in both substantive ethics and the theory of value. Chapter 1 explicates Ross's ethical pluralism, his moral epistemology, his conception of intuition, his theory of prima facie duties, and his conception of the resolution of conflicts between them. Ross's intuitionism emerges as a plausible position that well deserves its place as an important ethical theory.

The aim of Chapter 2 is to develop Ross's intuitionism by both additions and corrections. His legacy has suffered because of the stereotype of intuitionism as claiming that we "just see" moral truths, particularly but not exclusively those that are self-evident. Self-evidence is not widely understood even among philosophers, and Ross did little that clarifies it. I have explicated the notion and contrasted it with obviousness and other kindred notions easily confused with it. I distinguish hard and soft kinds of self-evidence. I also distinguish two concepts of reasoning to a conclusion and their application to making Rossian intuitionism psychologically realistic. One kind of reasoning is premise-based, and its conclusion is inferentially grounded on its premises. The other is non-linear and in a certain way global. It yields conclusions based on reflection rather than inference.

Beyond this development of Rossian intuitionism, I indicate the possibility of different versions of intuitionism, for instance empiricist forms as well as the more common rationalist kind; I address some special problems, such as incommensurability and irresoluble disagreement; and I show how intuitionism can account for our knowledge of reasons for action. By the end of the chapter, it is clear how intuitionism can accommodate reflective equilibrium as an aid to both moral decision and ethical theory. Intuitionism can thus be appropriately fallibilistic in accounting for error in intuitive judgment; it can be self-corrective in refining its formulations in the light of the search for an ever more inclusive, more stable equilibrium; and it can avoid rigidity and dogmatism.

Chapter 3 arises from a conviction that intuitionism and Kantianism are natural allies in a way that neither Kantians nor intuitionists have seen. Intuitionists may resist this idea because of an inadequate epistemology. Kantians may resist it because of a top-down conception of the determination of moral obligation. The chapter integrates the Rossian intuitionism developed in Chapter 2 with Kantian ethics. The task of integration is challenging. For whereas Ross stressed intuitive induction as our route from understanding concrete instances of duty to apprehending abstract principles, Kant resoundingly asserted that one could not do morality a worse disservice than to derive it from examples.

Kant's pronouncement, taken together with his presentation of the categorical imperative, has led some critics to regard his ethics as too abstract and unclear in its application to moral decision-making. However we evaluate that judgment, we may conceive Kantian theory as top-down. Ross, by contrast, has been viewed as taking individual duties—"examples," in Kant's language—to be more readily known than principles of duty, and on the basis of this conception and his associated ethical pluralism, some of his critics consider him insufficiently systematic. Whether or not that judgment is warranted, in its emphasis on intuitive induction from exemplary cases Rossian intuitionism may be conceived as a bottom-up theory. Chapter 3 shows how understanding of the categorical imperative may be enhanced by reflection on Rossian principles, and conversely. Rossian principles, understood as I represent them, help to guide the downward inferences and applications called for by the categorical imperative; that imperative, understood to require, in the ways described in Chapters 3 and 4, treating persons as ends and never merely as means, helps us in seeing how prima facie duties may be grounded and interpreted.

If I have been right, Kant and other philosophers who have produced major ethical theories built around a master principle have had too little faith in intuitive everyday moral judgment; Ross and other intuitionists have had too little faith in comprehensive ethical theory. Chapter 3 shows how the integration of a Rossian view with a Kantian theory yields the major benefits of both positions: the moral unification possible through Kant's categorical imperative and other notions prominent in Kantian ethics, and the relative closeness to moral practice of Rossian principles. This is a theoretical result. On the practical side, the chapter shows how Kantian intuitionism can help us deal with conflicts of duties and can be extended to professional and "applied" ethics. On both counts, in dealing with conflicts of duties and in helping us to formulate plausible principles in professional ethics, Kantian intuitionism does better than Rossian intuitionism while retaining its major strengths.

Chapter 4 pursues a perennially central question in ethics: the relation between the right and the good. Historically, utilitarian theories have taken the right to be derivative from the good, and Kantian and intuitionist theories have denied this and in places held positions close to the converse view. I maintain that neither of these views is quite right, but that Kantians and intuitionists should still try to give us something that both utilitarianism and virtue ethics can claim as a merit: an account of how morality serves human flourishing. The main work of Chapter 4 is to provide this account for Kantian intuitionism.

In showing how a Kantian intuitionism can be anchored in a theory of the good, I presented the core of a theory of intrinsic value. The theory connects value, including moral intrinsic and inherent value, which are central for human dignity, with reasons for action. The result is an axiological integration of intuitionist moral principles: internalizing and acting on those principles is reasonably taken to contribute to human flourishing and thereby to the realization of intrinsic value in our everyday lives. The fulfillment of moral obligation can be goodness in action; obligatory actions can not only produce good results but realize the good. Here moral goodness is an element in the right, and not, as Ross often conceived it, just in the motivational elements appropriate to doing the right or, as Kant characteristically conceived it for actions, in their grounding in a motive of duty or in good will itself.

This axiological integration does not entail subordinating moral principles, whether Rossian or Kantian, to considerations of value in the way utilitarians have. Indeed, I show how the value base I identify for those principles allows them to retain the kind of autonomy—intuitive knowability—most important for intuitionism. By the end of this chapter, then, Kantian, valuational, and intuitionist elements are brought together to yield a distinctive ethical theory: a value-based Kantian intuitionism. Rightness is not reduced to goodness, but Kantian intuitionism, though its plausibility does not depend on axiological grounding, receives support from that basis.

Chapter 5 extends the work of the previous four. It combines theoretical and practical ethics. Above all, it clarifies and extends the normative ethical theory set forth by Ross. It first sketches five strategies of ethical reflection, some of them considered earlier. They may proceed from the top down (as with Kant); from the bottom up (in a case-based fashion); from the inside out (as with virtue ethics, which takes traits of character as basic); from values to principles (as with utilitarianism); and they may work from middle axioms, as Ross's principles may be called.

My theory allows a certain kind of employment of each of these strategies, but does much in working from the middle: from Rossian principles upward to very general principles like Kant's categorical imperative; and downward from Rossian principles to "middle theorems." These theorems are principles less general than the Rossian ones, but general enough to have wide application, for instance to figure in codes of professional ethics. The theorems concern, for example, injury, justice, or veracity in contexts narrower than those Ross considered in formulating his principle of non-injury, say contexts of journalistic or legal ethics, in which injury has some dimensions peculiar to those domains.

The final chapter also shows how a value-based Kantian intuitionism advances our understanding of some major ethical problems that continue to occupy much attention in the field: the moral priority of reducing pain over enhancing pleasure; the nature of moral rights and their analogy to prima facie duties as understood by a plausible intuitionism; the relations between ideals and obligations; and the place of liberty, autonomy, and justice in the overall moral framework the book develops. The core of Ross's often admired formulations is retained, but the theory developed in the book is used to clarify, extend, and unify them.

Far more could be said about how a value-based Kantian intuitionism may enable us to derive—or at least to reach and to account for—conclusions in one or another area of practical ethics. But I hope it is now clearer than before that even apart from any general ethical theory, we can effectively conduct a great deal of day-to-day moral thinking, and much ordinary moral decision-making, using the middle axioms or middle theorems and the practical standards they indicate, and that in doing so we should consider not only principles, but also ideals and virtues. We may fruitfully appeal both to Kantian moral standards in dealing with serious conflicts of prima facie duties, and to lower-level considerations if they improve the reflective equilibrium we should seek in resolving such conflicts. We may also consider values that are relevant in a context of moral decision, particularly those, such as rationality and autonomy, which are in part constitutive of the dignity of persons. And we may interpret and integrate moral principles we rely on with reference to the Kantian demand to avoid treating persons merely as means and, positively, to treat them as ends.

In formulating practical ethical standards, such as codes and administrative policies, we should consider the overall framework of values and principles, together with factual considerations about the profession or the kind of human situation we are addressing. In the practical domain, as in theoretical ethics, respect for persons is the fundamental attitude appropriate to the dignity of persons, and the dignity of persons is the central higher-order pervasive value that encompasses the other values essential in grounding moral obligation.

Practical wisdom remains indispensable, both in theoretical and in normative ethics. It certainly is no less important in determining the appropriate manner of performance of our duties than in determining what they are. Its role cannot be quantified or made ideally precise; but that will hold for central elements in any approach in ethics. All of the plausible approaches require practical wisdom for their everyday realization. But we must also give due weight to the many ways in which theory can aid the application of practical wisdom. The value-based Kantian intuitionism developed here has the advantage of integrating many different interacting levels of reflection from which to understand practical affairs and guide conduct in everyday life. Moral judgment need not come from an appeal to a theory; but our capacity for it can be enhanced by theoretical knowledge. Moral intuition has an authority of its own; but it can be refined, and must sometimes be corrected, by theoretical reflection. Intuition must also respond both to the pressure of obligation and to the incentive of ideals. Our obligations require us to reach certain destinations on life's journey, and they prohibit others; our ideals call us to take harder paths and to go further than we must. Along the way, the manner of our actions—their style, their timing, their sensitivity to others—is also governed by obligations and ideals that reflect the value of persons. A sound moral theory integrates these two kinds of normative sources, the obligatory and the ideal. It guides moral judgment, it stimulates moral imagination, and it clarifies the values that we seek to fulfill. In these and other ways, it can help us to achieve the good in doing the right.

Notes

Chapter 1. Early Twentieth-Century Intuitionism

1. In the *Summa Theologica*, ques. 94, art. 2, e.g., Aquinas says, "The precepts of the natural law in man stand in relation to operable matters as first principles do to matters of demonstration. But there are several first indemonstrable principles. Therefore there are also several precepts of the natural law . . . both are self-evident principles." The claims of pluralism, self-evidence, and indemonstrability—unprovability in the terminology of twentieth-century intuitionism—are (as we shall see) all echoed in the early twentieth-century intuitionists.

2. Henry More, *Enchiridion Ethicum* (1667), John Balguy, *The Foundations of Moral Goodness* (1728–29), Samuel Clarke, *A Discourse Concerning the Unchangeable Obligations of Natural Religion* (1738), Richard Price, *Review of the Chief Questions and Difficulties of Morals* (1757), and Ralph Cudworth, *A Treatise Concerning Eternal and Immutable Morality* (1781) are among the significant figures here. For a brief account of the views of More, Clarke, and Price, see Henry Sidgwick, *Outlines of the History of Ethics* (1866; Boston: Beacon Hill, 1960). Some of these figures (particularly Cudworth) are treated in detail by Stephen L. Darwall in *The British Moralists and the Internal 'Ought': 1640–1740* (Cambridge: Cambridge University Press, 1995); and most of them are discussed in a wide historical perspective by J. B. Schneewind in *The Invention of Autonomy: A History of Modern Moral Philosophy* (Cambridge: Cambridge University Press, 1998). For a more recent treatment, including an interpretation of Thomas Reid as an intuitionist, see Mark Mathewson, "British Moral Intuitionism in the Eighteenth Century" (forthcoming).

3. Recent defenders of the overall view include David McNaughton, "Intuitionism," in *The Blackwell Guide to Ethical Theory*, ed. Hugh LaFollette (Oxford: Blackwell, 2000), 268–87; Berys Gaut, "Moral Pluralism," *Philosophical Papers* 22 (1993): 17–40; Mark Nelson, "Morally Serious Critics of Intuitionism," *Ratio* 12 (1999): 54–79; Philip Stratton-Lake's introduction to his *Ethical Intuitionism: Re-evaluations* (Oxford: Clarendon Press, 2002) and the papers in that volume by Thomas Baldwin, Roger Crisp, Berys Gaut, Brad Hooker, and David McNaughton. Many philosophers have defended some significant element in Ross, as I do below for a number of his points. For a wide-ranging and more eclectic presentation of some intuitionistic views, see Charles Larmore, *The Morals of Modernity* (Cambridge: Cambridge University Press, 1996).

4. Henry Sidgwick, *The Methods of Ethics* (London: Macmillan, 1907; reissued by the University of Chicago Press in 1962), 96. Most references to this book will hereinafter be parenthetically included in the text.

5. *Methods*, 96 n. 1.

6. Sidgwick shows an awareness of the issue of interpretation. See, e.g., his long note at the end of the chapter, 102–3.

7. It is not clear whether "perceptional" judgments can be of a narrow act-type as well as of an act-token, as where a deed already done (a token) is said to have been one's duty (or right or wrong). It would seem so, in part because both Sidgwick and earlier intuitionists would have considered prospective judgments eligible to count as particular, as where one judges that one must jump into a lake to save a drowning child. No matter how narrowly one understands the obligation, one's prospective conception of the act will allow for different kinds of tokenings, say one in which the left hand is used and one in which the right hand is used to grasp the child. However this matter stands for perceptional intuitionism, it may be that intuitions formed in considering act-tokens are in some way more basic than those formed in contemplating act-types. The same question arises in connection with Prichard, as will be evident even in the brief discussion later in this chapter. For detailed discussion of Sidgwick's account of perceptional and other kinds of intuitionism, see Thomas Baldwin, "The Three Phases of Intuitionism," in Stratton-Lake, *Ethical Intuitionism*. Cf. Larmore, *Morals of Modernity*, chap. 5.

8. One might think there is an entailment rather than a strong suggestion here, but I do not think that is clearly so: just as one can perceive a shadow without believing it to be one, one might perhaps perceive a truth yet not believe (or disbelieve), or accept or reject, that proposition. The issue is complicated, and nothing major turns on the more cautious interpretation I give.

9. G. E. Moore, *Principia Ethica* (Cambridge: Cambridge University Press, 1903). References to this book hereinafter are parenthetically indicated in the text.

10. I call this an epistemic reason rather than a logical one in part because Moore should not be taken to be denying that in a logical sense of 'inference' *every* true proposition can be an inference. Logically, it may be conjoined with any other true proposition; it will then be validly inferable from the conjunction.

11. This point might hold, for some people, regarding the distribution laws, one of which is that r & (p or q) ↔ (r and p) or (r and q).

12. H. A. Prichard, "Does Moral Philosophy Rest on a Mistake?" *Mind* 21 (1912); reprinted in his *Moral Obligation* (Oxford: Clarendon Press, 1949), 8, emphasis added.

13. H. A. Prichard, *Duty and Interest* (Oxford: Oxford University Press, 1928), reprinted in *Readings in Ethical Theory*, ed. Wilfrid Sellars and John Hospers, 2d ed. (Englewood Cliffs, NJ: Prentice-Hall, 1970), 694–95.

14. Moore's claim that for a self-evident proposition there is "no reason" would seem to support the unprovability claim directly if 'reason for' is understood epistemically, as it naturally would be where the epistemic notion of proof is in question; but I am not assuming that Prichard missed Moore's ontic interpretation of his claim.

15. It is interesting to compare Prichard's attack on the advantage thesis with his later attack on the wider "mistake" (which he attributes to Hastings Rashdall, J. Laird, and Moore) of "resolving obligation into something else . . . into what has to be called ought-to-existness . . ." See "Moral Obligation," in his *Moral Obligation*, 158. Here a central claim is that if there is "a common characteristic [of acts] the possession of which renders us bound to do the various acts which we are bound to do . . . [then] that to which we are referring when we say of ourselves that we ought . . . to do a

certain action is not even in the widest sense of the term a characteristic of ourselves, as the statement suggests that it is, but a characteristic of the action" (159). This will not apply to future actions, however, since "only something which is can be something which ought, or ought not, to exist" (163), yet "there can only be an obligation to do an action so long as it is not done" (163). It would take more space than I have here to appraise this argument.

16. C. D. Broad, *Five Types of Ethical Theory* (London: Routledge and Kegan Paul, 1930), reprinted by Littlefield, Adams (Paterson, 1959). Page references to this book will hereinafter be parenthetically included in the text.

17. This idea, which is surely at least implicit in Kant, is developed and defended in chap. 4 of my *Epistemology*, 2d ed. (London: Routledge, 2003).

18. If, however, we take Broad's intuitionism to be an intuitionistic version of consequentialism, we may find a successor in Brad Hooker's position (depending in part on what each of them builds into the relevant good consequences, e.g. on whether Broad's covers what Hooker calls fairness). See Brad Hooker, "Ross-Style Pluralism versus Rule-Consequentialism," *Mind* 105 (1996): 531–52, and *Ideal Code, Real World* (Oxford: Oxford University Press, 2000).

19. There is no uncontroversial way to define 'naturalism', but it might be encapsulated as the idea that nature is all there is, and the only basic truths are truths of nature (which some people consider to be the kinds of propositions amenable to scientific assessment). Detailed discussion and references to a wide range of relevant literature are provided in my "Philosophical Naturalism at the Turn of the Century," *Journal of Philosophical Research* 25 (2000).

20. See W. D. Ross, *The Right and the Good* (Oxford: Oxford University Press, 1930), reprinted by Hackett Pub. Co. (Indianapolis, 1988), esp. chap. 2, 16–39. (This book now appears again from Oxford University Press [2002], ed. Philip Stratton-Lake, who has added a highly informative introduction, an extensive bibliography, and some editorial notes, but retained the original pagination also appearing in Hackett's edition.) John Rawls finds the pluralism so important that he considers it the basic feature of ethical intuitionism, though he grants that intuitionism is usually taken to have other important properties. See *A Theory of Justice* (Cambridge: Harvard University Press, 1971), 34–35. According to Bernard Williams, in the 1950s and 1960s "it was taken for granted that intuitionism in ethics was an epistemological doctrine . . . the kind of view held, for instance, by W. D. Ross and H. A. Prichard." See "What Does Intuitionism Imply?" in *Human Agency*, ed. R. Dancy, J. Moravcsik, and C. Taylor (Stanford: Stanford University Press, 1988), 198. Williams credits Rawls with changing "our understanding of the term" so as to "restore an earlier state of affairs" (ibid.). For William K. Frankena, "An intuitionist must believe in simple indefinable properties, properties that are of a peculiar non-natural or normative sort, a priori or nonempirical concepts, and self-evident or synthetic necessary propositions." See *Ethics*, 2d ed. (Englewood Cliffs, NJ: Prentice-Hall, 1973), 103.

21. For Bruce Russell, at least, intuitionism need not be pluralist. See his "In Defense of Intuitionism," presented at the Pacific Division of the American Philosophical Association in 1999.

22. I am not alone in so conceiving the matter; see Walter Sinnott-Armstrong's valuable account of intuitionism in *The Encyclopedia of Ethics* (New York and London: Garland Publishing Co., 1992), 628–30.

23. See Ross, *The Right and the Good*, 21.

24. Ross often used 'actual duty' where I use 'final duty', but this is misleading: as explained below, even an overridden duty is actually possessed.

25. Ross himself spoke this way: "I suggest '*prima facie* duty' or 'conditional duty' as a brief way of referring to this characteristic . . . which an act has, in virtue of being of a certain kind (e.g. the keeping of a promise), of being an act which would be a duty proper if it were not at the same time of another kind which is morally significant" (*The Right and the Good*,. 19). The term 'pro tanto' has also been used, and it has the advantage of suggesting that duties vary in strength; but given Ross's point that a prima facie duty may not be strictly a duty at all, and given how well established the term 'prima facie duty' is, I will continue to use it.

26. He contrasts his view, e.g., with that of "Professor Moore and Dr. Rashdall, that there is only the duty of producing good, and that all 'conflicts of duties' should be resolved by asking 'by which action will most good be produced'?" 18–19.

27. Ibid., 29–30. Cf. Prichard, "Does Moral Philosophy Rest on a Mistake?" The mistake, as noted in a quotation in the text, is "supposing the possibility of proving what can only be apprehended directly" (16).

28. Ibid., 31 and 33. Ross's examples show that he is thinking of the possibility that an act has some properties in virtue of which it is prima facie right and some in virtue of which it is prima facie wrong, and he holds that in such cases "we come to believe something not self-evident at all, but an object of probable opinion, viz. that this particular act is (not *prima facie* right but) actually right" (33). The note on 33 admits his overstating the no-general-description claim; his point could be taken to be a version of the thesis that no (non-normative) factual description entails an *actual* obligation, but it might also be considered epistemic: no set of facts makes it self-evident, even if it does entail, that a specific act is one's actual duty. The crucial point is that Rossian intuitionism does not claim that intuition yields knowledge of what to do in conflict cases. For Ross it would be a mistake to say that "Intuitionism is so called because it says intuition is what tells us what duty prevails," as remarked by Joel Feinberg in *Reason and Responsibility* (Belmont, CA: Wadsworth, 1993), 445. Regarding what to do given conflicts of duty Ross cites Aristotle's dictum that "The decision rests with perception," which Ross did not identify with apprehension or the faculty of intuition, though he left open that it sometimes yields intuitions (*The Right and the Good*, 41–42).

29. *The Right and the Good*, 39–41.

30. The quotation is from 41; for the primacy of reflection on specific cases, see, e.g., 41–42. In *The Foundations of Ethics* (Oxford: Oxford University Press, 1939), Ross says, of "insight into the basic principles of morality," that it is not based on "a fairly elaborate consideration of the probable consequences" of certain types of acts; "When we consider a particular act as a lie, or as the breaking of a promise . . . we do not need to, and do not, fall back on a remembered general principle; we see the individual act to be by its very nature wrong" (172–73). Speaking approvingly of Aristotle, Ross said

of right acts that, while first "done without any thought of their rightness," when "a certain degree of mental maturity" was reached, "their rightness was not deduced from any general principle; rather the general principle was later recognized by intuitive induction as being implied in the general judgments already passed on particular acts" (170). The reference to induction is not meant to imply that the knowledge of "basic principles of morality" is inferential. As the later intuitionist A. C. Ewing put it in referring to intuitive induction, it "is not reasoning at all but intuition or immediate insight helped by examples." See "Reason and Intuition," *Proceedings of the British Academy* 27 (1941) reprinted in his *Non-Linguistic Philosophy* (London: George Allen and Unwin, 1968), 38 n. 1.

31. This is relevant to problems of euthanasia. I would stress that the absence of any a priori hierarchy does not prevent Ross's countenancing either prima facie generalizations to the effect that one duty is stronger than another or generalizations to the effect that under certain conditions a type of act, such as unplugging a respirator, is preferable to another, say a fatal injection. He says, e.g., "normally promise-keeping comes before benevolence," and then *roughly* specifies the conditions under which it does (*The Right and the Good*, 19). Intuitionism as such may leave open whether these comparative generalizations are a priori. For discussion of orderings of duties and the sense in which their conflicts can create moral dilemmas, see Walter Sinnott-Armstrong, "Moral Dilemmas and Incomparability," *American Philosophical Quarterly* 22 (1985).

32. This may be in part what leads R. B. Brandt (among others) to consider intuitionism as such committed to the possibility of intuitively grasping self-evidence, as opposed to truth. See *Ethical Theory* (Englewood Cliffs, NJ: Prentice-Hall, 1959), chap. 8. Cf. Jonathan Harrison: "According to this view [intuitionism], a person who can grasp the truth of ethical generalizations does not acquire them as a result of a process of ratiocination; he just sees without argument that they are and must be true, and true of all possible worlds." See "Ethical Objectivism," in *The Encyclopedia of Philosophy* (New York: Macmillan, 1967). It is noteworthy that John Rawls, in explicating Samuel Clarke, says, "First principles of more and less fitness are known by reason in the way the truths about numbers and geometrical figures are known: such truths are seen to be necessary and self-evident, at least in the case of axioms . . ." See *Lectures on the History of Moral Philosophy* (Cambridge: Harvard University Press, 2000), 73. (In the quotation from Clarke that follows, 'manifest' and 'clear' are used rather than 'self-evident' or 'necessary', but Rawls's reading certainly fits the passage and would be natural for later intuitionist readers as well.)

33. I do not think that this point is contradicted by Ross's *Foundations of Ethics*.

34. Moore, *Principia*, x. See also 145. Cf. Sidgwick's remark (cited earlier) that "by calling any affirmation as to the rightness or wrongness of actions 'intuitive', I do not mean to prejudice the question as to its ultimate validity . . . I only mean that its truth is *apparently* known immediately . . ." (211, my emphasis). For detailed explication of Moore and an ethical theory in the Moorean tradition, see Panayot Butchvarov, *Skepticism in Ethics* (Bloomington: Indiana University Press, 1989). For further pertinent discussion and a number of helpful references, see Caroline J. Simon, "The Intuitionist Argument," *Southern Journal of Philosophy* 28 (1990).

35. Such fallibility is not strictly entailed by the defeasibility of the justification of the intuition in question. An intuition of a logical truth could be defeasible—as where one finds what looks on careful reflection like a disproof—without being fallible; one could thus lose justification for the proposition even though, objectively, one's intuition, being of a logical truth, could not have been in error.

36. A common conception of intuitionism is echoed by J. L. Mackie when he says, "if we were aware of them [objective values], it would have to be by some special faculty of moral perception or intuition, utterly different from our ordinary ways of knowing anything else in the universe . . ." See *Ethics: Inventing Right and Wrong* (Penguin Books: Harmondsworth, Middlesex, 1977), 38. Roger Crisp calls this the "radar view" and argues against its attribution to intuitionism; see "Sidgwick and the Boundaries of Intuitionism," in Stratton-Lake, *Ethical Intuitionism*, 57–60.

37. I restrict discussion to *propositional intuitions—intuitions that*, intuitions of some proposition as true, as opposed to *property intuitions—intuitions of*, roughly, apprehensions of some property. Suppose, however, that the former must be based on the latter; e.g. an intuition that a triangle has three sides might have to be based on an intuitive grasp of the nature of a triangle (or, perhaps better, of the concept of a triangle). The points to follow concerning propositional intuitions will hold whether or not there is such an epistemic dependency. For a statement of a view taking intuitions to be seemings rather than cognitions of the kind I am describing, see George Bealer's contribution to *The Blackwell Guide to Epistemology*, ed. John Greco and Ernest Sosa (Oxford: Blackwell, 1998), and his "Intuition and the Autonomy of Philosophy," in *Rethinking Intuition*, ed. Michael R. DePaul and William Ramsey (Lanham, MD: Rowman and Littlefield, 1998). This volume also contains instructive papers by psychologists and philosophical accounts of intuition largely complementary to mine ("Minimal Intuition," by Ernest Sosa, 257–69, and "Southern Fundamentalism and the Ends of Philosophy," by George Graham and Terry Horgan, 271–92), as well as one which provides cognitive-psychological hypotheses that bear on the status of my account ("Philosophical Theory and Intuitional Evidence," by Alvin I. Goldman and Joel Pust, 179–97). Cf. William Tolhurst, "Seemings," *American Philosophical Quarterly* 35 (1998).

38. A. C. Ewing is explicit on the point, at least for basic intuitions. See, e.g., *Ethics* (London: English Universities Press, 1953), 136, where he says that "propositions, particularly in ethics but also in other fields of thought, sometimes present themselves to a person in such a way that he . . . knows or rationally believes them to be true without having reasons or at least seems to himself to do so . . . some ethical propositions must be known immediately if any are to be known at all." Cf. his *The Fundamental Questions of Philosophy* (London: Routledge and Kegan Paul, 1951), 48–49.

39. Ross even comments on the difficulty of determining exactly what a promise is (*The Right and the Good*, 35).

40. An intuition may also be caused by commitment to a theory, as where reflection on the theory leads one to explore a topic and one thereby forms intuitions about it. But this causal dependence of the intuition on the theory has no necessary bearing on the justificatory status of the former.

Chapter 2. Rossian Intuitionism as a Contemporary Ethical Theory

1. See, e.g., recent work of David McNaughton cited in Chapter 1, as well as many of the papers in *Moral Particularism*, ed. Brad Hooker and Margaret Little (Oxford: Oxford University Press, 2000) and Stratton-Lake, *Ethical Intuitionism*.

2. See *The Right and the Good*, 21.

3. Ross would probably have denied that there is even an empirical hierarchy among them. He held that conflicts of duties must be resolved "with no principle upon which to discern what is our actual duty in particular circumstances" (ibid., 23), he calls the duty of non-maleficence only "prima facie more binding" than that of beneficence (22), and this prima facie qualification seems representative of how he regarded the comparisons he makes between conflicting duties.

4. Ibid., 29–30. Cf. Prichard's "Does Moral Philosophy Rest on a Mistake?" which takes the mistake to be supposing the provability of what can only be apprehended directly. Philip Stratton-Lake notes that in "The Basis of Objective Judgment in Ethics," published three years before *The Right and the Good* in vol. 17 of the *International Journal of Ethics* (1927), "Ross explicitly states that 'the fact that something can be inferred does not prove that it cannot be seen intuitively'. If he thinks that some proposition can be inferred from (justified by) other propositions and be self-evident, he clearly thinks that its being self-evident does not rule out the possibility of a proof." See Stratton-Lake's introduction to *The Right and the Good*, xlix. I do not believe that this quotation casts doubt on Ross's meaning what he says in *The Right and the Good*. For one thing, not everything intuitive is "immediate," in the apparently Aristotelian sense Moore, Prichard, and others seemed to have in mind as a characteristic of the self-evident in the context of describing it as unprovable (cf. the quotation from Ewing referenced in n. 6 below). If, as Ross seems to hold, some singular moral judgments (and probably other non-self-evident judgments) can be intuitive, then not everything intuitive is even a priori. Second, I doubt that Ross was thinking of the "mathematical axioms" or "forms of inference" he referred to in the context of the unprovability claim as provable (or inferable in the relevant sense). Third, I would resist Stratton-Lake's apparent identification of the inferable with the justifiable and provable (xlviii–xlix). Inferability, even in the epistemic as opposed to logical sense, does not entail justifiability, which in turn does not entail provability.

5. Ross, *The Right and the Good*, 39–41.

6. Ewing, "Reason and Intuition," 39. He also brings Broad to mind in calling intuitions in the sense that concerns him "both non-empirical and immediate" (41).

7. As noted in Chapter 1, this may be in part what leads Brandt (in *Ethical Theory*) and others to take intuitionism to be committed to the possibility of intuitively grasping self-evidence, as opposed to truth. The view is parallel to the position that a priori justification is grounded in a grasp of the necessity of the proposition in question. On this traditional position, see Laurence BonJour's construal of the "traditional rationalist account of *a priori* knowledge as the intuitive grasp or apprehension of necessity" in his *The Structure of Empirical Knowledge* (Cambridge: Harvard University Press, 1985), 207.

8. In A. C. Ewing we find a similar conception of intuition, though in the context his subject is intuition of self-evident propositions. He says, regarding "the mode of cognition we are discussing . . . As to the third objection, to the effect that 'intuition' is merely a subjective criterion, we may reply that . . . it is not a case of inferring a necessary proposition from a contingent, empirical one about my state of mind . . . but of *seeing a proposition to be necessary* where of course the seeing is a subjective state of mind." See "Reason and Intuition," 54.

9. As Alvin Plantinga puts it, "the tradition . . . held that self-evident propositions — simple truths of arithmetic and logic, for example — are such that we can't even grasp or understand them without seeing that they are true . . . A better position, I think, is that a self-evident proposition is such that a *properly functioning* (mature) human being can't grasp it without believing it." See *Warrant and Proper Function* (Oxford: Oxford University Press, 1993), 108–9. The view developed in this chapter contrasts with both positions.

10. This is an issue discussed in some detail in my "Self-Evidence," *Philosophical Perspectives* 13 (1999).

11. This approach to skepticism is elaborated and defended in chap. 10 of my *Epistemology*, 2d ed. (London: Routledge, 2003).

12. For a quite different view of inference, see Nicholas L. Sturgeon, "Ethical Intuitionism and Ethical Naturalism," in Stratton-Lake, *Ethical Intuitionism*. His view of inference is wider than mine, which is a main reason he resists countenancing noninferential knowledge. It may be that some of the kinds of beliefs he considers conclusions of inference could be what I call conclusions of reflection.

13. It is not under just any conditions that the unobtainability of reflective equilibrium can undermine the justification of an intuition. Even if *some* such equilibrium can in principle be found for virtually any true intuitive judgment, undermining is expectable only when a certain kind of reasonable effort fails. It might seem that when a moral judgment has much practical importance, one is not justified in holding it except on the basis of finding such an equilibrium — or at least supporting premises — but this does not follow from the defeasibility acknowledged in this chapter and seems doubtful. Some of its plausibility may derive from failure to distinguish it from the idea that one should have justificatory reasons for *acting* on a moral judgment in an important matter; but this idea could be true in part because holding justified intuitive judgments or other intuitive cognitions *constitutes* having adequate reason. For an elaborate case for the view that non-inferential moral cognitions need support of the broadly inferentialist kind intuitionists think is often unnecessary, see Walter Sinnott-Armstrong, "Moral Relativity and Intuitionism," *Philosophical Issues* 12 (2002). For many of the kinds of examples in question, this chapter and the next two indicate how inferential support might, consistently with intuitionism, be forthcoming. The skeptical thrust of his paper, however, can be met only through arguments in general epistemology.

14. For a discussion of the justificatory role of reflective equilibrium in a pluralist ethics that is largely complementary to the sketch presented here (and in Chapter 3), see Berys Gaut, "Justifying Moral Pluralism," in Stratton-Lake, *Ethical Intuitionism*.

15. On the importance of this in ethics, see Margaret Walker's "Feminist Skepticism, Authority, and Transparency," in Walter Sinnott-Armstrong and Mark Timmons, *Moral Knowledge?* (Oxford: Oxford University Press, 1996).

16. Ross says, e.g., that "a great deal has been made of 'what we really think' about moral questions" (39); and that "The existing body of moral convictions of the best people is the cumulative product of the moral reflection of many generations, which has developed an extremely delicate power of appreciation of moral distinctions; and this the theorist cannot afford to treat with anything other than the greatest respect. The verdicts of the moral consciousness of the best people are the foundation on which we must build; though he [the theorist] must first compare them with one another and eliminate any contradictions they may contain" (41).

17. One might plausibly argue that a dispositionally held intuition *must* be formed experientially. But this is not obvious; apparently we can form beliefs without their ever being occurrent, and I am inclined to think that one which constitutes an intuition need not enter the mind as an occurrent intuition. (Nothing I say in this book will turn on this question.)

18. I am speaking only of intuitions *that p* (where *p* is a proposition), as opposed to property intuitions, intuitions *of F* (some property); the latter do not admit of justification or constitute knowledge in the same way.

19. Two qualifications will help. First, if the belief is based on anything *other* than understanding the proposition, that understanding must still be a *sufficient* basis (in a sense I cannot explicate now). Second, I take the relevant basis relation to preclude a wayward causal chain: the understanding must not produce the belief in certain abnormal ways. What is more controversial about my characterization is that—apparently—only a priori propositions satisfy it. Note, however, that the analysandum is self-evidence simpliciter, not self-evidence *for (some person) S*. There is some plausibility in saying that it is self-evident, for me, that I exist. I leave open whether such cases illustrate a kind of self-evidence, but the relevant proposition asserting my existence (assuming it is believable by others) is surely not self-evident.

20. Thomas Nagel is among the philosophers who apparently consider the self-evident invariably obvious. He says, "In arguing for this claim [about reasons], I am somewhat handicapped by the fact that I find it self-evident. Since I can't find anything more certain with which to back it up, I face the danger of explaining the obvious in terms of the obscure." See *The View from Nowhere* (Oxford: Oxford University Press, 1986), 159–60. He *may* also be taking the self-evident to be in some sense unprovable; but if so, he does not take this to preclude arguing for it in some way. Cf. 162. Nothing I have said precludes everything self-evident's being obvious to *some* possible mind; I am thinking about obviousness in relation to normal adult literate speakers of a language like English.

21. Further discussion of the relevant notion of understanding is provided in my "Self-Evidence."

22. There is no avoiding the notion of "an appropriately wide range of cases" here because the central concepts in question are vague. Someone who understands the concepts of redness and greenness quite well enough to know that nothing is red and green all over at once need not be disposed to infer, regarding a certain shade of red close to the orange side of the spectrum, either that it is or that it is not orange. Compare aesthetic cases, such as the notion of being a poem.

23. There is no way to make a sharp distinction here; but we do not want to say unqualifiedly that one is justified in believing *p* where one would have to work one's

way to it by reasoning from various things one does believe or one would come to believe in the course of exploring the grounds one might have for p. I might actually be justified, by what I now believe, in believing not-p, yet able to come to see, by reflection—with no new information coming through my senses or any external source—that I am mistaken in believing not-p and should instead think that p. In this second case, I would have what, below, I call structural justification. If, however, one justifiedly believes some proposition that self-evidently entails p and is easily seen to entail it—as with the compound proposition that q, and if q then p—we normally would want to speak of dispositional justification for believing p.

24. I explicate structural justification in a paper of that title in *The Structure of Justification* (Cambridge: Cambridge University Press, 1993). To mark the contrast with cases in which, if one thought about whether a proposition is true, one would form new beliefs—possibly giving up standing ones in the process or even gaining beliefs by consulting friends or otherwise acquiring new evidence—we might speak of *conditional justification*. The proposition is *justifiable* for one and under the specified conditions one would justifiedly believe it; but one does not have justification apart from meeting the condition. The distinction in question is not sharp and is only outlined here; in the paper it is clarified further.

25. The term 'normal adults' is vague, but begs no questions here; the problem is largely eliminable by relativizing, making the basic notion that of the mediately self-evident *for S*, or for adults with a certain conceptual sophistication.

26. See the *Groundwork*, secs. 428–29. He also says, however, "We come to know pure practical laws . . . by the necessity with which reason prescribes them to us," and that "one cannot ferret it out from antecedent data of reason." See the *Critique of Practical Reason*, trans. Lewis White Beck (Indianapolis: Bobbs-Merrill, 1958), secs. 29–31.

27. This matter is more complex than it may seem. Even supposing a *proof* can be given for any knowable proposition, it is not clear that any given knowable proposition can be known (wholly) on the *basis* of a proof. I doubt that I could believe that if x = y, then y = x wholly on the basis of a proof, as opposed to seeing that it follows from self-evident premises. Still, for at least a huge proportion of knowable propositions, someone could be led to doubt any one of them by a clever skeptical argument, and could *then* come to know the proposition in question on the basis of a cogent argument for it.

28. Recall that Ross said (e.g., in the quotation given from *The Right and the Good*, 29–30) that his principles do not admit of proof, and that Moore went so far as to say that in calling propositions intuitions he means "*merely* to assert that they are incapable of proof; I imply nothing whatever as to the manner or origin of our cognition of them." *Principia*, x. See also 145. Cf. Ewing on logical intuition in "Reason and Intuition," esp. 39 and 45–52. Moore's claim does not preclude one's *arriving at* an intuition by inference; but he is ruling out one's premises' yielding a proof, and he apparently thinks that if one believes a proposition constituting an intuition inferentially, one does not believe it intuitively.

29. I have defended this claim more concretely in chap. 12 of my *Moral Knowledge and Ethical Character* (Oxford: Oxford University Press, 1997). A different and largely

compatible kind of defense is given by Hooker in "Ross-Style Pluralism versus Rule-Consequentialism" and in *Ideal Code, Real World*.

30. One might think that the term 'rational intuitionism', used by John Rawls to refer to Samuel Clarke's position and later versions of intuitionism, implies a recognition that intuitionism can be developed along empiricist lines. This recognition is at least not prominent in Rawls's writings, however, nor in later work (perhaps influenced by him) in which the term occurs. See his *Lectures on the History of Moral Philosophy*, esp. 69–77. Cf. the section headed "Rational Intuitionism" (49–54) in Stephen L. Darwall, *Philosophical Ethics* (Boulder, CO: Westview, 1998). As to the term 'moral sense', although in the text I compare this to sense perception, one could be both a moral sense theorist and a rationalist, as Reid was (though I find nothing in Reid that commits him to taking *singular* moral judgments, as opposed to moral principles, to be a priori). For discussion of Reid's moral epistemology, see Mathewson, "British Moral Intuitionism in the Eighteenth Century."

31. This is not to say that no beliefs of empirical propositions can be indefeasibly justified. Special cases are my beliefs that I have a belief and (arguably) that I exist. Detailed discussion of defeasibility is provided in my *Epistemology*, chap. 3, and, for a priori cases, "Self-Evidence."

32. I have critically compared the merits of these two approaches to justification in "Justification, Truth, and Reliability," in *The Structure of Justification*.

33. I have discussed the supervenience of moral on natural properties in "Ethical Naturalism and the Supervenience of Moral Properties," chap. 5 in *Moral Knowledge*.

34. I discuss this issue in detail (and briefly defend the rationalist view) in my *Moral Knowledge*, chap. 5, "Ethical Naturalism and the Explanatory Power of Moral Concepts." For a defense of non-reductive naturalism, see John F. Post, "Global Supervenient Determination: Too Permissive?" in *Essays on Supervenience*, ed. Elias Savellos and Umit Yalcin (Cambridge: Cambridge University Press, 1995).

35. For a portrait and defense of contextualism in moral epistemology, see Mark Timmons, "Outline of a Contextualist Moral Epistemology," in Sinnott-Armstrong and Timmons, *Moral Knowledge?*, and *Morality without Foundations* (Oxford: Oxford University Press, 1999). Cf. the contextual particularism of Jonathan Dancy's view in *Moral Reasons* (Oxford: Blackwell, 1993), esp. chaps. 4–6. Some of Dancy's views are considered in sec. 5.

36. A similar objection is voiced and partially answered by J. R. Lucas, in a paper defending Rossian intuitionism against objections by P. F. Strawson and others. See "Ethical Intuitionism II," *Philosophy* 46, no. 175 (1971): 1–11, 5.

37. One might perhaps say 'civilized' rather than 'thoughtful'. It might be objected, however, that we have no way to identify people as civilized apart from their accepting certain moral standards. I would agree that the notion is vague, but I have in mind mainly complexity of life forms, especially including institutions such as universities and orderly government, activities like the creation of literature and the other arts, and a high level of literacy. Civilized people, conceived as participating in such forms of life, can surely be identified without presupposing their agreement on specific moral standards and probably with at most minimal presuppositions about their moral standards or lack thereof. Even supposing, however, that certain kinds of tribal societies

are not civilized in the sense in question, *within* those societies there may still be adherence to all or most of the principles Ross articulated. It is toward *outgroups* of one kind or another that history has seen the grossest departures from those principles.

38. Compare Judith Jarvis Thomson's distinction between explanatory and object-level moral judgments, e.g. between the judgment that capital punishment is wrong because it is intentional killing of someone who poses no threat, and the judgment that capital punishment is wrong. See *The Realm of Rights* (Cambridge: Harvard University Press, 1990), 30. I suspect that some resistance to Rossian intuitionism may derive from insufficiently detaching his object-level principles of prima facie duty from his explanatory gloss—prominent in his introduction of the basic duties—construing each as having a particular ground.

39. The position defended here is instructively compared with a suggestion of Ruth Chang's: "Every justifying reason, I wish to claim, has its justifying force in virtue of a comparison of the alternatives." See her introduction to *Incommensurability, Incomparability, and Practical Reason* (Cambridge: Harvard University Press, 1997), 12. If this is applied to a reason for an action chosen in preference to another, it is plausible. Much action is like that, but not all of it is. The fact that one *has* an alternative to an action one performs does not entail that one chooses to perform the action in preference to the alternative (particularly if the alternative is simply not doing the thing in question). No alternative need enter one's practical thinking at all, as I have argued in detail in chap. 4 of *Practical Reasoning* (London: Routledge, 1989). On the other hand, *showing* that a reason *is* justifying and, commonly, justifying an action, presumably do depend on some comparison, as suggested by my discussion in the text. A reason can justify one in an action, however, even if one is not able to show that or how it does.

40. I might even be capable of knowing the proposition non-inferentially, say through a global sense of the bearing of the information in the context. Here some would say that I dispositionally believe it. I do not think that follows, for the kinds of reasons detailed in my "Dispositional Beliefs and Dispositions to Believe," *Nous* 29 (1994), which indicates various kinds of cases in which there is much we are disposed to believe but do not in fact believe.

41. Chang's collection, *Incommensurability, Incomparability, and Practical Reason*, contains many valuable discussions of the comparability problem. For support of the kind of comparability thesis I suggest here, see, e.g., her essay cited earlier and Donald Regan's more ambitious defense, "Value, Comparability, and Choice," 129–50. Further support is found in Sinnott-Armstrong. "Moral Dilemmas and Incomparability," 321–29.

42. For valuable discussion of the kind of supervenience I have described here, see Frank Jackson, Philip Pettit, and Michael Smith, "Ethical Particularism and Patterns," in Hooker and Little, *Moral Particularism*.

43. See, e.g., Stephen C. Pepper, *Ethics* (New York: Appleton-Century-Crofts, 1960), 237. BonJour, *Structure of Empirical Knowledge*, 209, notes a similar range of objections.

44. He says that "even before the implicit undertaking to tell the truth was established [by a contract] I had a duty not to tell lies, since to tell lies is *prima facie* to do

a positive injury to a person," *The Right and the Good*, 55. This seems to countenance a derivation of a duty of fidelity (Ross conceived honesty as fidelity to one's implicit agreement in speaking) from one of non-injury.

45. Here I leave aside the possibility of someone's holding that promise-breaking is not intrinsically prima facie wrong; my interest is in a denial of the general moral bearing of promising-breaking, not in affirmation of possible exceptions to its prima facie wrongness, such as Jonathan Dancy takes to exist. See *Moral Reasons*, chaps. 4–7, and his critique of Moore, "Are There Organic Unities?" *Ethics* 113, no. 3 (2003). For discussion of the obligation to keep promises, see David McNaughton and Piers Rawling, "Unprincipled Ethics," in Hooker and Little, *Moral Particularism*, e.g. 267–69. Cf. Hooker's claim that "Promises obtained under coercion or deception are without force." See his "Moral Particularism: Wrong and Bad," in Hooker and Little (9). This is plausible, but a defender of the invariant force of promising might claim that either genuine coercion to "promise" makes promising impossible or extracting promises by coercion eliminates any right by the coercer to have the promise kept but may not eliminate all prima facie obligation to keep it (e.g. where an innocent person is the beneficiary), even if it provides an excuse for non-performance.

46. Cf. John Lucas: "If I was arguing with a man, and he did not allow that causing pain was *a* reason for an action's being wrong, that is, he did not see the relevance of the fact that the action caused pain, I think I should break off the argument with him . . . the problem is what weight to attach to such considerations . . . sadists . . . need to be cured rather than convinced" ("Ethical Intuitionism II," 9–10).

47. I neglect noncognitivism here; I believe it encounters serious problems of its own, but it is a significant contender. See, e.g., Allan Gibbard, *Wise Choices, Apt Feelings* (Cambridge: Harvard University Press, 1990). For criticism of Gibbard's position, see Walter Sinnott-Armstrong, "Some Problems for Gibbard's Norm Expressivism," *Philosophical Studies* 69 (1993): 297–313, and James Dreier, "Transforming Expressivism," *Nous* 33, no. 4 (1999): 558–72, which shows how a plausible generalization of the view tends to undermine its claim to expressivist as opposed to cognitivist status. I also neglect R. B. Brandt's modified instrumentalism in *A Theory of the Good and the Right* (Oxford: Clarendon Press, 1979). I have appraised Brandt's overall view of rationality in "An Epistemic Conception of Rationality," in *The Structure of Justification*.

48. Some empiricists might claim that it is analytic, say because to have a reason for action just *is* to have such a basic desire and set of beliefs. But this is at best highly controversial, in part because it simply begs the question against intuitionism and other prominent views.

49. For a recent discussion of this kind of issue, see Peter Railton, "On the Hypothetical and Non-Hypothetical in Reasoning about Belief and Action," in *Ethics and Practical Reason*, ed. Garrett Cullity and Berys Gaut (Oxford: Oxford University Press, 1997), 51–79. Railton speaks of the inference from 'E is an end of mine' and 'means M would secure E' to 'There is that much to be said deliberatively in favor of my doing M or against my having E' as if its cogency no more depended on an added premise than that of modus ponens depends on adding a corresponding conditional of the argument as a premise—something Lewis Carroll famously showed we must not de-

mand, on pain of regress. It is not clear how far Railton takes the analogy to go, e.g. whether he considers the first inference form (non-formally) valid; but it is difficult to see how to avoid so construing it; and if this is its status, the validity in question does not appear to be empirical. Nor, indeed, does its apparent cogency. See esp. 76–79.

50. For a plausible case that rational judgment and action can go against morality, see Bruce Russell, "Two Forms of Ethical Skepticism," in *Ethical Theory*, ed. Louis P. Pojman (Belmont, CA: Wadsworth, 1989). Cf. Bernard Gert's view, in *Morality: Its Nature and Justification*, 2d ed. (Oxford: Oxford University Press, 1998), that even if moral action is not always rationally required, it is always rationally permitted (see, e.g., 70). My own views on the status of moral reasons in relation to other practical reasons are given in part in *The Architecture of Reason* (Oxford: Oxford University Press, 2001), esp. chap. 6.

51. This motivational internalist assumption is appraised in detail, and with many references to the relevant literature on the question, in my "Moral Judgment and Reasons for Action," chap. 10 in *Moral Knowledge*.

52. See Broad, *Five Types of Ethical Theory*, 282.

53. Methodological particularism and other kinds are distinguished by Walter Sinnott-Armstrong in "Some Varieties of Particularism," *Metaphilosophy* 30 (1999): 1–12. A strong version would hold that adequate moral reasoning *must* properly attend to particular cases.

54. Jonathan Dancy holds both forms of normative particularism; see, e.g., *Moral Reasons*, 60–62, and 66–68. For detailed and informative discussion of the status of particularism, see Mark C. Timmons, *Moral Theory* (Lanham, MD: Rowman and Littlefield, 2002), 245–66.

55. For Dancy, "The leading thought behind particularism is that the behaviour of a reason . . . in a new case cannot be predicted from its behaviour elsewhere . . . I borrow a book from you, and then discover that you have stolen it from the library . . . It isn't that I have *some* reason to return it to you and more reason to put it back in the library. I have no reason at all to return it to you" (ibid., 60).

56. The problem of *Schadenfreude* and the related organicity of intrinsic value are discussed in some detail in chap. 11 of my *Moral Knowledge* and further in my "Intrinsic Value and Reasons for Action," *Southern Journal of Philosophy* 41 (2003).

57. Cf. Dancy (*Moral Reasons*): "Since I recommend a particularist understanding of the rightness or wrongness of the action [public executions of convicted rapists if the event would give pleasure both to the executioner and to the crowds], I recommend a particularist approach to the rightness or wrongness of any resulting pleasure" (61). This is not quite to deny that one can be a holist about final duty and not about prima facie duty, but Dancy seems to think it at least unnatural to hold the former without the latter view. I cannot here do justice to the richness of his discussion of the overall question of particularism. For a later statement of Dancy's views, see his "The Particularist's Progress," in Hooker and Little, *Moral Particularism* (which also contains many other positions concerning particularism). For a critical response to Dancy's case, with special reference to both Aristotelian and Rossian resources, see Roger Crisp, "Particularizing Particularism," in Hooker and Little. Further criticism of particularism is found in Baldwin, "The Three Phases of Intuitionism."

58. This distinction is developed in chap. 4 of my *Structure of Justification*, which defends a moderate foundationalism that incorporates what I consider the most plausible elements in epistemological coherentism.

59. For discussion of the resources of Rossian intuitionism regarding comparisons of duty, see McNaughton's (1996) paper in Stratton-Lake, *Ethical Intuitionism*.

60. This is not to deny that one could develop a coherentist intuitionism, but I think the two kinds of theories pull in different directions, e.g. because of the kind of non-inferential justification to which intuitionism is committed. Dancy's particularism comes closer to a coherentist intuitionism than any view I know.

61. In chap. 10 of *Epistemology*, I have produced arguments of this kind concerning some representative skeptical theses.

62. My main concern here is academic as opposed to Pyrrhonian skepticism, where the former is a thesis about the epistemic status of one or another kind of cognitive claim and the latter is roughly a refusal to accept *or* deny various kinds. For an elaboration of the distinction and a defense of Pyrrhonian skepticism in ethics, see Walter Sinnott-Armstrong, *Limited Moral Skepticism* (forthcoming).

63. In the *Grundlegung* Kant claims or at least implies that except where one is acting against inclination, one cannot know one is acting from duty. See, e.g., sec. 407.

64. Unlike Kant, I unequivocally allow that one can be acting from duty even if a different motive cooperates, provided one's motive of duty actually explains the deed. (I leave open that the *overall* thrust of Kant's position is consistent with allowing this.) If overdetermination is ruled out, the skeptical view is more difficult to resist. I discuss this range of issues in "Causalist Internalism," in *The Structure of Justification*. For some of Ross's views on the question, with some critical interpretation of Kant, see *The Foundations of Ethics*, e.g. 304–10.

Chapter 3. Kantian Intuitionism

1. The reference is to the closing passages of chap. 2 of *Utilitarianism*.

2. See Henry Sidgwick, *Practical Ethics* (London: Swan Sonnenschein & Co., 1909), 8. For an indication of the importance of middle axioms, see Sissela Bok's introduction to her edition of this book (Oxford: Oxford University Press, 1998) and her *Common Values* (Columbia: University of Missouri Press, 1995).

3. In *The Foundations of Ethics*, at least, Ross contrasts middle axioms with self-evident principles. Of "periods in which mankind appears to sink to a lower moral plane" he says, "What is questioned in such periods is not the fundamental principles of morality but the *media axiomata*, the rules for which no *a priori* evidence can be claimed but which rest partly on circumstances that have ceased to exist, and partly on opinions . . . that have been given up" (21). This makes it seem that he takes such "axioms" to be at best theorems that are not self-evident. Later, moreover, he attributes to utilitarianism the view that "*Media axiomata* such as 'Men should keep their promises' have come to be accepted as true as if they were self-evidently true, and people habitually judge acts to be right on the strength of the *media axiomata*, forgetting the method by which the *media axiomata* have been established" (69), namely, determination that the kind of act in question is or is not "optimific." Again we find a contrast

between self-evident principles like his own and "middle axioms." And later he says, of intuitionism, "With regard to all *media axiomata*, which are attempts to apply these general principles [the "general principles which it regards as intuitively seen to be true"] to particular situations, it preserves an open mind . . . new circumstances sometimes abrogate old claims . . ." (190). In this case (assuming that abrogation entails falsity) it appears that a middle axiom need not even be a theorem (at least if a theorem cannot be false).

4. Given some of the things that, in Chapter 1, I cited Sidgwick as saying in support of philosophical intuitionism, and given his notion of utilitarianism as in some way systematizing the kinds of principles "dogmatic" intuitionists maintained, one would expect some exceptions to the tendency, even among philosophers sympathetic to intuitionism, to overlook the possibility of systematizing Rossian principles by appeal to a more general standard. Sidgwick spoke not only of "middle axioms" but of *subordinate* ones: after making the important point that we might have to qualify an apparently self-evident formula, he adds that we may wonder "whether we have not mistaken for an independent and ultimate axiom one that is really derivative and subordinate." See *Methods*, 341. Whether or not in response to Sidgwick, at least two philosophers have noted the possibility of intuitionists' appealing to a wider standard. Christine Swanton, in a rigorous defense of intuitionism, says that "there is no reason why an intuitionist could not appeal to such a conception in grounding both the first-order principles of the system and the second-order principles for resolving conflict . . . a conception of human flourishing founded on an Aristotelian system of human virtue . . . Alternatively, the underlying moral conception could be contractualist, involving an understanding of the point of morality as a system which renders possible co-operation amidst conflict of interest." See "The Rationality of Ethical Intuitionism," *Australasian Journal of Philosophy* 65 (1987): 175. This line is not, however, developed in relation to any account of self-evidence nor shown to be an option for Ross in particular. See also Sinnott-Armstrong's entry on intuitionism in *The Encyclopedia of Ethics*, 628–30, for a formulation of the consistency of intuitionism with a kind of derivability.

5. Ross apparently did distinguish evidencing and proving, as where he called the proposition that an act, "*qua* fulfilling a promise," is prima facie right "self-evident . . . evident in itself, without any need of proof, or of evidence beyond itself" (*The Right and the Good*, 29). But he nowhere considers what evidence there might be for such propositions—which is not surprising given that he compares them to mathematical axioms and the validity of forms of inference (20–30)—and when he says they "cannot be proved" (30), he does not go on to deny that they can be evidenced.

6. As pointed out in Chapter 2 (n. 44) Ross seems to take the duty of fidelity as derivable from one of non-injury, "since to tell lies is *prima facie* to do a positive injury to a person," ibid., 55. Cf. his remark that bringing about the "proportionment of happiness to virtue . . . with beneficence and self-improvement, comes under *the general principle that we should produce as much good as possible*, though the good here involved differs from any other" (27, my italics).

7. Ewing, "Reason and Intuition," 57. Recognizing the defeasibility of intuition, he later says, "We cannot dispense with intuition, but its results can be tested by coherence with other propositions. The intuitionist is wrong if he will not admit that his apparent

intuitions may have all degrees of certainty . . . the advocate of the coherence theory is wrong if he denies or ignores the need for intuition over and above any coherence test" (ibid., 59).

8. Even if systematization did require proof, there is a notion of proving that does not entail the use of self-evident premises, as where we prove a complicated theorem from other complicated ones that are not self-evident. There is also the everyday use of 'proof' in which one may prove the guilt of a criminal from known facts. Here we may not even have a valid deduction and will have contingent premises. A related case is *behavioral proving*, e.g. proving that a device works by demonstrating its operation. All of these varieties of proof deserve more attention than they are usually given. Cf. John Stuart Mill's notion of proof in a wide sense; see, e.g., the introduction and chap. 4 of *Utilitarianism*.

9. Ross, *The Right and the Good*, 16.

10. These points are in ibid., chap. 2. See esp. 41–42.

11. Three points should be noted here. First, the "kinds" of deeds in question must be specified in a general way; we cannot, e.g., list every kind of promise, say marital or professional. Second, normative completeness does not entail the correctness of the theory in question; our terminology allows that an ethical theory plausible in the indicated way is normatively complete in the sense of "covering the relevant territory." The better the theory, the more readily it gives us a basis for knowledge as opposed to just plausibility. Third, since my concern here is ethical theories, I am ignoring the point that a normative theory need not be specifically moral; it might, e.g., be directed to what we ought rationally to do, and might or might not take one's doing this to entail acting morally.

12. The ontic and the epistemic dependences in question (which were noticed by Ross and are widely accepted by ethical theorists) are explicated in my "Ethical Naturalism and the Explanatory Power of Moral Concepts," in my *Moral Knowledge*. The epistemic dependence is ultimate because one can of course acquire moral knowledge through testimony; but the attester (or someone in the testimonial chain) must acquire it from the relevant non-moral grounds.

13. He introduces the list of duties "without claiming completeness of finality for it" (*The Right and the Good*, 20).

14. This point is argued and illustrated in some detail in my "The Axiology of Moral Experience," *Journal of Ethics* 2 (1998): 355–75. I should add that in saying there need not be recognition of the relevant grounds, I do not imply that there need be no *awareness* of them; the point is that they need not be conceptualized, or even conceived, under moral concepts or *as* grounds, even if, as is likely, the agent is *disposed* to conceptualize them as such given certain kinds of reflection or the prompting of a challenge to the judgment.

15. Accounting for a duty disjunctively might be conceived as distributing duties over actions, whereas an ordinary disjunctive duty, say a duty of charity requiring one to give to cause *x* or to cause *y*, might be conceived as distributing actions over duties.

16. Ross, *The Right and the Good*, chap. 2. He implies, however, that "the rival theory" is in no better position, which confirms that his preoccupation here is with Moore. He seems not to be considering Kantianism as providing an answer.

17. Since I am only sketching a normative theory, I largely ignore the point that one may have conflicting *sets* of duties, say two pulling one way and two pulling another. Moreover, I take a set of duties to A that conflicts with a set of duties to B (where A and B are incompatible) to be final only if the deontic weight of the first set is *greater* than that of the second. If they are equally weighty, presumably one is morally free to A and to B (though the choice may be difficult or even in some way tragic). Cf. David O. Brink, "Moral Conflict and Its Structure," *Philosophical Review* 103, no. 2 (1994): 215–47, critically discussed by Walter Sinnott-Armstrong in "Moral Dilemmas and Rights," in *Moral Dilemmas and Moral Theory*, ed. H. E. Mason (Oxford: Oxford University Press, 1996).

18. Since the notion of completeness in question can apply at still higher orders, what I call overall completeness is not the most comprehensive kind possible; what is said about it here will, however, suggest how one might proceed to characterize progressively higher-order completeness.

19. I refer to Kant's widely known view, suggested in the *Groundwork of the Metaphysics of Morals* and other work of his, that a perfect duty, such as the duty to keep a promise, always outweighs an imperfect duty, such as the duty to help someone in distress. Since perfect duties can conflict, even if Kant were right about the former case, he would presumably need to appeal to the categorical imperative, in the way suggested in the text, to deal with those conflicts.

20. Kant apparently regarded these as equivalent, even if not *identical*, in content. I provisionally assume that if only because the intrinsic end formulation provides the main materials needed for interpretation of the universality one, the equivalence claim is plausible. The falsity of this claim would not, however, substantially alter my project here. Similar points seem to hold for the autonomy formulation: stressing that "A rational being must always regard himself as making laws in a kingdom of ends which is possible through freedom of the will" (*Groundwork*, sec. 434), Kant says, "the principle of autonomy is 'Never to choose except in such a way that in the same volition the maxims of your choice are also present as universal law' " (sec. 440). Among the helpful discussions of the equivalence question are those in Rawls's *Lectures on the History of Moral Philosophy* and Onora O'Neill's "Rationality as Practical Reason," in *Rationality*, ed. Alfred R. Mele and Piers Rawling (forthcoming from Oxford University Press). For an account of the differences in function of these formulations, see Mark C. Timmons, "Decision Procedures, Moral Criteria, and the Problem of Relevant Descriptions," *Jahrbuch für Recht und Ethic* 5 (1997).

21. Kant, *Groundwork*, 89.

22. I insert 'rationally' to capture Kant's intention and because it is in any case not plausible to think the requirement concerns either psychological or strict logical possibility—as is well known, in the *Groundwork* Kant grants that there is no inconsistency in universalizing the maxims corresponding to failure to do good deeds and to develop one's talents. In the application at hand we could be more cautious and say 'could not reasonably resent', but this may not be necessary for a sound maxim in such cases. The notion of what is reasonable in such a case is by implication clarified in many parts of this book. A similar notion is illuminatingly discussed by T. M. Scanlon

in connection with contractarian justifications. See, e.g., his "Contractarianism and Utilitarianism," in *Utilitarianism and Beyond*, ed. Amartya Sen and Bernard Williams (Cambridge: Cambridge University Press, 1982), and his *What We Owe to Each Other* (Cambridge: Harvard University Press, 1998).

23. Kant, *Groundwork*, 96. Some translations use 'merely' rather than 'simply', and since 'merely' seems more appropriate to the relevant notion as expressed in English, I will generally prefer it.

24. I am here assuming that even logically equivalent propositions need not be identical, and where the equivalence is in addition synthetic, which is presumably what Kant intended, this assumption seems plainly warranted.

25. The notion of reasonableness intended here is not specifically moral and I do not think its use begs any questions crucial here. I have explicated this notion at some length in chap. 6 of *The Architecture of Reason*. Other accounts are given by Rawls and Scanlon.

26. A brief account of how maxims should be formulated, with special emphasis on intention, is given in chap. 3 of my *Practical Reasoning*. A much more detailed treatment of the question in given by Derek Parfit in his forthcoming Tanner Lectures on Kant's ethics. For a valuable short treatment, see Jens Timmerman, "Kant's Puzzling Ethics of Maxims," *Harvard Review of Philosophy* 8 (2000). Also instructive is Barbara Herman, "The Practice of Moral Judgment," *Journal of Philosophy* 82 (1985).

27. These points about treating as ends vs. treating merely as a means are based on a detailed account given in my "Treating Persons as Ends" (forthcoming).

28. I leave open the prospects for developing a prior notion from a Kantian perspective. My own approach (in chap. 11 of *Moral Knowledge*) allows taking certain moral values as basic and using them to clarify the content and application of both the categorical imperative and the Rossian duties. As will be apparent shortly, this approach also allows that our axiological and deontic concepts may be mutually clarifying.

29. The reason I am not treating general moral propositions, such as Rossian principles or principles that follow from them, as grounded in natural facts is that—though in some sense held *in the light of natural facts* (the sense that goes with intuitive induction)—they are best conceived as at least broadly a priori. To be sure, 'moral judgment' standardly has reference to singular judgments, but the clarification may still be needed.

30. This is a reference to the supervenience of moral properties, widely discussed in recent literature and explored in chaps. 4 and 5 of my *Moral Knowledge*. The relevant passages in Ross are mainly in chaps. 2 and 4 of *The Right and the Good*. See esp. 33, 105, and 121–23.

31. Ross, *The Right and the Good*, 21. Cf. Ross's affirmation of a duty to produce as much good as we can (27) and Sidgwick: "The Utilitarian doctrine . . . is that each man ought to consider the happiness of any other as *theoretically* of equal importance with his own, and only of less importance *practically*, in so far as he is better able to realise the latter)," *Methods*, 252. Clearly, this leaves problems about how to decide what we are better able to do and what degree of priority that determination has.

32. Ross, *The Right and the Good*, 21 and 17–18.

33. Kant says, e.g., "The *autonomy* of the will is the sole principle of all moral laws
. . . the moral law expresses nothing else than the autonomy of the pure practical
reason, i.e., freedom." See the *Critique of Practical Reason*, sec. 33 (34–35).

34. This approach to a Kantian intuitionism goes well with Bernard Gert's idea that
what are commonly called obligations of beneficence are not moral duties but *moral
ideals*. See *Morality*, chap. 10. The suggestion I am exploring could be put in these
terms: there is no *basic* prima facie duty of beneficence, as opposed to a basic beneficent
moral ideal, but in any normal human life such duties are incurred at least implicitly.

35. Here one may think of a contractualist account of why the duty of beneficence
is so often overridden. See, e.g., Scanlon, *What We Owe to Each Other*, e.g. 213–18.
This is not to suggest that it is *obvious* that we may reasonably reject any principle
requiring beneficent deeds that seems intuitively too demanding; indeed, Scanlon is
understandably vague in specifying what counts as reasonable rejectability in a moral
standard. But if that notion is understood in part on the lines developed in this chapter,
e.g. as satisfied by a principle that would have us use people merely (or even mainly)
as means, rejectability of the intuitively over-demanding beneficence principles is what
we might expect.

36. One might also hold that the duty of beneficence (or some other) has priority
over any number of other normative considerations, but there is no need to consider
other possibilities here. For a brief account of various views on the strength and
varieties of moral and other reasons for action, see *The Architecture of Reason*, esp.
162–64.

37. One worry is that in practice we can extract only such vague principles as 'In
cases like this, prefer spending money on educating one's children over saving children
abroad', where at best we can be specific by listing so many circumstances that the
principle is unlikely to reapply. As suggested earlier, moral decision is often guided
by discriminations that are readily generalizable and, on reflection, can be roughly
formulated. But there is no need to deny that there is a problem of formulation in
such cases. It seems, however, to confront any plausible comprehensive ethics.

38. *Groundwork*, sec. 423, emphases added. The parenthesized point *may* indicate
that Kant is thinking of the duty as restricted in scope depending on one's capacities
and other factors. Cf. his point that "To help others *when we can* is a duty" (sec. 398,
emphasis added), and his remark that in "practical beneficence (benevolence) . . . I
can, without violating the universality of my maxim, vary the degree greatly according
to the different object of my love." See *The Doctrine of Virtue*, trans. Mary J. Gregor
(New York: Harper and Row, 1964), 119 (sec. 451).

39. This point applies to any plausible moral theory that countenances supererogation, as most versions of utilitarianism, e.g., apparently do not.

40. I refer to the setting out of the prima facie duties on 21; on 35 he expresses the
duty of justice differently and positively, as that of "producing a distribution of goods
in proportion to merit."

41. In *Through the Moral Maze* (New York: Paragon House, 1994), Robert Kane
discusses the nature of treating people as ends and not as means; and although he does
not systematize duties under precisely the categorical imperative (for one thing, he

omits the 'merely' in the Kantian phrase 'merely as a means'), his treatment of the issues can be fruitfully compared with this one. See esp. chap. 2.

42. It is helpful to compare the detailed case for a justification of Rossian duties from rule-consequentialism made by Hooker in "Ross-Style Pluralism versus Rule-Consequentialism." This paper is critically discussed by Philip Stratton-Lake in "Can Hooker's Rule-Consequentialist Principle Justify Ross's Prima Facie Duties?" *Mind* 106, no. 424 (1997): 751–58. A reply by Hooker follows in the same issue, 759–60, and Hooker's position is defended further in his *Ideal Code, Real World*.

43. In the light of these points we can see that the Kantian intuitionist (or even the theoretically enlightened Rossian intuitionist) could reply to Christine Korsgaard's worry that, to the question whether one must face death rather than do a certain deed, "The realist's answer to this question is simply 'Yes'. That is, *all* he can say is that it is *true* that this is what you ought to do. This is of course especially troublesome when the rightness of the action is supposed to be self-evident and knowable through intuition, *so that* there is nothing more to say about it." See her *Sources of Normativity* (Cambridge: Cambridge University Press, 1996), 38. The emphasis on 'so that' is added to indicate an apparent presupposition that the self-evident is ungroundable.

44. I do not mean to put much weight on the clarity of the distinctions between positive and negative duties and between perfect and imperfect ones. The (perfect) duty to keep promises, e.g., can be taken to be the duty not to break them, though it is more natural to express its content positively. If it is positive, then a positive duty would be perfect. The Kantian distinctions partially developed in this chapter may be a better basis for classifying duties than such elusive terms as 'positive' and 'negative' taken independently of them.

45. I omit consideration of Kant's two-worlds view. Interpreting this is a major task, and so far as I can tell my position in this book is compatible with at least some plausible interpretations of it. As to the notion of constructivism as applied to Kant, helpful discussion is provided by Rawls in his *Lectures on the History of Moral Philosophy* and "Kantian Constructivism in Moral Theory," *Journal of Philosophy* 77 (1980), reprinted in revised form in his *Political Liberalism* (New York: Columbia University Press, 1993); by Korsgaard in her *Sources of Normativity*; and by Onora O'Neill in "Kantian Constructivism," in *The Cambridge Companion to Kant*, ed. Samuel Freeman (Cambridge: Cambridge University Press, forthcoming).

46. The second and third points are supported by a number of considerations developed in chap. 11 of *Moral Knowledge*. I should add here that taking dignity to be part of what underlies autonomy rights is compatible with considering the *property* of autonomy—roughly, a kind of capacity of self-government—to be a basis of dignity.

47. Kant says, e.g., "Suppose there were something *whose existence* has *in itself* an absolute value, something which *as an end in itself* could be a ground of determinate laws; then . . . in it alone, would there be the ground of a possible categorical imperative." See the *Groundwork*, sec. 428. There is of course controversy about just how, in or outside Kant's work, the categorical imperative is grounded. For a sustained attempt inspired by Kant, see Alan Gewirth, *Reason and Morality* (Chicago: University of Chicago Press, 1975).

48. David McNaughton might have been thinking of such passages in saying, "I am more skeptical than Audi about the possibility of any other theory providing independent support for a list of duties of Ross's kind. Kantianism, for example, appears to hold that some principles are exceptionless, and not *prima facie*." See "Intuitionism," 283.

49. It is an interesting question whether the two injunctions in the intrinsic end formula can conflict. Could one face a situation in which avoiding treating someone merely as a means requires failing to treat someone else as an end, or in which treating someone as an end requires treating someone else merely as a means? This is not clearly impossible, but is arguably avoidable. To resolve this we may need an account of the two central notions; I attempt one in "Treating Persons as Ends" (forthcoming); and I address the related question whether there are non-trivially specifiable absolute obligations in "Ethical Generality and Moral Judgment" (forthcoming from Basil Blackwell in *Contemporary Debates in Ethical Theory*, ed. James Dreier).

50. I leave open whether adequate non-moral concepts of treating people as means and of treating them as ends may be devised from a Kantian perspective, so that application of the categorical imperative does not require independent moral standards. If this is not so, then the Kantian framework in question needs supplementation by, for instance, an intuitionist perspective such as the one presented here.

51. Complex epistemological issues arise here. A major source of the common— though by no means universal or uncontested—view that the confirmatory use of reflective equilibrium implies a coherentist epistemology is Rawls, *A Theory of Justice*. The use of it I suggest comports *better* with moderate foundationalism. Reasons for this are suggested in the next paragraph but I explain them in detail in chaps. 1 and 2 of *The Architecture of Reason*.

52. Justification from above and from below are discussed in some detail in my "Intuitionism, Pluralism, and the Foundations of Ethics," in Sinnott-Armstrong and Timmons, *Moral Knowledge?*. (The metaphor may be appropriately reversed depending on what is to be emphasized, and in stressing, e.g., comprehensiveness I find it natural to speak of "overarching" principles.) For discussion bearing on how coherence considerations can contribute to reflective equilibrium and on the kinds of coherence considerations pertinent in this context, see Geoffrey Sayre-McCord's paper in the same volume.

53. It is noteworthy that in at least one place Ross spoke of "Kant's form of Intuitionism, in which it is held [contrary to Ross] that the rightness or wrongness of an individual act can be inferred with certainty from its falling or not falling under a rule capable of being universalized." See *The Foundations of Ethics*, 189.

54. I distinguish between the theory Kant presented and his pronouncements in interpreting it. I cannot, e.g., see that anything fundamental in the categorical imperative framework makes all suicides immoral, as Kant is commonly read as holding. See, e.g., *The Doctrine of Virtue*, 84–87 (secs. 421–23).

55. It is noteworthy that Kant ties respect not only to "consciousness of the direct constraint of the will through law" (*Critique of Practical Reason*, sec. 117, p. 121), which I take to be consciousness of a major aspect of autonomy, but also to dignity, conceived as grounded in the worth of persons: "man regarded as a *person* . . . is exalted above any price . . . He possesses, in other words, a *dignity* (an absolute inner worth)

by which he exacts *respect* for himself from all other rational beings: he can . . . value himself on a footing of equality with them." See *The Doctrine of Virtue*, secs. 433–34, p. 99. For related discussion of how, for Kant, moral action is motivated and connected with feelings and valuational attitudes, see Jeanine M. Grenberg, "Feeling, Desire and Interest in Kant's Theory of Action," *Kant-Studien* 92 (2001).

56. See the *Groundwork*, sec. 408.

57. This is only a summary formulation of Ross's particularism. That view and the stronger particularism defended by Jonathan Dancy are discussed in detail above in Chapter 2.

58. Sidgwick made it quite clear that the master principle does not have the reciprocal kind of relation that, for a Kantian intuitionism, holds between the categorical imperative and Rossian principles. He held, e.g., that "Utilitarianism . . . must be accepted as overruling Intuitionism and Egoism" (*Methods*, 420) and "must show to the Intuitionist that the principles of Truth, Justice, etc. have only a dependent and subordinate validity . . ." (421, footnote omitted).

59. I use 'practical ethics' here rather than the more common 'applied ethics' because ordinary moral decision-making and everyday moral appraisals need not be applications of any ethical theory and (I assume here) do not presuppose any particular theory.

60. If one wonders why moral judgments should not *always* be grounded in factual ones, I suggest that sometimes the former are *non-inferential* responses to facts, somewhat as perceptual judgments are. I discuss this possibility in some detail in "The Axiology of Moral Experience."

61. These terms are found in Ross, *The Right and the Good*, 21 (emphases added). This may be a good place to reiterate that a Kantian intuitionism is not committed to following Kant or even to consistency with him on every major claim it makes. Kant did not, for instance, take beneficence to entail trying to make others better in respect of virtue. See *Doctrine of Virtue*.

62. Some writers place a great deal of weight on the notion of a thick moral concept. David McNaughton and Piers Rawling, e.g., say, regarding Ross's list of the "duties of reparation, gratitude, fidelity, justice, self-improvement, beneficence, and non-maleficence," that "These are all terms for thick moral concepts," which they then suggest are central (and perhaps essential) in grounding moral reasons. See "Unprincipled Ethics," 266–67. The intuitionism they favor is a thick variety, in which these and other "thick" terms play an essential role. Cf. Margaret Little's view (in "Moral Generalities Revisited," in Hooker and Little, *Moral Particularism*) that "Thick moral features differ from nonmoral ones precisely because, so identified, they are guaranteed of carrying a given valence of moral significance" (289). The question I am pursuing concerns, in large part, how we can identify such features without presupposing moral judgments, and this question does not seem to have been adequately dealt with either by Ross or by the various writers who make major use of the notion of thick moral concepts.

63. I have already suggested how a kind of exploitiveness can be understood non-normatively, in terms of using someone in a merely instrumental way. I doubt that the relevant notion of treating someone as an end is explicable non-normatively; but its explication may not require using *moral* concepts, and if so it can still help in clarifying

Rossian duties without moral presuppositions and, to some extent, in terms of the factual grounds of the non-moral kind of good treatment implied in treating a person as an end. These questions are addressed in detail in my "Treating Persons as Ends."

64. For a treatment of the dualism of practical reason that is highly pertinent to this book and contains critical discussion of the positions of Shelly Kagan and Samuel Scheffler on the problem, see Roger Crisp, "The Dualism of Practical Reason," *Proceedings of the Aristotelian Society* 96 (1996): 53–73. Another pertinent discussion is John Deigh's "Sidgwick on Ethical Judgment," in his *The Sources of Moral Agency: Essays on Moral Psychology and Freudian Theory* (Cambridge: Cambridge University Press, 1996).

Chapter 4. Rightness and Goodness

1. See, e.g., Sidgwick, *Methods*, bk. 4, chap. 1, where he calls utilitarianism the theory that "the conduct which, under any given circumstances, is objectively right, is that which will produce the greatest amount of happiness on the whole" (411); and Moore, e.g. *Ethics*, where he says that "the total consequences of right actions must always be as good, intrinsically, as any which it was *possible* for the agent to produce under the circumstances" (98).

2. For a brief account of such values and their relation to reasons, see chap. 11 of my *Moral Knowledge*. A recent volume bearing on many of the difficult issues here is Chang, *Incommensurability, Incomparability, and Practical Reason*; her instructive introductory essay bears particularly on the organic element in value and reasons for action discussed in this chapter. It should be evident that I am allowing that an intrinsic good might "provide" a reason without *constituting* one. Suppose, e.g., that we adopt T. M. Scanlon's "buck-passing" view of goodness and value (hence presumably also of basic reasons for action), on which reasons are constituted by the specific things in virtue of which something is good—say, being enjoyable—not by its goodness as such. See *What We Owe to Each Other*, esp. 95–100. We can still speak of intrinsically good things as providing the reasons, though in *virtue* of their grounds. We could also distinguish between elements' directly and indirectly constituting reasons and between specific and general reasons. I might do a thing because (for the reason that) it is good even if I think it is good only *on account of* some particular property of it. Suppose, moreover, that I do it only because I believe you when you tell me it will be good. It would appear that even if, given an inquiry into the status or basis of my reason, I would pass the buck to you, my generic reason—to do something good—is where the buck stops for me. Granted it stops there *on* your authority; but that does not make my reason *doing what you suggest*.

3. Here I draw on chap. 11 of my *Moral Knowledge*.

4. See Noah Lemos, *Intrinsic Value* (Cambridge: Cambridge University Press, 1994) for a systematic discussion of the nature and bearers of intrinsic value. His own candidate for basic bearer is a kind of obtaining state of affairs, which he identifies with a fact, as did Ross in *The Right and the Good*, 113. I would not identify facts with obtaining states of affairs, but there is no need to go into that here. For supporting discussion of Ross's view on bearers of intrinsic value, see Michael J. Zimmerman,

"Virtual Intrinsic Value and the Principle of Organic Unities," *Philosophy and Phenomenological Research* 59 (1999): 653–66.

5. *The Right and the Good*, 86.

6. I take it that an intrinsic property need not be an essential one, i.e., one the thing in question has in any world in which it exists; but some have conceived intrinsic properties that way, and I leave open the possibility that properties of a *particular experience* in virtue of which it has (positive or negative) intrinsic value are essential to it. This issue is discussed in some detail in my "Intrinsic Value and Reasons for Action."

7. Two points may help here. First, it is plausible to conceive the bearers of intrinsic value as experience *tokens* such as a specific enjoyment of a symphony by a given person at a particular time. Second, I believe we can achieve the same substantive results using property talk, but it does not seem as natural for the purpose and I leave it aside to avoid making matters more complex.

8. As William K. Frankena has done: he says, of the items on a very diverse list, "all of them may be kept on the list, and perhaps others may be added, if it is understood that it is the *experience* of them that is good in itself. Sidgwick seems to me to be right on this point . . . truth is not itself intrinsically good . . . what is good in itself is knowledge or belief in the truth." *Ethics*, 89. Actually, knowledge and belief are not experiences, and a page later Frankena corrects the apparent oversight here, saying that "knowledge, excellence, power, and so on are . . . valueless in themselves unless they are experienced with some kind of enjoyment or satisfaction."

9. I say 'normally' here because there is a sense in which reasons can be repressed or otherwise "unconscious." This does not imply that they cannot enter consciousness, but their doing this may require special efforts or techniques—and, if they do enter consciousness, the subject may not take them for what they are.

10. There is of course a relational notion of experience in which, if one is hallucinating a tree, one is not experiencing one at all. But note the naturalness of saying, e.g., 'The experience was so vivid I expected to feel the lush foliage'. If the two can be intrinsically indistinguishable and arguably have the same intrinsic value, they need not (and in general would not) have the same inherent value. There would then be less reason to bring the hallucinatory experience about, other things equal, and some prima facie reason not to bring it about at all. This issue is discussed in some detail in chap. 11 of *Moral Knowledge* and, further, in "Intrinsic Value and Reasons for Action."

11. This is the kind of thing Moore said in criticizing Sidgwick's experientialist hedonism in the theory of value. See *Principia*, esp. 83–85.

12. Appropriately experiencing something "for its own sake" does not entail viewing or otherwise relating to it for any particular *purpose* or indeed for any reason at all. One can happen upon a lovely landscape and view it in the relevant non-instrumental way, for instance aesthetically, in terms of its intrinsic properties. Moreover, I include among those intrinsic properties *internal relational properties* such as one color's complementing another.

13. The term 'inherently valuable' was C. I. Lewis's term for things whose (proper) contemplation is intrinsically valuable. See *An Analysis of Knowledge and Valuation* (LaSalle, IL: Open Court, 1946), 391 (Lewis, like Sidgwick and other hedonists, defended an experientialist view of the bearers of intrinsic value). I take it that inherent value is possessed on the basis of intrinsic properties and leave open whether *every*

instance of appropriate experience of them for their own sake has intrinsic value or whether there is simply a tendency for this to occur. Frankena characterizes the notion similarly; see his *Ethics*, 82 and 89.

14. See bk. 1 of the *Nicomachean Ethics* 1097a, esp. 25–30 ff., where Aristotle says, "We call that which is pursued as an end in itself more final than an end which is pursued for the sake of something else" (trans. Martin Ostwald [Indianapolis: Hackett, 1962]). Cf. Terence Irwin's translation, 2d ed. (Hackett, 1999), which uses 'complete' in place of 'final'.

15. Someone drawing on Brentano's view that we should love the good and hate the bad might argue that insofar as we *can* experience others' intrinsically good or intrinsically bad experiences, the relevant second-order experiences should be correspondingly good or bad. I suspect that the most one could say is that there is a prima facie appropriateness here, particularly if we think of cases in which thoroughly malicious people are having very good experiences that ill-befit their character. The question of what experiential responses are appropriate to various kinds of contemplation or experiences of the good or bad experiences of others is quite complicated, and I cannot pursue it here.

16. Why should we not say that pleasure is only prima facie good? We *may* say this so long as we take prima facie goodness to be a kind of intrinsic goodness: the pleasure cannot fail to be good qua pleasure, even though the whole of which it is an aspect can fail to be intrinsically good, just as an action cannot fail to be obligatory qua promised even if other facts about it prevent it from being obligatory on the whole. This kind of defeasibility does not imply a relational status; that pleasure does not necessarily make the experience it characterizes intrinsically good *overall* does not imply that the pleasure itself is good only in relation to something else, *or* only when certain conditions are met. Cf. Ross's potentially misleading comment that "Pleasure seems, indeed, to have a property analogous to . . . conditional or *prima facie* rightness . . . a state [episode, in my terms] of pleasure has the property, not necessarily of being good, but of being something that is good if the state has no other characteristic [besides its pleasurable aspect] that prevents it from being good [overall]" (*The Right and the Good*, 139). He goes on to speak of pleasure as "*prima facie* good in itself," which suggests that it is not intrinsically good, without squaring this with his view that it is intrinsically good. Distinguishing between the episodic and aspectual uses of 'pleasure' (in the way implied by the bracketed expressions) helps us to reconcile these two remarks.

17. Even if the suffering were hallucinated, the *property* of suffering—which is a clearly bad-making characteristic—is essential to the content of the pleasurable experience and is thus intrinsic to it. The reference to hallucination is intended to suggest a problem for experientialism: that it seems to deprive us of a ground for taking veridical experience of (e.g.) doing something enjoyable to be better than hallucinatory experience with the same intrinsic qualities. This problem is explored at length in chap. 11 of my *Moral Knowledge* and in "Intrinsic Value and Reasons for Action."

18. Frankena saw this point. See *Ethics*, 90, for valuable discussion of how the "total [intrinsic value] score" of an experience containing pleasure can be negative.

19. In the same passage (*Groundwork*, sec. 393) Kant places happiness in the same category as other items in being possibly "bad and hurtful," though the overall context does not warrant taking him to consider it *intrinsically* bad.

20. This objection was suggested to me by Michael Zimmerman.

21. I refer to the higher-order experience of it because I take it that the period of prosperity in question is not an experience but a series of experiences, hence not a candidate for intrinsic, as opposed to inherent, value on the view in question. The higher-order experience need not be painful but will tend to be colored by disapproval: considering it in itself, one would rather not have it, though given that one sees such cruelty, one may intrinsically want to feel disapproval of it. Lemos (*Intrinsic Value*, 42–44) defends the idea that the overall badness of the relevant kind of state of affairs is best understood on the assumption of the (essential) intrinsic goodness of the pleasure, but he sees this as preferring Moore's view over that of Kant and Ross, whereas I am suggesting that Kant, at least, is not best read as denying the value of the relevant pleasure taken by itself (not, anyway, in the *Groundwork*). Another experientialist reading of the example would construe the overall experience (rather than the state of affairs experienced) as *inherently* bad; this would still satisfy Kant's basic demand: that it merits disapproval.

22. At one point Ross says, of pleasure, "a state of pleasure has the property, not necessarily of being good, but of being something that is good if the state has no other characteristic that prevents it from being good. The two characteristics that may interfere with its being good are (a) that of being contrary to desert, and (b) that of being a state which is the realization of a bad disposition" (138). Ross's view here is fruitfully compared with that of Franz Brentano, which is explicated and critically discussed in R. M. Chisholm, *Brentano and Intrinsic Value* (Cambridge: Cambridge University Press, 1986). Chisholm notes, for instance, that "Brentano mentions with approval Fechner's view according to which 'every sensory pleasure, regarded in and for itself, is good, and that such pleasure can be said to be bad only to the extent that it is aroused by one's being pleased with what is detestable' " (31). Presumably such a pleasure is a "realization of a bad disposition," as would be displeasure in what is good (something Brentano took to be intrinsically bad); it would be "contrary to desert" on the assumption that non-persons can have desert.

23. The content in question is described as intentional because the person taking pleasure in the bad might be mistaken in thinking that the bad thing, e.g. the other's suffering, is actual. But taken in itself, *as* pleasure, the overall experience is as bad as it would be if the suffering were real.

24. See, e.g., Moore's *Ethics* for his distinction between the intrinsically and the ultimately good, which he also called "good for its own sake." The former term is misleading in suggesting that even when something is good overall, it may not be good, "in the final analysis," when his meaning is quite different (he simply wants a term to rule out what has one or more intrinsically bad elements). A splendid thing, such as the viewing of a great artwork with an almost indiscernible imperfection, could have some bad elements and, intuitively, is ultimately good, and certainly good "for its own sake," despite them.

25. Among the most plausible objections to its intelligibility is the idea that something can be good only qua *kind* of thing, pressed by, e.g., Judith Jarvis Thomson in "The Right and the Good," *Journal of Philosophy* 94 (1997). I accommodate what is plausible in this in "Intrinsic Value and Reasons for Action."

26. This is not the place for a detailed account of reasons for action, and many kinds of things bear that description. I have, however, provided a detailed account in

The Architecture of Reason, esp. chap. 5. See also Scanlon's *What We Owe to Each Other* and Derek Parfit's "Reasons and Motivation," *Proceedings of the Aristotelian Society,* supp. vol. (1997) and his forthcoming *Practical Realism.*

27. One reason he holds this is that his principles would then be derivable from an overarching consequentialist one. Another is that he does not regard the question of what to do as in any sense quantitative, or at least quantitative in this way.

28. *The Right and the Good,* 132.

29. Ibid., 140.

30. Kant says, e.g., that "an action of this kind [helping others from a "sympathetic temper" and an "inner pleasure in spreading happiness"], however right and however amiable it may be, has still no genuinely moral worth." See the *Groundwork,* sec. 10. He also says, of a sufferer from gout, that when he acts from "the law of furthering his happiness, not from inclination, but from duty; . . . his conduct has for the first time a real moral worth" (secs. 12–13). But he also closely connects the moral worth of actions with "the worth of character" which he calls "a moral worth and beyond all comparison the highest—namely that he [a man with "a good-natured temperament"] does good, not from inclination, but from duty" (sec. 11). Nonetheless, he apparently countenances the possibility that actions may be good in themselves. See, e.g., secs. 414–15. For detailed discussion of Kant's position on moral worth, see Phillip Stratton-Lake, *Kant, Duty, and Moral Worth* (London: Routledge: 2000).

31. The notion of well-being is in any case of great importance in ethics for James Griffin; see, e.g. his *Well-Being* (Oxford: Clarendon Press, 1986).

32. As William Frankena put it, "morality was made for man, not man for morality." See *Ethics,* 44. I take Frankena to be referring here, as I am in the text, to the paradigms of moral conduct. Nothing I say precludes applying moral notions to the treatment of animals and other non-persons.

33. Ross says, e.g.,"The first thing for which I would claim that it is intrinsically good is virtuous disposition and action, i.e., action, or disposition to act, from any one of certain motives of which at all events the most notable are the desire to do one's duty, the desire to bring into being something that is good, and the desire to give pleasure or save pain to others." See *The Right and the Good,* 134. He is not excluding *moral* virtue from his comment or even taking it as less valuable than non-moral virtue.

34. I here ignore the point that these might be better construed as *inherent* goods (i.e., goods that, though not necessarily intrinsic, are such that an appropriate experience of them has intrinsic value, as in the case of viewing a beautiful painting with aesthetic pleasure) since nothing in this chapter turns on the distinction. I also cannot attempt here to develop an account of the varieties of appropriateness or to distinguish moral from non-moral value. This is a difficult matter, but in this book I am assuming that moral values are above all those that contrast (if not always sharply) with hedonic and aesthetic ones and that are reflected in the content of the Rossian duties, perhaps most clearly those of justice, fidelity (including veracity), non-injury, and reparation.

35. We can also leave open the possibility of a noncognitivist account. A noncognitivist could accept my points and then try to explain why what we express by calling a deed good, or good qua according people respect, is more basic than what we express by saying simply that we have a reason to do it. For a full-scale account of noncognitivism, see Allan Gibbard, *Wise Choices, Apt Feelings.*

36. Ross says, e.g., that "when we think of an act as right we think that either something good or some pleasure for another will be brought into being" (*The Right and the Good*, 162), but the good in question need not be moral, nor is Ross implying that the strong association here affirmed between the thoughts of rightness and of goodness implies that actions can be morally good in virtue of anything concerning their rightness as such. Ross seems to hold the view he approvingly ascribes to Kant, that "virtue alone is morally good" (136), though he also says that "an action or feeling is morally good by virtue of proceeding from a character of a certain kind" (155; cf. 156–57). His considered view seems to be (in part) that morally good actions are only *derivatively* so.

37. This is argued in detail in "The Axiology of Moral Experience."

38. Whether indignation provides a moral reason, as opposed to a more general practical reason, say on account of its unpleasantness as calling for relief, depends on whether, from the moral point of view, it has an appropriate basis. I have illustrated both indignation that evidences wrong-doing and indignation that is perversely determined by perceiving a good deed.

39. Moore was unwilling to call these complex wholes good "for their own sake," since he restricted this term to what is "ultimately good," i.e., intrinsically good and containing no parts that are not intrinsically good. See *Ethics*, esp. 47–48. He apparently took "for its own sake" to entail goodness throughout, but the phrase is not naturally given that interpretation; and although his distinction is worth making, the indicated usage has not prevailed for either that phrase or 'ultimately good'.

40. What, then, of the case in which he enjoys what he falsely takes to be causing someone pain (and just vividly hallucinates doing this)? Here it remains true that his enjoyment is intrinsically good, but the complex state of affairs, his enjoying the experience *as of* causing someone pain, may still be both intrinsically and inherently bad. (This might depend on, e.g., whether he believes the person has masochistically asked for the painful action.)

41. Moore formulated a "principle of organic unities" in *Principia*, e.g. 28, and reiterated a version of it in *Ethics*. In the light of an understanding of the organicity of value, one can see how Kant could both countenance intrinsic goods other than good will (including happiness) and yet say that "a rational and impartial spectator can never feel approval in contemplating the uninterrupted prosperity of a being graced by no touch of a pure and good will . . ." (*Groundwork* 393).

42. Deontological reasons and, more generally, the connection between intrinsic and inherent value and reasons for action are discussed in some detail in my "Intrinsic Value and Reasons for Action."

43. This is a reference to the supervenience of moral properties, widely discussed in recent literature and explored in chaps. 4 and 5 of my *Moral Knowledge*. The relevant passages in Ross are mainly in chaps. 2 and 4 of *The Right and the Good*. See esp. 33, 105, and 121–23.

44. This would be quite all right for an externalist, reliabilist account of moral justification, but even then the relevant property must be *causally* discriminated, whether inaccessibly to consciousness (without outside help) or not.

45. Sometimes a *proposition* is said to be "an inference" from one or more other propositions. This can mean that it cannot be *known* (or perhaps justified) except on

the basis of the other(s), in which case the point is epistemic and general, or that the former is actually (or appropriately) held on the basis of the latter, in which case the point may be either epistemic or psychological, and either general or about someone specified in the context. My threefold distinction in the text usually provides a better way to make one or the other of these points and related ones.

46. One may wonder whether a cognition of a proposition that is epistemically dependent does not *have* to be inferentially grounded. It does not. One can *have* a justification for a proposition, and even justifiedly believe it, without that justification's leading to having a justified belief of a premise for it. This would be a case of what, in Chapter 2, I called structural justification; this is possible for a belief of a principle without that justification's figuring in any premise or being an inferential ground of the principle.

47. There is an oddity in saying that persons have intrinsic, and particularly absolute, worth, since some are so very bad—people can apparently even be "no damned good." The reference is to Nicholas Sturgeon's "Moral Explanations," in *Morality, Reason, and Truth*, ed. David Copp and David Zimmerman (Totowa, NJ: Rowman and Allanheld, 1984), where moral properties are taken to have explanatory power in a sense that is partly causal. The approach of this chapter is compatible with elements of the moral realism defended by Sturgeon (which allows for a causal-explanatory notion of value); the chief difference is apparently in the epistemology of the two, but much of what I say could be detached from the rationalist epistemology that I am taking to be most natural, as well as historically dominant, for intuitionism. Indeed, at least most of my main points in this book could be true even if moral properties turned out to be identical with natural properties. A similar compatibility with my view might hold for the moral realism of Richard Boyd's related "How to Be a Moral Realist," in *Essays on Moral Realism*, ed. Geoffrey Sayre-McCord (Ithaca: Cornell University Press, 1988).

48. See the *Groundwork*, sec. 428 (Paton trans.). This is one among other passages in Kant, particularly in the *Groundwork*, that do not lend themselves readily to a constructivist interpretation of his ethics. For discussion of this perspective on Kant and in contrast with realism, see Korsgaard, *Sources of Normativity*; and Berys Gaut's "The Structure of Practical Reason," in Cullity and Gaut, *Ethics and Practical Reason*.

49. This is not to say that there are no other good candidates to play the indicated roles. Moreover, dignity is presumably a higher-order value in the sense that beings have it on the basis of their capacity to realize other values, such as moral satisfaction, pleasure in contemplating goodness and beauty, and suffering in experiencing injustice to others or themselves.

50. I leave open that some live births may be an exception to this, say of anencephalic infants; but I assume that basic human dignity is not necessarily lost by normal human beings even when they fall into irreversible coma.

51. This maximization emphasis comes out in *Ethics*, e.g. in the optimality description of right action cited above.

52. This is not to suggest that explicating this distinction is easy for any moral theory or that consequentialists have no resources for dealing with it. Chapter 3 contains some discussion of the problem for Kantian intuitionism.

53. See *Principia*, 149. Space constraints prohibit my discussing Moore's overall ethics in detail in this book; a thorough treatment should take account of his Preface to the Second Edition of *Principia*, reprinted, with an instructive introduction, by Thomas Baldwin, in the latter's revised edition (Cambridge: Cambridge University Press, 1993).

54. This is reminiscent of the error in epistemology of inferring, from the capacity of incoherence to defeat justification, that coherence is the ground of justification. Rejecting the fallacious inferences here does not, of course, commit one to denying that we should even try to maximize or that coherence never plays a positive role in justification. Analysis of the epistemological case is provided in my *Structure of Justification*, esp. chaps. 3–4.

55. Ross notes this in connection with the duty of self-improvement. See, e.g., *The Right and the Good*, 25–26.

56. The truth of Rossian moral propositions, in which supervening moral properties figure essentially, is presumably consequential on natural properties in a derivative way. But it is no easy task to specify how the two kinds of dependency, that of properties and that of truth values, are connected, and the task need not be undertaken for our purposes here.

57. Ross characterized intuitive induction in more than one place. See esp. chap. 2 of *The Right and the Good*. A similar notion is characterized by Broad in a passage quoted in Chapter 1. I might add that the particularism referred to here is not the strong kind defended by Jonathan Dancy in *Moral Reasons* and appraised in Chapter 2.

58. The notion of the self-evident is also defended against many objections by Laurence BonJour, *In Defense of Pure Reason* (Cambridge: Cambridge University Press, 1998), and for a more moderate account and other clarificatory moves, see my "Self-Evidence."

59. In chap. 4 of *Epistemology*, I have argued in some detail for the possibility of knowledge of substantive a priori propositions and indicated a number of other works relevant to the issue.

60. The kind of view in question is what Robert Nozick calls a "side-constraints view": it "forbids you to violate these constraints in the pursuit of your goals; whereas the view whose objective is to minimize the violation of these rights allows you to violate the rights (the constraints) in order to lessen their total violation in society." See his *Anarchy, State, and Utopia* (New York: Basic Books, 1974), 29. In partial summary of this view he says, "Individuals are inviolable" (31); but cf. his cautionary note on 30, apparently allowing exceptions for "catastrophic moral horror." Philip Pettit contrasts this side-constraints view with what he calls a "goal-centered theory." For recent critical discussion of Nozick's side-constraints view, see Pettit's "Non-Consequentialism and Political Philosophy," in *Robert Nozick*, ed. David Schmidtz (Cambridge: Cambridge University Press, 2002).

61. I have not argued in this book for the general priority of the duty of non-injury over that of beneficence, but in "The Moral Rights of the Terminally Ill," in *Contemporary Issues in Biomedical Ethics*, ed. John W. Davis, Barry Hoffmaster, and Sarah Shorten (Clifton, NJ: The Humana Press, 1979), I have defended a version of the view at length.

62. It is not easy to say just what the force of 'merely' is in 'merely as means' here; this problem is discussed in detail in my "Treating Persons as Ends."

63. A different approach to accommodating deontological constraints is taken by Brad Hooker in his defense of rule consequentialism. See esp. chap. 3, sec. 2, and chap. 4, secs. 2 and 6, of *Ideal Code, Real World*.

64. Even in this case there might be possible exceptions: perhaps in some far-off possible world, *temporary* enslavement might be necessary to overcome some condition that has impaired, and will otherwise kill, those enslaved; and the desperate "rescue" might be possible only if those doing it caused themselves to be motivated by self-aggrandizement.

65. A detailed treatment of various kinds of relativity is provided in chap. 7 of my *Architecture of Reason*, which stresses (among many other kinds of relativity) relativity of reasons to grounds. Thomas Nagel has extensively discussed agent relativity; see, e.g., his *The View from Nowhere*, esp. chap. 9.

66. I take this objection from Rawls, "Kantian Constructivism"; see esp. 91–92. The first objection is echoed by John McDowell in "Projection and Truth in Ethics," The Lindley Lecture (Lawrence: University of Kansas, 1987), reprinted in *Moral Discourse and Practice*, ed. Stephen Darwall, Allan Gibbard, and Peter Railton (Oxford: Oxford University Press, 1997), 215–25. It is interesting to note the lengths to which Rawls went in criticizing intuitionism; perhaps this is in part because, as a kind of intuitivist, he shared some important intuitionist ideas. He says, e.g., in *Justice as Fairness: A Restatement* (Cambridge: Harvard University Press, 2001), "A second reason the ideal cannot be fully attained is that the balance of reasons itself rests on judgment, though judgment informed and guided by reasoning . . . we must rely on judgment as to what considerations are more or less significant, and when in practice to close the list of reasons" (134). Even in *A Theory of Justice*, there is at least one place where he seems to allow, as an intuitionist would, for possible exceptions to the priority of the liberty principle over the difference principle (45).

67. Ross notes defeasibility when he compares moral convictions with sense-perceptions, *The Right and the Good*, 41.

68. The idea that for intuitionism we "just see" what our duty is can be found in Mackie's discussion of intuitionism in *Ethics: Inventing Right and Wrong* as well as in a number of other writers.

69. This objection to intuitionism also comes from Rawls's "Kantian Constructivism"; see 91–92 of *Political Liberalism*.

70. This is treated by David McNaughton, "An Unconnected Heap of Duties?" *Philosophical Quarterly* 46 (1996): 443–47; Hooker, "Ross-Style Pluralism versus Rule-Consequentialism," and others. See also David McNaughton and Piers Rawling, "On Defending Deontology," *Ratio* 11, no. 1 (1998): 37–54, both for interpretation of Rossian intuitionism and for criticism of an attempt (quite different from the approach outlined here) to derive a related deontological standard from considerations of value.

71. This can give rise to a circularity problem if there is no way to understand the notion of dignity apart from the duties, but that is not so; nor is it the only basis for knowledge of those principles (as it could not be if they are self-evident).

Chapter 5. Intuitionism in Normative Ethics

1. Significant support for this point is provided in a recent wide-ranging study of the continuity among many different religious and cultural traditions; see Brian Lepard, *Rethinking Humanitarian Intervention* (College Park: Penn State University Press, 2002).

2. A widely known paper that well illustrates a case-based method is Judith Jarvis Thomson's "A Defense of Abortion," *Philosophy and Public Affairs* 1 (1971). In an instructive treatment of a position that seems both intuitionist and perhaps mainly consistent with the one developed in this book, F. M. Kamm draws on cases in formulating and in appraising moral principles in a way that, in places, also well illustrates a case-based method. See her "Nonconsequentialism," in LaFollette, *The Blackwell Guide to Ethical Theory*.

3. For discussion of how virtues may be conceived in relation to moral standards governing conduct, see my "Acting from Virtue," *Mind* (1994), reprinted in *Moral Knowledge*, chap. 8. For a critique of virtue ethics that supports my conclusions favoring an intuitionist approach, see Robert N. Johnson, "Virtue and Rights," *Ethics* 113, no. 4 (2003). Contrasting conceptions of virtue ethics are provided by Alasdair MacIntyre, *After Virtue*, 2d ed. (Notre Dame, IN: University of Notre Dame Press, 1981), and Rosalind Hursthouse, *On Virtue Ethics* (Oxford: Oxford University Press, 1999).

4. Philippa Foot has instructively sought to specify what kind of thing counts as an injury in what appears to be a broadly factual way. See her "Moral Beliefs," *Proceedings of the Aristotelian Society* 59 (1958–59): 410–25.

5. To be sure, treating persons as ends is *also* a sufficient condition for avoiding treating them merely as a means. If one keeps a promise to someone where one sees it would be lucrative to break it and thereby gain, one serves moral aims. But the negative and positive notions in question are distinct, particularly in that failure to treat as an end does not imply treating merely as a means.

6. For a view on which beneficence, like other "imperfect duties," is really only an ideal in my sense, see Gert, *Morality.*

7. Here, however, one must view duty as calling for production of just distributions, as Ross sometimes does, not simply as requiring rectification of unjust distributions. (I assume that Ross may include punishment under the wide meritarian sense of 'distribution' he employed in specifying the relevant duty.)

8. In stressing the need for moral psychology here, I concur with G.E.M. Anscombe's call for "an adequate philosophy of psychology." See "Modern Moral Philosophy," in *Virtue Ethics*, ed. Roger Crisp and Michael Slote (Oxford: Oxford University Press, 1997), 26–44. See also Philippa Foot, "Virtues and Vices," in her *Virtues and Vices and Other Essays in Moral Philosophy* (Oxford: Blackwell, 1978), 1–18, in which a good deal of moral psychology is brought to bear on virtue ethics.

9. I explain and argue for this in "Self-Evidence." In part the point is that no amount of understanding of the content of the conditional must necessarily lead to one's discovering the needed intermediate premise(s). That may require imagination. As with scientific hypotheses, validation is one thing, discovery another. That there is

a clear proof of *T* given *A* which one could see to be sound when presented with it does not entail that it will occur to one on reflecting ever so long on the conditional, 'If *A*, then *T*'.

10. This point is supported by many critiques of consequentialism, especially utilitarianism. For an indication both of some of the intuitive objections to consequentialism and of how to qualify it to block them, see Hooker's *Ideal Code, Real World*. A number of good examples showing deficiencies in unrestricted consequentialist views are given in Derek Parfit's *Rediscovering Reasons* (forthcoming).

11. There are theistic perspectives in which being created by God is central for the kind of dignity I refer to. I am supposing that there is an priori basis for such dignity in our human capacities but of course do not rule out a theistic account of the origin and sustenance of these capacities.

12. Gert's *Morality* is in part a defense of the moral importance of avoiding evil over promoting good. I do not go as far as he in taking moral obligation not to include duties of beneficence, but I hope here to contribute to explaining the plausibility of his judgment of priority. For detailed discussion, see my "Reasons and Rationality in the Moral Philosophy of Bernard Gert," in *Rationality, Rules, and Ideals: Critical Essays on Bernard Gert's Moral Theory*, ed. Walter Sinnott-Armstrong and Robert Audi (Lanham, MD: Rowman and Littlefield, 2002).

13. I am presupposing a distinction between the exercise of freedom and the mere performance of a free action; and I am taking the former to carry a kind of experience of exercising freedom. This does not require thinking of the action under that description or indeed under any particular one. Part of what I have in mind is a familiar sense of controlling what one is doing and of having options. My main points concerning the exercise of freedom could be sustained, however, even if it were to have just inherent, rather than intrinsic, value.

14. This point has far-reaching implications in the domain of church-state relations and of the balance of religious and secular reasons in individual political decision. For extensive discussion of these issues, see my *Religious Commitment and Secular Reason* (Cambridge: Cambridge University Press, 2000).

15. Here I presuppose a detailed account of autonomy, given in chap. 9 of *Moral Knowledge*, that develops these ideas.

16. What it is to act from a motive, and particularly from moral virtue, and the connection of such notions with that of moral worth are discussed in detail in my "Acting from Virtue," in my *Moral Knowledge*.

17. Two clarifications are important here (and even then the formulation remains rough). First, where the (moral) right is to have a promise or agreement honored, the protection from coercion is twofold: from being forced to relinquish one's claim and from being prevented from asserting it. Second, we might also consider moral rights ineradicable provided we distinguish eradication from other kinds of elimination, such as forfeiture and alienation. (This is not to say that there are not rights that cannot be forfeited or alienated, such as, perhaps, the right not to be enslaved.)

18. Much has been written on rights, and I cannot here treat even a representative sample of the literature. The work of John Rawls, Joel Feinberg, and Judith Jarvis Thomson is instructive here. See, e.g., her *The Realm of Rights*.

19. For an extended defense of the view that there are moral expectations which we have a right not to fulfill but ought to fulfill in a sense implying criticizability, see Gregory Mellema, *The Expectations of Morality* (forthcoming from Rodopi in 2004).

20. This is essentially the view defended by Gert, *Morality*.

21. We have a choice here: we can say, e.g., that if an injury or harm is fully excusable, the principle is violated but the agent is not blameworthy, or that because a prima facie obligation is overridden by a sufficient moral consideration, the principle is *not* violated but simply does not *prevail*. It seems best to speak of excuses only where we still should say that a wrong was done, and of a principle's not prevailing—or the obligation it expresses being overridden—where we should not speak of a wrong. There are many variant terminologies; but nothing of importance in this book turns on the terminological details in question, and I cannot pursue them here.

22. Gert, *Morality*, has much of value to say about deprivations of ability, freedom, and pleasure, and he indeed takes the prohibition of these as morally basic, whereas I am taking deprivation of ability to be a harm and the other two to be in general injustices. Particularly given my attempt to ground middle-level axioms in something wider, I am not mainly concerned with which among the candidates for middle axioms are the closest to being conceptually independent.

23. I think that we also have a prima facie obligation to contribute to the welfare of non-human animals, but I do not include this here. It raises questions I cannot take time to address here and has a lesser claim to be in any way self-evident.

24. An interesting question here is whether a good deed's *grounding* an obligation of gratitude must be roughly well-intentioned or at least not ill-intentioned, or whether its being ill-intentioned simply defeats the obligation. I think the latter more plausible, but cannot argue the point here. If the deed is well-intentioned but morally wrong, defeat will at least tend to occur; but I do not think that the relevant deed's being morally permissible is a part of the *ground* of the duty of beneficence. If it is, that ground is of course not morally neutral. For a full-scale discussion of the nature and ethical significance of gratitude, see Terrance McConnell, *Gratitude* (Philadelphia: Temple University Press, 1993).

25. Whether, given certain information, rational persons must recognize such duties or even act in accordance with them is discussed in detail in my *Architecture of Reason*, esp. chap. 6.

Index

accessibility, internal, 58, 124
amoralism, 67
Anscombe, G.E.M., 235n.8
apprehension, 15, 25, 29. See also intuitive induction; reflection
a priori, the. See self-evidence
Aquinas, St. Thomas, 5, 161
Aristotle, 27, 76, 77, 116, 123, 126, 144, 148, 161, 198, 206nn. 28 and 30, 228n.14
autonomy, 95–97, 99, 106, 142, 178, 184, 194, 224n.55; of ethics, 54, 149–51. See also freedom
axiological experientialism, 124–30, 136, 228n.17. See also value
axioms, 9–10, 54, 80–83, 106, 203n.1; middle, 80–83, 187, 217n.3

Baldwin, Thomas, 203n.3, 204n.7, 216n.57, 233n.53
Balguy, John, 203n.2
Bealer, George, 207n.37
beauty, 122–23, 125
Beck, Lewis White, 212n.26
beneficence. See duty: of beneficence
Bentham, Jeremy, 86
bias, 9, 37, 38
Bok, Sissela, 217n.2
BonJour, Laurence, 209n.7, 214n.43, 233n.58
Boyd, Richard, 232n.47
Brandt, R. B., 207n.32, 209n.7, 215n.47
Brentano, Franz, 228n.15, 229n.22
Brink, David, 220n.17
Broad, C. D., 17–20, 23, 26, 42, 62, 69, 70, 126, 205n.18, 233n.57
Broome, John, x
Butchvarov, Panayot, x, 207n.34
Butler, Joseph, 16

Carroll, Lewis, 215n.49
categorical imperative, the, 52, 80, 90–94, 102–3, 108, 142, 144, 170, 191. See also dignity; intutionism: Kantian; Kant, Immanuel; respect for persons

causal dependence, 208n.40
Chang, Ruth, x, 214nn. 39 and 41, 226n.2
Chisholm, R. M., 229n.22
Clarke, Samuel, 203n.2, 207n.32, 213n.30
codes of ethics, 170, 201
cognitivism. See noncognitivism
coherentism, conceptual, 73–74
coherentism, epistemological, 73–74, 111, 218–19n.7, 233n.54. See also justification
completeness, epistemic, 85–87, 115
completeness, normative, 85–87, 89, 117, 220n.18
consequentialism, 97, 99, 121, 131, 146, 147, 152, 163. See also deontology; utilitarianism
consequentiality, 55–56, 57, 58, 74–75, 86, 139, 140, 213n.33
constructivism, 105, 223n.45
contractualism, 218n.4, 220–21n.22, 222n.35
creditworthiness, 133, 180
Crisp, Roger, x, 203n.3, 208n.36, 216n.57, 224n.64
Cudworth, Ralph, 203n.2
Cullity, Garrett, x

Dancy, Jonathan, x, 213n.35, 215n.45, 216nn. 54, 55, and 57, 225n.57, 233n.57
Darwall, Stephen L., x, 203n.2, 213n.30
defeasibility, 31–32, 36, 45, 64–65. See also epistemic dependence; justification; reflective equilibrium
Deigh, John, x, 226n.64
deontological constraints, 138, 151–53
deontology, 131, 134, 138, 146, 147, 152, 163, 171. See also consequentialism; duty
DePaul, Michael, x
dependence, causal. See causal dependence
dependence, epistemic. See epistemic dependence
dependence, inferential. See inferential dependence
dependence, normative. See normative dependence
desert, 191–92, 229n.22